WINDOWS ON THEOLOGY

FENSTER ZUR THEOLOGIE

for students past and present of
Black Christian Studies
at the Queen's College Birmingham

and for all who are claiming the inheritance

John L. Wilkinson

Church in Black and White

The Black Christian Tradition in "Mainstream"
Churches in England:
A White Response and Testimony

Saint Andrew Press
Pahl-Rugenstein Verlag Nachfolger

First published 1993 by Pahl-Rugenstein
and Saint Andrew Press.

Pahl-Rugenstein Verlag Nachfolger GmbH
Breite Str. 47, 53111 Bonn
Tel (0228) 63 23 06 Fax (0228) 63 49 68
Bundesrepublik Deutschland
ISBN 3-89144-301-3

Saint Andrew Press
121 George Street
Edinburgh EH2 4YN
Scotland, UK
Tel (031) 22 55 72 2 Fax (031) 22 03 11 3
ISBN 0-86153-154-X

Die Deutsche Bibliothek - CIP-Einheitsaufnahme

Wilkinson, John Laurence: Church in Black and White
The Black Christian Tradition in "Mainstream" Churches in England: A
White Response and Testimony / John Laurence Wilkinson. - Edinburgh :
Saint Andrew Press; Bonn : Pahl-Rugenstein, 1993 (Windows on Theology
/ Fenster zur Theologie)
ISBN 3-89144-301-3 (Pahl-Rugenstein)
ISBN 0-86153-154-X (Saint Andrew Press)

British Library Cataloguing in Publication Data:
A catalogue record for this book is avaible from the British Library

Printed in Hungary by Interpress

Contents

Foreword
Redeeming a Tragic History: A Call to Conversion

John Wilkinson's book is likely to be read by many black Christians belonging to different denominations and traditions in this country, including the independent black-majority churches. After all, it deals with a story that they all share to a larger or lesser extent.

When black Christians came to these islands with the great immigrations that started in the early 1950s', an alarmingly large number of them felt they were being 'frozen out' of the local, preponderantly 'white-membership' churches to which they thought they belonged. Those who went through that traumatic experience responded in two different ways. A certain number opted to walk out of these churches and to form independent Christian congregations in which they could feel at home and could create the kind of christian experience that responded to their needs. These are the independent 'black-majority' churches which have become such a marking feature of present-day British christianity. But an equally significant number chose to remain in their denominations of origin and to carry on from the inside the demanding task of helping to create visibly multi-cultural and multi-racial congregations such as would prove the truth of Paul's declaration: 'For (in Christ) . . . there is neither Jew nor Greek, there is neither slave nor free, there is neither male nor female (and add: neither white nor black)' (Galatians 3:28)

This book sets out to listen to the story of this section of black Christians. It does far more than that: it goes on to propose what the author feels should be the appropriate and constructive response, on the part of the white membership of those churches, to the prophetic challenge thrown by their black brothers and sisters. Indeed Wilkinson makes it very clear that this book is meant to be 'a white response and testimony'. In that sense it surely is a brave and daring exercise, and one wonders what kind of reception his book will get from those it seeks to engage in dialogue.

In this dialogue the black Christians themselves are simply in the position of interested observers, waiting to see what will be the reaction of their white brothers and sisters to this testimony coming from their own midst. It may be interesting, however, to hear how these black Christians are likely to think about such a book. I do not presume to claim that my own personal feelings are necessarily representative in this case, nor does it make sense for me to want to speak for other black christians. And after all, the story is really about the Church of England of which I am not a member.

There are several reasons, however, that encouraged me to accept the kind invitation to contribute my own reflections along with those of Professor Hollenweger. What happened, and is still happening, in the Church of England in the area of race relationships is not completely unique to that Church. Black Christians in other mainstream churches in this country could vouch for the validity, as regards their own denomination, of much that Wilkinson describes in this book. This is evident from the exchanges that go on in such ecumenical forums as the Association of Black Clergy (ABC), 'Claiming the Inheritance' (CTI), and 'Evangelical Christians for Racial Justice' (ECRJ), or in denominational movements like the Catholic Association for Racial Justice (CARJ), and similar organizations, e.g. in the Methodist Church. It should be helpful, therefore, to hear other voices joining the one in the Church of England. On the other side, my involvement in the work of the Centre for Black and White Christian Partnership makes it quite natural for me to be specially interested in a work of this type.

Despite its apparently calm and irenical tone, this little book is very challenging and demanding; and yet at the same time it succeeds in proposing a positive message of liberation and hope. The author courageously puts the finger on the real source of uneasiness in the relations between white and black members in the same church, namely that, because of a long past history, one group represents the side of oppressor while the other represents the side of victim. It is not helpful to want to simply brush aside or throw a blanket of innocent forgetfulness over this painful history, for the quite important reason that it has left deep and lasting marks that account for individual and especially group actions and reactions even in our present times. There are deep-seated assumptions and images of superiority and inferiority, feelings of guilt and insecurity, hidden fears and prejudices, which are the unconscious motivations of customs, ways of thinking and doing things, rules of conduct, even explicit regulations that govern the relationships between the two sides. The centuries of slavery and colonialism, added to the ongoing interactions of neo-colonialism, account for much of these strained relationships.

The book rightly prescribes the courage to lay bare these hidden roots of history, for without that there is no hope in dealing with the relationships in an effective way. Two things are necessary. The first is to dare to admit and look carefully into the differences that separate blacks from whites. For indeed the two sides are not in the same situation: every day experience proves that. It is painful and insulting to hear well-meaning folk say: 'I see no difference between white and black: for me, we are all human beings'. Surely we are. But this does not mean that in real life it makes no difference whether you are black or white. We must dare to call black 'black', and white 'white', lest we forget what history has set in motion, and risk to just go on as if everything was alright. The second is to go beyond the consideration of merely individual responsibility, and take in the tremendous importance of inherited and group responsibility. In such matters as race relations there is enormously more than simple personal malice or good intentions. Even the most well-intentioned and nice people can be part of an effectively oppressive and unjust system, and their apparently innocent actions can produce much suffering and destruction without the persons themselves intending or wishing to do so. That is why it is important to reach back to the roots of our present life if we want to struggle effectively with such things as racism. Racism is more than a matter of being morally and consciously bad. It is much more a question of unfair distribution and exercise of power and privilege sustained by racist prejudice, whether conscious or not.

In the book the author makes two very helpful points. One is that the evil of racism becomes apparent and challenging only if the victims are given voice and listened to. For they are in the right position to say what is wrong, and why. Hopefully this book will encourage people to listen to the groaning of the victims, even if that is a painful and disconcerting experience. It need not lead into a negative and hopeless guilty conscience. But it can and should lead towards what the author calls 'conversion' or turning around. This important notion, which for me is the central message of the book, represents the point at which hope is possible. What our human history has built, it is possible to dismantle. We can today redeem our history, if we have the courage to single out the past roots of the predicament we are in today, and then consciously denounce and renounce them. By so doing we make it possible to struggle effectively with the evils that still bedevil our present relationships. I hope and pray that readers of this book will feel the challenge to engage in this healing adventure, and will want to respond courageously.

Rt Rev P.A. Kalilombe M.Afr.
The Centre for Black and White Christian Partnership,
Selly Oak Colleges, Birmingham.
May 1992

Acknowledgements

I wish to thank the many people – individuals, Black groups and organizations, church communities and funding bodies – who have contributed to this book through sharing experiences and critical reflection, by offering hospitality and support and by undertaking practical tasks.

In particular I must thank the following people: my wife Renate who has shared insights and ideas making this book in so many ways a shared enterprise; our children Martin, Jennifer and Samuel who have helped us all survive the disruption it has inevitably brought; Walter Hollenweger, Louis-Charles Harvey, Patrick Kalilombe, David Moore, Roderick Hewitt, Peter Harvey, Dan O'Connor and other friends who have shared their distinctive visions and given encouragement; the congregations of St. James' Aston and St. George's Newtown, Birmingham, the *Claiming the Inheritance* Committee and everyone who took part in the 'Living Faith' Project who have taught me by sharing their faith and experience, and colleagues at Queen's College who have given support and advice.

Also: Queen's College, Birmingham which offered me the College's Research Fellowship for the year 1984–85; the St. Peter's Saltley Trust, St. Gabriel's Trust, the Foundation of St. Matthias, the Culham Educational Foundation, the Hockerill Educational Foundation, the St. Augustine's Foundation, the Ecclesiastical Insurance Group, the Church of England Board of Mission and Unity and U.S.P.G. who all gave financial support; Black Christian Studies students at Queen's College who allowed me the privilege and stimulation of being involved with their theological education, and colleagues in the Caribbean, the United States and Canada who gave generous hospitality and opened the way for memorable occasions of sharing in study, reflection and worship during sabbatical leave in Autumn 1990.

And finally: Klaus Stoll of *Windows on Theology*; Michael Walpole as well as numerous volunteers who have done proof reading; and Paul and Barbara Llewellyn, Jeanette Estridge, Carolyn Gumbley and Jenny Hutton who have been patient and careful in typing the manuscript.

John Wilkinson

Preface
Encounter Between Black and White

Several publications have appeared recently on black-led churches in the United Kingdom.[1] Some people find these black-led churches interesting and challenging, some think they are not really necessary because the church should not be divided along racial lines. Why do they not simply join the mainline churches, they ask?

In his uncomfortable 'Testimony', John Wilkinson describes what happens if blacks remain in their Anglican church, for many of them were Anglicans before they came to the United Kingdom. This is first of all a reason for joy. It is greatly encouraging for us to learn that these blacks accepted Christianity in great numbers, but also deeply humbling. They accepted the religion of their exploiters,[2] the oppressors who called them 'black dogs' and opposed their baptism. One does not baptize horses, so why should one baptize black people? (p. 19). Nevertheless there was perhaps enough Christian substance in the Anglican witness (or alternatively God's grace was greater than our sin) for many of the victims to accept the religion of their oppressors.

However, the encounter between black and white is not without its problems. Dangerous memories lurk in the dark. The two cultures do not easily mix. Special grace, considerable cultural, theological and liturgical skill is needed on both sides to make this encounter successful.

When these black Christians came to England they found that their British passports were not really honoured, nor were their Anglican Communicant cards (p. 78). Sometimes people even lifted a black child's robe at Baptism to see if it had a tail (p. 174). Fortunately Wilkinson spares us the more cruel and disgusting stories of this ignorance and describes the meeting of white and black Anglicans as an encounter of historic oppressor and victim. When they meet in the presence of the Risen Christ, the promise of a new common life in the Church emerges.

For this to happen, a number of pre-conditions must be fulfilled. The encounter has to be properly staged and organized. It does not take place spontaneously. For instance Black Anglican music is only just being recognized. There is also very little material for Junior Church with which black youngsters can identify. Encounter also means that white youngsters are exposed to black Junior Church material.

Black theological education is only in its early days. Reports of liturgical and theological contributions by black Anglicans are very sparse. Nevertheless the problem has been recognized – at least by some.

Wilkinson sees it as his task to encourage this process and to articulate the promise of such an encounter within the Church, even if it is painful and uncomfortable. But if we want to be (or to become) the Church of Jesus Christ, it has to be tackled. That this task has not merely psychological but also theological and liturgical implications, is one of the most debated issues.

Many think that theology is objective and pure, untainted by colour or culture. Unfortunately this is not the case. We theologians could have learned this a long time ago if we had listened to our colleagues from other university departments. We have to realize that all we say and do in theological matters is also informed by our own cultural and racial interests. A theology which considers itself neutral on these matters continues to act as a subtle instrument of oppression. White theology is not more objective than black theology. Since we realize this only in encounter with theologies from other backgrounds, this encounter is a theological necessity. It must be properly reflected upon and integrated into our curriculum. Wilkinson has made a beginning for such reflection. He will be opposed because nobody likes to be told that he or she cannot continue in 'the old proven ways'. Since the Anglican community is now a black-majority Church worldwide (p. 6), we need to listen to this majority.

Dr Walter J. Hollenweger
Prof. em. University of Birmingham
CH-3704 Krattigen
Switzerland

1

A New People is Born

It is Sunday morning in a Church of England parish church in inner-city Birmingham in the spring of 1983. For an older member, a settler from the Caribbean island of Nevis of some twenty-five years standing, it is the Sunday before she leaves for her first ever visit home. To mark the occasion, she asks the Vicar whether she and another more elderly woman might sing a song during the Parish Communion. Instinctively he hesitates. He knows he should be pleased she feels free to sing but is anxious about the quality of what might be produced. He overcomes his hesitation, however, and during the service, after the sermon, the women lead the congregation into the period of intercession with a rendition of 'When I Travel'. It is an old Sankey revival song, but sung by the two women, in harmony and without introduction or accompaniment, it is transformed by the sharp cutting edge of the Black tradition of worship. It has a self-evident power and spiritual authenticity and not a few members of the congregation are moved to tears. And afterwards the Vicar ponders: for how many years more might the spiritual gifts of those Black Christians have remained hidden had not the exceptional circumstances of a long awaited visit home released them?

It is now nearly five hundred years since the first Africans were captured and brought as slaves to Europe.[1] More soon followed, and in far greater numbers, to newly established colonies in North and South America and the islands of the Caribbean. It is now nearly fifty years since the relatively small Black communities of Britain, France and Holland were swollen by the arrival of Caribbean settlers responding to the post-war labour shortage of their respective 'mother countries'.[2] The first slaves were African in religion, language and culture; whereas the twentieth century settlers had long since espoused the Christian religion, the English, French or Dutch language, and the European culture of their colonizers. And yet,

1

throughout the pain and the triumphs of their long journey, the people of the African Diaspora have been nourished by their African roots. They have been formed by a unique experience; resisting the demands of the European captors whilst adapting and appropriating their culture. The two women were singing praise to God out of that pain and that triumph; I was the Vicar who very nearly suppressed them.

Afro-Caribbean people, and hence the Afro-Caribbean-British, are the relatively recent offspring of a forced liaison between Europe and Africa. Indeed, it is not an exaggeration to speak of them as children of rape, of the forceful and violent assault of a European 'father' on the African 'mother'. As always in such abuse, hurt reaches deep into the consciousness of all concerned, and can be repressed or ignored only at the cost of personal wholeness and authenticity. It is necessary for all deliberately to face the past, not for its own sake nor to indulge in shame and guilt, but to establish a new future on the basis of healed memories. Facing the past has a special sharpness for Christians, and never more than when the violated 'mother' and her 'children' break the Bread of Life and share the Cup of Salvation with their 'assailant' at the Lord's Table. But the hope and the joy of Christians is so much the greater, since our trust is in the power of God, shown in the death and resurrection of Jesus, to bring good out of evil and light out of darkness.

THREE STORIES

How is the past to be deliberately faced so that a new future might be possible? It is the aim of this book to begin to answer that question. I shall begin with *three stories or narratives*, for it is within the account which individuals or communities give of their history and experience that their values, their self-understanding and, in the case of Christians, their theology are uncovered. The first is *my own story* (Chapter 2); how I discovered the significance of my own identity as a White priest of the Church of England through ministry to Black Afro-Caribbean people. Mine is an Anglican story, but I believe it will illuminate the stories of White people, clergy and laity, in all 'mainstream' or 'White-led' denominations. The second, which follows from the first, is my understanding of *the story of the Christian community to which I belong*, the Church of England, in respect of its relationship to the history of Black people (Chapter 3). It should likewise illuminate the story of other 'mainstream' churches. In both these stories I describe that of which I am a part.

The third story is that of *Black Christianity*, in particular Black Anglicans of Afro-Caribbean origin (Chapters 4 and 5). Here I describe from the outside that of which I can never be a part. So at some points I will simply report and summarise the work of well-known Black scholars. I hope this summary will be helpful to Black as well as to White readers; and in any case no other such summary is as yet available. But my sources can easily be checked and my summary challenged if need be. At other points I will bear witness to that which I have seen and heard. My experience is so vivid, and the hope uncovered is so much greater than the not inconsiderable pain, that I can do no other. My interpretation owes much to American Black theology and I am aware that there are as yet few precedents for thus linking the British and American stories.[3] However, I do venture to claim that it is a methodology which has already been profitably used by Black students training for ministry. The testimony is always self-consciously White; I have tried hard to avoid attempting to be a White voice for Black people.

'UNDERSIDE OF HISTORY'

Some important words and phrases will recur in the book. I will speak, for example, of the *underside of history*.[4] History is usually written by the victors, by those powerful enough to make their understanding of events prevail and impose it on the vanquished. Thus when Afro-Caribbean settlers arrived in Britain they were better acquainted with the history of the British Empire than of their own countries, let alone Africa; Caribbean history syllabuses were not introduced until the 1960's.[5] Christian history is likewise usually written by missionaries and by the 'sending' churches, by those whose culture, priorities and categories of interpretation prevail. Thus when Afro-Caribbean Anglicans arrived in Britain they were far better instructed in the ways of the Church of England than in the religious heritage of Caribbean Black people.

Those whose story has been ignored and has thus remained unwritten constitute the 'underside' of history. Those Christians whose song, story and prayer has not been recognised constitute the 'underside' of Christian history. The culture and context in which they first became Christians (in the case of Afro-Caribbean Christians, their African roots and the 'crucible' of slavery) have been counted as of no positive theological significance; it was as if salvation depended on identification with the dominant church and cultural forms. In recent years, however, this has begun to change; the recipients are beginning to tell their own story and to write their own theology.[6] In Europe itself, nowadays, theology students must quickly master theological labels such as 'Feminist', 'Black', 'African', 'Min-jung' or 'Liberation' which were unheard of only twenty-five years ago.[7]

'COLLISION'

I will also speak of the *collision* of stories or of narratives, and of the interaction between them being *dialectical*. It would of course be more comfortable to use other words to describe the relationship between the White and Black stories, words like 'mutually enriching' or 'complementing'. But this would be to pass too quickly over a history which is self-evidently one of violent collision, and to ignore the way the dominant story has been used actually to suppress the self-understanding of the victims. That is to say the White story is 'ideological', for it gives a misleading *eidos* (= 'image' in Greek) of Black experience. It presents Black experience in a form which makes it recognizable to White people but at the same time mis-understands and conceals the real historical relationship between themselves and Black people.[8]

For a better and more nearly mutually acceptable story to be formed, it is necessary for the two stories to 'collide', to react with each other, like two chemicals in a chemistry experiment. When this happens, something of each has to be destroyed or *negated*: some-thing of each continues, is *preserved*, and something new is created, a *transformation* of what previously existed. Also, there is usually a release of heat and energy; perhaps costly and painful, but necessary to the act of new birth.

'BLACK' MEANING OPPRESSED

I have already made use of the word *Black* to denote a particular history and thus the community to whom that history belongs, hence the upper case. 'Black' is a complex term; it carries a reference to skin colour which is rarely an accurate description of pigmentation; it carries a reference to the scientifically undefinable concept of 'race', – our present 'races' being the product of varied movements of human beings.[9] And it carries a reference to culture but does not necessarily denote a clearly definable ethnic group. Fundamentally, 'Black' refers to the historical relationship between White European power and consciousness (slavery, colonialism and myths of racial superiority), and the Black people who were subjected to them. Since White power and consciousness still determine the relationship of White to Black in Britain, the use of the word takes us into a painful area, namely the existence of a *White oppressor* and a *Black victim*.

Many people, not having understood or accepted this definition, find the term 'Black Christianity' objectionable.[10] They fear it will 'create divisions', forgetting that division was long since created by White assault. They claim it 'divides Christ', forgetting that Christ in his incarnation had to assume a particular racial and socio-political identity, (Jesus the brown man of Galilee, a first-Century Jew, killed by the imperial occupying power in collaboration with the ruling class of his own people), and bear its consequences.

Christian faith, the system of belief, worship and cultural and religious characteristics which grew up around Jesus, has similarly to assume cultural and socio-political identities and bear their consequences. There is no other way to be 'in the world'. Of course, in practice it may not be so difficult to accept plurality of cultural expression, for example that there is 'Indian' or 'Polish' Christianity and that the two are different. But to speak of 'Black Christianity' is much more disturbing because it necessarily refers to a particular history of oppression and struggle; its meaning lies there. In examining it, both Black and White people have to reckon with the 'collision' of their two stories and journey through the 'heat' of the interaction between them; the reluctance is to that extent understandable.

The Black American theologian, Gayraud Wilmore, defines Black Christianity as 'the particular appropriation which Afro-Americans made of the religion that was first delivered to them by White Americans'.[11] By 'delivered' is meant not conventional missionary activity but the subjection of Black slaves to 'Christian' owners. Remembering that the thirteen American states were once British colonies like Jamaica or Barbados, we may add to 'American' the *British* rule of the Caribbean. We then have a workable definition of Black Christianity: *the particular appropriation which African people, brought into slavery in the historically British territories of North America and the Caribbean, made of the religion that was first delivered to them by White British or American people*. Black Christianity is the 'incarnation' of Christianity in the experience of Black people.

'BLACK' MEANING AFRICA AND THE NEW WORLD

At the same time I use 'Black' to denote 'Afro-American', 'Afro-Caribbean' or Afro-Caribbean-British people – those for whom the determining factors in their cultural and religious identity are their African heritage, slavery and subsequent White oppression. This accords with United States usage, as in the expressions 'Black Theology', 'Black Pride' or 'Black Consciousness'.[12] In Britain today, however, 'Black' often denotes all 'non-White' people, thus expressing the political solidarity between people of Asian, African and Afro-Caribbean origin, all of whom experience White racism. In later chapters, where I write of Britain today, this wider usage is inevitably encountered; for example 'Black Anglicans' include Afro-Caribbean-British people and others of a different inheritance not conditioned by slavery.

I have tried to recognise that there is ongoing debate among Black people on this issue,[13] and of course to acknowledge the right of people to name themselves. But in this book I limit my concern to Black Afro-Caribbean-British people; I do not examine the inheritance of other 'underside' people, for example the East Indian-Caribbean-British. They may, however find parallels with their own story.

'MAINSTREAM'

Finally, I follow common practice in using *mainstream* to denote the historic, White-led, established denominations. *Black-led* is a convenient term for the newer Pentecostal and Holiness churches with mainly Black congregations. However, 'mainstream' does not imply superiority or an ecclesial norm. I am aware that some White leadership is to be found in 'Black-led' churches, and that some 'mainstream' denominations, though majority-White as British churches, are majority-Black as world churches, whilst the reverse is true for some 'Black-led' denominations. No terminology is available which is entirely accurate and non-judgemental.

2
Discovering Black Christianity

If I, in telling my own story as a White priest of the Church of England, speak of 'discovering' Black Christianity, I do so in order to testify to a spiritual journey – to testify indeed to a kind of second conversion. It is not that I discovered some new phenomenon, a strange sect in an obscure backwater, but that I found a new significance within the familiar. As a V.S.O. teacher in the Caribbean country of Belize, I had already experienced how the history of the oppression of Blacks by Whites was still 'live' history, still an issue needing to be worked through and resolved: the attentiveness and 'body language' of the children in class had changed markedly when we left the 'dead' history of the Arawaks and Sir Francis Drake and turned to study the Slave Trade. But, although I worshipped each Sunday with a Black Anglican congregation and counted its members among my friends, I only perceived at that time Anglicans who happened to be Black. It was the time of the Civil Rights struggle in the United States, the progress of which I had followed carefully on television; even so I was not at that time really able to name the concept of a Black Christianity. The 'discovery' came in Birmingham, in ten years spent as one of the clergy of the Church of England parish of St. James, Aston, Birmingham.

AN INNER RING PARISH IN THE 1960's

The parish of St James', Aston had undergone in the post-war years a pattern of social change typical of many inner-ring churches in larger cities in Britain. The pattern consisted of a long period of slow decline, then a rapid acceleration of exodus and decline in response to Black immigration, the failure of the church to understand the significance of social change, increasingly desperate attempts to maintain existing congregational life, lack of resources for the development of new strategies of mission, an overtly racist general atmosphere (though with individual exceptions) and in spite of it all, the 'planting' of a small Black presence in the congregation.[1]

By the early 1950's, Aston had already assumed the character of an inner-ring area, home for skilled and unskilled working class people, of whom the more aspiring were moving out to the new municipal and private housing in the suburbs. Nonetheless, the 1954 St. James Annual Church Meeting was able to report a good number of thriving church organisations; there was a new Envelope Giving Scheme, a new Lay Reader and a popular new monthly Parish Communion service. There were 146 Easter Communicants, 83 Baptisms (including one Black child) and 29 Marriages (including six Black couples). Six years later, however, demolition and 'White flight' had brought first slow and then rapid change and decline in church life. Easter Communicants had declined by a third and some church organisations had closed. Also by 1961 'immigration' had become such an issue that the monthly tabloid *Birmingham Christian News*, sold city-wide by the Anglican diocese, produced a special issue on the topic. St. James', which normally sold something over 1,000 copies, ordered 5,000 of this issue for distribution.

At the 1962 Annual Church Meeting the Vicar, describing the parish as 'an exciting one due to its vast and inter-racial population,' exhorted members to 'realise the needs of the situation'. It is hard to imagine, however, how the dwindling congregation, already feeling threatened, could have responded to this call without the stimulus of outside resources and advice. The Vicar was in effect calling for a new strategy for mission, yet the outside resources hardly existed. (The Bishop of Birmingham had appointed The Revd. Paul Burrough as 'Chaplain to Overseas People', but he was too detached from main diocesan structures, too hard pressed supporting the ministry of a large number of parishes and too busy sustaining a much valued pastoral ministry with a formidable caseload, to enable parishes to develop new strategies).[2] An overtly racist general climate in the West Midlands, as highlighted in the Smethwick Election campaign of 1964, was certainly reflected in congregations despite the welcoming ministry of a few individuals.

In 1964 St. James' held a Stewardship Campaign. Though a considerable success both financially and in bringing new members into active church life, in retrospect it must be seen as an attempt to shore up the superstructure of a form of church life which was being eroded by social change. Within four years of the Campaign pledged income had halved and Parish Magazine sales were rapidly declining.

By 1972 we find a reduction of Easter Communicants to only 20% of their 1954 total, inability to manage the Church Hall, lack of volunteers for the office of Churchwarden, and choirboys so unruly that their complete dismissal was proposed at one Church Council meeting. Two extracts from Church Council minutes in 1971 and 1972 tell their own story:

> The Treasurer remarked that the financial outlook was not very bright, and the Vicar agreed. Manpower was, he said, very badly needed, and much needed to be done to the fabric of the church. Yet all the money from the Christmas Fair was needed to keep our heads above water.
>
> The Vicar said that some measure of misbehaviour was inevitable from the type of boy now coming forward and we had a duty to try to show a Christian outlook. He thought that until we had some adults in the choir the position would not improve. Members were not very happy about the situation at all. The Vicar mentioned the difficulties of the rising generation of coloured children, and that there was a danger of separation of white and coloured people. The church had a duty to help these people but was hampered by a great shortage of assistants. Mrs. W----suggested that one or two of the older members of the church sit with the choir during services, but the Vicar would only agree if these people robed in order to identify themselves with the choir.

However, even in these bleak years there were signs of life available to a church that could change – a church with which Black Anglicans could identify. Half of the 900 children baptised between 1962 and 1972 were Black, whilst almost half of the 190 marriages were of Black or mixed-race couples. Within the life of the congregation itself, seventeen out of nineteen people confirmed in 1972–3 were Black; there were two Black sidesmen, and two Black Church Council members – at least for one year. Two Black women taught in the Sunday School.

Basically, though, the Black presence was timid and peripheral, whilst the White congregation, mainly elderly, was reduced to a pitiful demoralisation, unable to manage or maintain its buildings, pay its way, or even keep the choir in order during divine service. It is a sad and moving story, painful and bewildering to live through, and one can only admire the tenacity and devotion of those both Black and White who survived it.

A BLACK-MAJORITY CONGREGATION

The new clergy team, John Austen, myself and my wife Renate (an ordained minister of the German Protestant Church), arrived at St. James in September 1974 together with three committed lay people. We were unaware of the heritage we were to have the privilege of harvesting. For behind the faithfulness of our predecessor through the years of rapid social change, and the ministry of Paul Burrough in the 1960's, lay the life of the Anglican Church in the Caribbean, and behind that the whole tradition of Black Christianity. At first, in the 'old church', intensely cold in winter with its broken windows, leaking gutters and the newspapers stacked in the north aisle for recycling, came a number of initiatives from both clergy and congregation: the re-forming of the choir by a number of Black youngsters, the introduction of a regular Parish Communion, the starting of a Junior Church and Youth Fellowship, as well as the beginnings of social outreach activities. It was, however, the tragic death of the single parent of four children, the youngest only eight, which brought our first vivid encounter with the Black Christian Tradition. At the funeral service over four hundred of the church's six hundred places were filled by mourners who rendered the traditional hymns with the free guttural tone characteristic of Black singing. Children and relatives sang and wept. Slowly the entire congregation, resplendent in the dignity of its formal funeral attire, took leave of the deceased as they filed past the open coffin. At the graveside the women again wept as the men filled in the grave and we all sang, 'We loved thee well, but Jesus loves thee best, Goodnight, Goodnight, Goodnight'. Afterwards crowds gathered at the family home, and the clergy led prayers before the serving of food and drink. It was our first Black funeral, taken because of the circumstances with perhaps especial care. Next Sunday the adult congregation doubled to 70 worshippers.

In the following three years, a new mainly Black congregation rapidly came into being. Organisational and pastoral structures were developed, and the first steps were taken towards the replacement of the ailing church building. A pre-school Playgroup and a parish Advice Centre, the latter mainly serving the Bangladeshi community, opened as church responses to local community need. But I still had little conceptual grasp of the history and content of Black Christianity. Naively, I believed that overcoming both the recent rejection of Black people and the fears of Black and White by means of welcome and fellowship would lead to the formation of a congregation whose life would then not be particularly different from a White one. And so it seemed for most of those first four years; a time of growth, consolidation and structuring.

By 1979, however, we were being forced to reckon with indications of the cultural difference between Black Anglicans and White Anglicans, the spiritual expression of that difference, and its grounding in the historical relationship of White to Black, namely that of oppressor to victim. Some indications were very positive: we experienced the power and articulateness of the Black tradition of free prayer, especially at prayer meetings, Bible study groups and in times of open intercession and thanksgiving at the daily Morning Prayer. We heard the Black style of singing revealed in certain hymns in particular, and were embraced by the warmth and openness of the Black community at family celebrations and observances such as Baptisms, birthdays, times of sickness or death. We learned more of the sharpness of the unexpected rejection by the 'mother country' and the 'mother church', the very image of 'mother' showing how deeply that rejection had injured the self-understanding of a people. Young people responded to Confirmation preparation and youth work which at least attempted to take their identity and experience seriously. They shared something of the struggles, from home, school and work, of growing up in a society which gave ambiguous and contradictory messages of its expectations. There was from so many people an unforgettable quality of love for me and my family, despite both my mistakes and the never-ending racism of the wider society. Above all, there was the sheer faith, gratitude and openness to God of Afro-Caribbean Christians.

Some indications were disturbing however: some young people, apparently settled in church life, left not only church but home as well at the age of sixteen to become Rastafarians. Black parents anxiously pressed the clergy to 'do youth work' but their ideas of what that would entail sprang more from the Caribbean past than from an understanding of the difficulties of young Black people growing up in a complex and White-dominated society. With one or two exceptions, responsibility and leadership were taken up only slowly, and despite the efforts of the clergy it was not until 1982 that Blacks were equally represented with Whites on the Church Council, although the congregation had been Black-majority since 1976. Even the happy emergence of the Black Tradition more openly in the life of the church, as with the two women mentioned in the last chapter, served to demonstrate the spiritual riches that had previously been suppressed and stifled. At times it was necessary to challenge the apparently conservative firmly-held theology of older Black members in the interests of responding to problems and questions raised by their children.

No doubt my 'discovering' was a gradual process, the fruit primarily of pastoral ministry, of years of listening to the hurts and afflictions of Black people, during which time I had been constantly surprised and inspired by the spiritual resources which the Black Christian Tradition brought to their suffering. But it was two overseas theologians who gave me the vital conceptual framework with which I could begin to make theological sense of my experience. Their work has remained for me a vivid demonstration of the importance of 'committed' academic theology to the practice of mission and ministry, for without it I would have soon reached the point of simply not knowing what to do. The first was the German theologian Gerhard Kamphausen from Hamburg who in 1982 gave the annual Cadbury Lectures at Birmingham University. He introduced me to the key category 'Black Christianity', and to its story.[3]

The second was the American Black theologian Gayraud Wilmore. In 1983 he led a consultation, *Black Religious Experience in a Cross-Cultural Perspective*, at Overstone College, the New Testament Church of God college near Northampton. He painted a picture of the Black Christian Tradition, a part of the Christian story which, as he told us, is missing from almost all White scholarship. He outlined its history, theology, and religious and liturgical characteristics. He then described Black-British Christianity (or 'Afro-Caribbean – British Christianity') – the story of the Afro-Christian stream entering a new stage of the Black Diaspora. This was marked by the 'collision' of what was brought, including membership of mainstream churches and the Afro-Christian heritage now much influenced by North American Pentecostal/Evangelical Christianity, with the British situation, especially the 'shock' of meeting racism and decaying Christianity in Britain and the 'shattering experience' of rejection in British Churches.

So Black Christianity developed in Britain its own institutions, the Black-led churches. But these were to be understood as far more than simply a response to rejection. Black Christianity, now finding open expression in these churches, was a positive heritage fashioned in suffering and rooted in Africa, and was therefore characterized by a pervasive sense of God as a living force, by attractiveness, joy, liveliness and warmth, and by worship characterised by the 'experiential rise of the human spirit to meet the descending grace of the Divine'. Black British Christians inherited a vision of the church as people rather than building or hierarchy and maintained a universal vision with little division between sacred and secular. Their use of Scripture should not be mistaken for the fundamentalism of White conservative evangelicals; the Bible was rather a 'storehouse of information' about human relationships and God's work of liberating His people, a work in which the Exodus, Exile, Cross and Pentecost were the key and definitive events. This was a rich heritage; it could be offered, but not sacrificed, to the wider church.

It was immediately clear that, although members of our congregation had opted to remain in a 'mainstream' church and in many cases had their own criticisms of 'Black-led' churches, this description resonated with, and indicated an explanation of, the spiritual tradition that was manifesting itself through – or was it in spite of? – its Anglican form.

BLACK CHRISTIANITY

Further study showed me that this dynamic Christian tradition was alive wherever the African diaspora of the Caribbean and North America had settled. It was a tradition which had developed through interaction with White oppression, a process through which an enduring and tested inheritance had emerged. This inheritance may be summarized under five headings, the five 'plumblines' (Amos 7[7]) or measuring rods (Revelation 21[15]) of authentic Black Christianity.

Firstly, Black Christian faith is rooted in *Africa*, in God's creative act in fashioning the peoples of Africa, and in the revelation of himself which he has given to Africans, and which they have appropriated in the 'primal vision' of African traditional religion.[4] This world view, which pre-dates the coming of Christianity,[5] has been sustained and transmitted in story, song, dance and ceremony, without written liturgy, creed or scripture. Africans have developed a profound belief in the continuous involvement of the spirit world in all the affairs of daily life. Yet behind the sacrifice and spirit possession, dances, dreams, visions and the mediation of the 'medicine-man' and the ancestors, there is the belief in the one High God, Creator and sustainer of the universe, provider and healer of his people. African traditional religion is about experiencing the spiritual power of God, and appropriating it for life.[6] It is this African heritage which first corrected and purified White Christianity. It constitutes for Black people the cultural and historical roots of their own humanity; essential source material for their theology of creation.

Secondly, Black Christian faith is rooted in an encounter with a new name, the 'name above all names' which was hitherto unknown to Black people, the *name of Jesus*. Jesus, 'de Lawd', was encountered as One who could give divine power to the believer, which the slaves appropriated to affirm their 'somebodiness',[7] their dignity as human beings. With the help of Jesus they were able to survive the traumas

13

of bondage ('nobody knows but Jesus'[8]); with his help they could struggle to be free. The slaves firmly believed that, as the spiritual says, 'God will make a way out of no way'[9]. The Jesus encountered in Black faith is the Jesus of history who took upon himself the fullness not only of humanity but of *oppressed* humanity. Born human, he was also born poor; living on earth he also had 'nowhere to lay his head' (Lk.9[58]); dying the death of a human being, he also died the death of a tortured political criminal. This same Jesus is risen from the dead, triumphing over the forces of death and 'destroying the works of the devil' (1 John 3[8]). He is present in the worship of the Black Church, giving believers the strength to survive, walking with them in their suffering. And he will come again to consummate their struggle for liberation. Because of the victory he has already won and his presence with his people now, the struggles for justice are directly related to the coming judgement. Without this Christology rooted in the full humanity of the historical Jesus, Black Christian religion would be, as the Black American theologian James Cone puts it, 'nothing but an account of black people's subjective fantasies.'[10]

Thirdly, Black Christian faith is a *religion of the Spirit*. It is by the Spirit that God possessed the first believers and gave them the 'liberated zone' of ecstatic worship, with its song, dance, testimony and other expressions of the feelings of deepest sorrow and joy. Black worship, theology and church structures are therefore not dependent on White church tradition, however time-honoured, and do not require White authentication. In this sense they are, like the Gospel which Paul received, not a 'human invention, not received or taught by any man' (Gal.1[10]) but revealed in the Spirit. Without the Spirit who is freedom, Black Christianity would still be under the 'law', the life-denying ordinances, including ecclesiastical ones, of White domination.

Fourthly, Black Christian faith is a *liberation faith* arising out of necessary response to concrete historical experience. It rejects any separation of Christian faith from history. Its truth is disclosed not through speculative theology but through participation in the suffering and struggles of the oppressed. It rejects any doctrine of salvation which is divorced from the liberation of the oppressed, and it rejects any spirituality consisting of 'spiritual practices' or 'spiritual method' which claim to give contact with a spiritual world separate from history.[11] Its liberative praxis is a praxis of love, rooted in the Black affirmation of the love of God. Martin Luther King makes clear that 'strength to love' is a constant element in the tradition:

> By its very nature hate destroys and tears down; by its very nature love creates and builds up. Love transforms with redemptive power.[12]

14

Equally, a constant element is the demands of love on others, as the preacher of Maya Angelou's childhood, expounding 1 Cor. 13, makes very plain:

> 'As I understand it, charity vaunteth not itself, is not puffed up.' He blew himself up with a deep breath to give us the picture of what Charity was not. 'Charity don't go around saying, "I give you food and by rights you ought to thank me."'
>
> The congregation knew whom he was talking about and voiced agreement with his analysis. 'Tell the truth, Lord.'
>
> 'Charity don't say, "Because I give you this job, you got to bend your knee to me."' The church was rocking with each phrase. 'It don't say, "Because I pays you what you due, you got to call me master." It don't ask me to humble myself and belittle myself. That ain't what Charity is.'[13]

Lastly, Black Christian faith has a *vision of a new future*; though historical, it is not bound by history. We see this in the use made of the idea of 'heaven', which was, as James Cone tells us, judgement on White oppression and an affirmation of humanity in spite of oppression.[14] But it was more than that; it was an anticipation of future freedom now, and the certainty that that freedom would be achieved. For there will be an inescapable time of judgement, which the community of believers can welcome with confidence, when a verdict will be given against the wicked. Who constitute this 'beloved community'? The answer is: the oppressed community struggling for its freedom in faith. And this is not ultimately a matter of skin colour. For whilst some Black people may betray the struggle, there is a place for Whites who, in James Cone's words, 'undergo the true experience of conversion wherein they die to Whiteness and are re-born in order to struggle against White oppression and for the liberation of the oppressed'.[15]

A PERSONAL RESPONSE

How could I respond to my 'discovery'? It took only a little reflection to see the extent to which the Church of England (and other 'mainstream' churches) had failed to understand the distinctive identity of its Black members. I began to realise how deprived Black people are in the Church. In theory the resources of the Church were available for all. In practice, however, there was an important sense in which they were not usable by Black people; they were available in a meaningful way only for people who could identify as White. For example, appropriate Junior Church materials did not exist; musicians able to co-ordinate and lead the yearning of Black youngsters in our congregation to praise God in the tradition of Black Christian music could not be found. It was little use going to Diocesan officers or other established church resources for help, as they had normally little or no experience of Black culture or spiritual tradition. The basic lack, however, was of Black Anglican community, theology and consciousness. Black Anglicans had not come together to 'name' themselves, to acknowledge each other as a historic community of faith with a distinctive experience and distinctive resources. Therefore there could be no articulation of an appropriate theology: nowhere in Britain was it then possible for 'mainstream' Black Christians to study theology on the explicit basis of a Black identity.[16] Pastoral ministry had shown me that Black identity is confirmed and Black Christianity lived every day in the life of Black people, using the resources of the Tradition to combat and overcome their on-going experience of White racism. But what did this mean for Black people in the Church of England? Without a self-conscious community and an articulated theology arising out of it, how could they have a future? It now became clear why Black Anglicans in Britain had thus far produced so few candidates for full-time ministry.

My response took two forms. Firstly, realising that there was little prospect of Black ministerial leadership being available through the normal channels of full-time ministry, I called together a group from St. James' and from the wider church to create a post for a Black lay pastoral assistant. This post would involve training 'on the job', being rooted in the local situation and devised specially for it. The parish subsequently employed a young woman from the congregation as 'church neighbourhood worker'. Her funding came from the Birmingham Inner City Partnership and from the Church Missionary Society, not from diocesan sources. Simon Barrington-Ward, General Secretary of C.M.S., wrote of her:

> This young woman and others like her must have a vital future in the church and be encouraged to enable scattered or battered black Church [of England] members to rise up and challenge the Body of Christ in Britain.[17]

My second response was to apply for the position of Research Fellow at Queen's College, an ecumenical theological college in Birmingham. I had already written *Black Anglicans in Birmingham*, a history of the response of the Diocese of Birmingham to the arrival of

Anglicans from the West Indies in the post-war period, and in 1984 my wife Renate completed *A Chance to Change*, a sociological study of the present position of Black people in the Church of England in the Diocese. These works showed that there was both a heritage and a present constituency (one in ten of all adult Anglicans in the Birmingham Diocese being Black) worthy of further study. The Fellowship allowed me time to lay the foundations for this book in which I reflect on what it means to be a church of Black and White people, and seek to uncover the living voice of Black Anglicanism.

3

English Christianity and Black People

FROM PREJUDICE TO RACISM

The second story is that of the Church of England and of 'main-stream' White English Christianity in relation to Black people. To understand the story, we must set it within the history of British expansion into Africa and British acquisition of territories in North America and the Caribbean.

Why did the British begin to enslave Africans and carry them to the New World? Firstly, it was made possible by the European tradition of race prejudice against Black people which sixteenth-century Britain, like the rest of Western European Christendom, had inherited. For almost a thousand years Christian Europe had found itself threatened by Moslem 'blackamoors', just as the Vandal and Vizigoth barbarians had once threatened the Roman Empire. The story of that Empire remained the model for White European identity, power and 'civilization', whilst Blackness was associated with the 'uncivilized' outside the gate who threatened to conquer and destroy. Furthermore, as Peter Fryer describes in his monumental *Staying Power: The History of Black People in Britain*, Blackness 'traditionally stood for death, mourning, baseness, evil, sin and danger', and was the colour of the Devil himself.[1] These images mingled with ancient bizarre and fantastic tales to produce images of beasts, monsters and savages, physically strong, lustful, treacherous, idle and cannibalistic. At the same time there developed the contra-dictory, image of the 'noble savage' and 'grateful Negro'. As Fryer observes, these prejudices, including those allegedly based on observations in Africa, 'tell us more about the White men – and women – who did the writing than about the Negroes who did the suffering'.[2] John Griffin, a White American who in the 1960's dyed his skin black and lived as a Negro, found many of these folk fantasies

18

alive and well in the oral tradition of White America.[3] White European and North American prejudice about Africans has ancient roots. All this explains why Black people were seen as inferior beings, at best marginal to the human community. Rationally examined, it is shown to be a scrappy and self-contradictory orally transmitted bundle of traditions, a classic folk *superstition*.

A second reason, namely the *drive for wealth*, is necessary to explain why British merchant capitalists first sought human captive labour in Africa. Of course other European nations also took part in the slave trade; indeed all countries which took part in colonial expansion from the end of the fifteenth century onwards were at some point slave traders. However, since by 1700 British imperialism was already in the ascendant over its main rival, Spain, Britain became the country whose name is most linked with slavery, from which it profited hugely. The great ports of London, Bristol and Liverpool grew prosperous on the profits of slavery, whilst the capital and the banking institutions which financed the Industrial Revolution came substantially from the same source.[4] As the merchant Joshua Gee wrote in 1779:

> The supplying our Plantations with Negroes is of that extraordinary advantage to us, that the planting of Sugar and Tobacco, and carrying on Trade there could not be supported without them, which Plantations . . . are the great Cause of the Increase of the Riches of the Kingdom . . . All this great Increase of our Treasure proceeds chiefly from the Labour of Negroes in the Plantations.[5]

The need for wealth, planted in the fertile soil of racial prejudice, gave rise to a relatively systematic and internally consistent *dogma* about race, which was structured and transmitted to a great extent through the printed word. This dogma is called *racism*.[6]

The second half of the seventeenth century saw the first written evidence of *plantocracy racism* – not so much in the planters' own writings as in the quotation of their views by religious opponents. The aim of these Christian writers was not to oppose slavery as such, but to establish the humanity of Black people and their fitness for conversion and baptism. Outstanding among them is Morgan Godwyn, a priest in Barbados, author of *The Negro's and Indian's advocate* (1680). He quotes planters who equal Black people with animals, as in the case of the slaveowner who cried, 'What, those black Dogs be made Christians? What, shall they be like us?' and asked whether the minister would start baptizing horses.[7]

Peter Fryer examines a key passage from Godwyn, which, he says, tells us five things about this early stage of English racism: first of all, racist ideology was created by the planters and slave-merchants out of 'avarice'; second, it was spread at first in whispers, furtively; third, by 1680 it had become respectable enough for its propagators in England to have come into the open, though not yet in print; fourth, opponents of racism were as yet few and uninfluential; and lastly, one of racism's functions was to justify the planters and merchants in their own eyes as well as in the eyes of the rest of society. Godwyn says it stopped them feeling guilty about what they were doing to their slaves.[8]

These Christian writers were not yet abolitionists, but they raised the first serious voice against the racism that was at the root of slavery, whilst exposing its foundations as not simply prejudice, but lust for power and wealth.

Before long openly racist writing began to appear. The two great empiricist philosophers, John Locke (1632–1704) and David Hume (1711–1776) both supported slavery. Both were racially prejudiced whilst Hume had a crudely racist understanding of the innate inferiority of Black people.[9] It is, however, Edward Long whom Fryer cites as the 'father of English racism'. In his *History of Jamaica* (1774) Long gives an account of the allegedly sub-human status of Black people in which political, social and sexual fears, which pre-figure modern racism in striking detail, are made clear. It is not only an appalling diatribe of prejudice and misinformation; it fits into and supports the overall economic argument which underlay slavery and its handmaid ideology, racism. The editor's introduction to a modern reprint of Long's book includes a convenient summary of Long's views on slavery:

That the trade in slaves and in goods produced by slaves was immensely profitable, not only to the West Indies, but to Britain itself and that it greatly enriched Englishmen in all walks of life; that West Indian slavery was, on the whole, a mild and benevolent institution and that slaves were better off than the lowest classes in Britain; that negro slavery was inevitable and necessary in certain regions of the world; that the slave trade benefited and helped to civilise Africa; that virtually all the slaves were originally convicted criminals; that in every mental and moral way negroes were absolutely inferior to white men, and that the most constructive thing which could happen to them was to be compelled to work productively.[10]

20

Fryer traces the development of racism from this plantocracy racism to the '*pseudo-scientists*', writers who, in an age when Britain was facing the new task of ruling territories with 'natives' in them, produced grossly subjective classifications of the human race. Some scientists are now seen to have played an important part in the development of biological science, a fact which makes their racism the more grotesque. The Swedish botanist Linnaeus, for example, who laid the basis for the modern classification of plants and animals, also produced the following descriptions which first appeared in English in 1792:

> *H. Europaei.* Of fair complexion, sanguine temperament, and brawny form . . . Of gentle manners, acute in judgement, of quick invention and governed by fixed laws . . .
> *H. Afri.* Of black complexion, phlegmatic temperament, and relaxed fibre . . . Of crafty, indolent and careless disposition, and are governed in their actions by caprice. – Anoint the skin with grease.[11]

Racism was therefore not the preserve of a cranky or extreme minority. On the contrary, Fryer claims that 'virtually every scientist and intellectual in nineteenth-century Britain took it for granted that only people with white skin were capable of thinking and governing.' But however would-be 'scientific' racism became, it remained linked to its primary function, namely, the pursuit of wealth and power. 'Racist' rhetoric was also commonly employed against the 'lower orders' at home, both English working people and the Irish.[12]

Fryer gives eight broad headings under which nineteenth-century racism may be understood, which it is important to note, as the attitudes developed in this period have shaped the outlook of the present century.[13] *Phrenology*, the pseudo- science by which people's characters are told from the shape of their skulls was used to detect the 'inferiority' of Black people, whilst a *teleological* argument, sometimes linked to the 'curse of Ham' theory, affirmed that Black people were created to be servants of Whites.[14] A kind of racial *evolutionism* held that 'lesser races' could not withstand the White race, and were destined to die out. As one anatomist wrote,

> Destined by the nature of their race, to run, like all other animals, a certain limited course of existence, it matters little how their extinction is brought about.[15]

Anthropologists meanwhile found 'evidence' that Black people were nearer to apes than to Europeans, whilst *social – Darwinists* distorted the theory of evolution to show that the White race was 'fittest' to survive. 'White' was narrowed to 'British' by what Fryer terms *Anglo-Saxonists*, those who believed that Britain had a God-given destiny to rule the world, of which the theologically dubious jingoism of 'Rule, Britannia!' is a well-known example. At first sight less repugnant was *trusteeship*, the belief that power should be exercised over colonial peoples for their ultimate benefit. It was an ideal which no doubt tamed the worst excesses of Empire and inspired behaviour which, at an individual level, could be considered self-sacrificial. But trusteeship provided a moral justification for colonialism, which, whilst preferable to slavery, was blind to the culture and identity of the 'natives'. Fryer comments:

> the British who ruled them owed a special obligation, not unlike the obligation that decent Englishmen owed to women, children and dumb animals.[16]

Trusteeship is summed up in Kipling's famous verse, 'The White Man's Burden':

> Take up the White Man's burden,
> Send forth the best ye breed.
> Go, bind your sons to exile
> To serve your captives need;
> To wait in heavy harness,
> On fluttered folk and wild –
> Your new-caught, sullen peoples,
> Half devil and half child.[17]

Finally, Fryer describes the *vulgar racism* and prejudice with which Black people were described in popular literature, including children's books, where humanity was divided into three 'races': 'us', 'foreigners' (non-British Whites, including the Irish) and 'niggers'.

The British Empire is now part of history, but the final phase of its expansion, in which some of the most extreme expressions of racist ideology were formulated, took place only a hundred years ago. Though the conditions which gave rise to that era of racism have disappeared, 'these dead ideas went on gripping the minds of the living.'[18] They helped to shape the church life of Black people in colonial churches, as well as the White response to the British subjects, Anglicans and others, who arrived from the Caribbean in the years following 1948.

FROM 'REPLACEABLE TOOL' TO 'CHILD OF EMPIRE'

How did English Christianity, and in particular the Church of England, respond to slavery and to racism? Since the Church of England was most bound up with the ruling classes, its involvement with slavery is deeper, more thorough and longer-lasting than that of other denominations. However it should be noted that all denominations in Britain had members who owned or traded in slaves; this includes even Quakers: 84 Quaker slave-traders were operating in London in 1756.[19]

The radical nature of the de-humanization involved in Protestant English slavery may be understood from a comparison with its Catholic equivalent. Spanish and Portuguese slavery at least involved some recognition of the humanity of its victims. Baptism and consequent eternal salvation were regarded as sufficient compensation for loss of freedom. S.M. Elkins writes:

> It was not a question of the planting class 'permitting' the slave under rigidly specified conditions to take part in divine worship. It was rather a matter of the Church's insisting – under its own conditions – that masters bring their slaves to church and teach them religion.[20]

The Spanish Slave Code, though not always adhered to, obliged a master to instruct slaves and have them baptised within their first year of residence in Spanish territory. Thus it was assumed that slaves were more than property, that in the end they shared the spiritual identity and destiny of their masters. The Code established a slave's rights and position in society, including a variety of ways in which freedom could be obtained. Marriage was permitted, and the integrity of the slave family protected. A substantial class of free Blacks and mulattoes arose, some gaining considerable prominence in society.[21]

Protestant slavery, however involved a radical denial and destruction of Black people's humanity. We have noted above the radical nature of the racism of the English planters. Its consequence was a denial of the humanity of Black people, the refusal of Baptism, and the almost absolute power of the master over a slave's body, with virtually no restriction on punishment. The integrity of the family was ignored and slave marriage had no moral or legal standing. Such laws as existed were the product of the local planters' legislature, not the British Government – let alone the Church – and their enforcement depended more on the planters than the Governor. The laws aimed to prevent only extremes of cruelty, as in the case of Antigua's 1724 act against the 'murdering, maiming and castrating of slaves'.[22] Fines were light and not always imposed. Later, the killing of a slave did become a capital offence but conviction was rarely secured. Basically slaves were 'things' – in the words of a 1674 Jamaican law, 'goods and chattels'. A slave had no soul, no culture, no humanity. As Gayraud Wilmore puts it:

> Black slavery . . . was a deliberate system of cultural and psychological genocide. Every connection with the past was to be obliterated and the slaves were so thoroughly dehumanized and brainwashed that they would forget that he or she had been anything other than Nigger John or Nigger Mandy created by God, as the early slave catechisms taught, 'to make a crop'.[23]

Identity, in short was to be destroyed, and to be replaced by nothing except the identity of 'replaceable tool'.

The teaching and practice of the Church of England did not seriously challenge this state of non-being, of invisibility except as 'necessary implement'. On the other hand, the Church as such did not actually teach such a negative doctrine, and was never entirely without witness to Black people's status as human beings made in the image of God. We have already noted the writings and ministry of Morgan Godwyn. Eighteen years earlier, the 1662 Book of Common Prayer had made incidental mention of Black people as potential candidates for Baptism; as the Preface explains:

> An office for the Baptism of such as are of Riper Years . . . by growth of Anabaptism . . . is now become necessary, and may always be useful for the baptising of Natives (*sic!*) in our Plantations.

Charles II's 1660 instructions to the Council for Foreign Plantations commended the conversion, baptism and Christian instruction of the slaves as 'being to the honour of our Crowne and of the Protestant Religion'.[24]

In practice, however, God sailed with the White English, who denied their slaves even the knowledge of that God. Cape Castle, in what is now Ghana, was built in 1664. Its thirteen grim dungeons in which slaves awaiting transportation were kept survive to this day for visitors to inspect. A grill from the roof of a dungeon leads through to the floor of the chapel.[25] The film series 'Roots' depicts the rape of an African woman by the captain of a slave-ship. Above his bed, a Bible lies on the shelf, vividly illustrating the situation in which many Black women were first brought face to face with a symbol of the Christian religion.[26] For years very few slaves were baptised, not least because of the popular rumour that the sacrament conferred freedom. The Church, however, was clear that it did not. Planters and missionaries alike agreed with the infamous affirmation of Thomas Sherlock, later Bishop of London, that 'Christianity and the embracing of the Gospel does not make the least difference in civil property'.[27]

The Church of England's commitment to, or even interest in, the slaves was therefore fragmentary and ineffectual, and among its ordained clergy the best that could be found were occasional attempts at evangelism and the affirmation that Black people were at least human beings. However, its ministry among the planters was scarcely more commendable. In 1740 Leslie in his *History of Jamaica* describes the clergy as 'except for a few . . . generally the most finished of our debauchers'.[28] As late as 1822 there were only twelve clergy of the Established Church on the island of Jamaica. As a modern Caribbean writer puts it, 'The Church of England was a White man's church, but he usually gave it only a nominal allegiance'.[29]

Such evangelising of the slaves as did take place was largely the work of the Society for the Propagation of the Gospel in Foreign Parts (S.P.G.), founded in 1701 on the initiative of Thomas Bray.[30] S.P.G. sought to minister to the colonists of the West Indies and North America, and to *instruct* the Indians and Negroes. 'Instruction' or *catechesis* involved teaching the basic doctrines of the Christian faith, including the Creed, the Lord's Prayer and the Ten Commandments, 'and to baptize them as soon as they are sufficiently instructed and willing to receive baptism.'[31] And indeed, examples of slave baptisms and catechesis are found here and there. Thus Ebenezer Taylor, who worked in South Carolina from 1711 to 1717 records hearing a number of slaves give a good account of their Christian faith, as well as rehearsing the Creed, the Lord's Prayer and the Ten Commandments by heart. 'They were so desirous to be baptized', he adds, 'that I thought it my duty to do it on the last Lord's Day.'[32]

Such developments depended, of course, on the goodwill of the slaveowners. Those who thus co-operated in the evangelising catechesis of their slaves were at least granting them a status, minimal indeed, but above that of 'replaceable tool'. Raboteau quotes Frank Klingberg:

The complete cycle of a sacramental progression from baptism to burial, with a special training of each successive step between, including the learning of the white man's language, might not be a legal emancipation, but was nevertheless a participation in the white man's folk ways amounting to something like a tribal adoption.[33]

He adds that this 'stepbrotherhood' could result in situations of religious reciprocity. At best it was a kind of socialisation into White social order and religious practices, and, compared to denial of Black humanity, it was a step forward.

The Codrington estate in Barbados is the best example of the possibility of this method. In 1710 Christopher Codrington, a leading planter left his estate, including its slaves to S.P.G. who then attempted to run the estate with (as a Barbadian historian remarks) 'the same social order, but new values'.[34] Blacks were included in the missionary work of conversion, and allowed positions of trust and responsibility. These policies aroused opposition from planters and local clergy, foreshadowing the struggles of the bishops of Barbados in the next century, not least the interpretation of Codrington's will.

Generally, however, *catechesis* was not a successful method of Christianization. Most planters were hostile and most slaves were suspicious and apathetic, as the religion preached by the Church had little to offer either side. For the planters, even the most minimal admission of spiritual fellowship could have revolutionary implications, not least because some slaves believed that Baptism conferred freedom. For the slaves it was quickly exposed as offering little as a religion of survival, and nothing at all as a religion of hope for liberation in this life. It validated rather than restricted the slave-masters' total and arbitrary power. It wasted time on Sunday which could be better spent in rest, leisure activities, or in working on small plots of land allotted to them. It failed to bring even the minimum protection which might be expected: for example, lifelong Christian marriage was not available to slaves so long as planters retained the power to separate slave families. This was partly because it taught submission to the existing system (as one former slave complained, 'The White preacher, just tell us not to steal master's chickens; they never preach the Lord to us.'), and partly because it totally ignored the slaves' African heritage which remained the repository of their human identity. For this reason they would not give up their drumming, obeah, myalism and other marks of their African past.[35]

We shall later see, however, that the emergence of authentic Black Christianity owed little to Anglican *catechesis* except in the important (if mainly negative) sense that it convinced the slaves that locked away within the Scriptures and the tradition of the Church was a truth which was being withheld from them. This truth they later discovered for themselves, often at great personal risk. Black Christianity's debt to White Christianity is rather to the Great Awakening in North America and to the Non-conformist missionary enterprises in both North America and the Caribbean which flowed from the Evangelical Revival in eighteenth-century Europe. The attempt to subjugate the intellect by *catechesis* was no match for the engagement of the whole personality in the fervour of the camp-meeting Revival with repentance and conversion.

Towards the end of the Eighteenth century new currents began to flow in the Church of England itself as the Evangelical movement became established there. This development was part of a much broader movement for social and political change in Britain which was to blossom fully in the reforms of 1828 to 1836. One of the most powerful signs for both Church and state was the Abolitionist movement which included Wilberforce and other leading Church of England Evangelicals. The Abolition of the slave trade in 1807, the attempt at a policy of Amelioration of slavery in 1825 and the three major slave uprisings of this period (in Barbados, 1816; Demerara, 1823 and Jamaica, 1831) were sure signs of the approaching end of the era of *slavery*, and of the new era of *colonialism* which was to replace it.

The British government's Amelioration policy led to considerable conflict between the Colonial Office and the West Indian planters' Assemblies. The Colonial Office therefore sought to reform and strengthen the Church for the new era. In 1824 Canning made the long overdue appointment of two Bishops for the West Indies: Christopher Lipscomb for Jamaica, Bahamas and Honduras, and William Hart Coleridge for Barbados, the Leeward Islands, Trinidad and Guiana.[36] Both Bishops took a stand against racial discrimination and against the defenders of slavery when the controversy was at its height. These appointments signalled the end of the old slavemaster Anglicanism. For the next twenty years the Church Missionary Society made a major effort to provide schools on the plantations. In Barbados S.P.G. and Coleridge's successor, Parry, won a famous victory over the planters in successfully maintaining the terms of Codrington's will, namely that a school and college should be established for the mission of the Church and the benefit of the people, rather than as a grammar school for planters' sons. Bishop Mitchinson (1873–81) carried reforms even further, applying the principles of Britain's Education Act of 1870 to Barbados. Even so late in the nineteenth century, however, he found it necessary frequently to reprimand not only the apathetic upper classes, but also lazy clergy.[37]

Barbados has remained a predominantly Anglican island, unique in that it specifically established the Anglican Church at a time when dis-establishment was taking place in other islands; an arrangement which lasted until 1969, three years after independence. Strong Anglican churches have developed in the Leeward Islands, which there as in Barbados have managed to include a relatively wide social spectrum in their membership. This is possible within the confines of small territories with modest populations and little free land available outside the plantations. Jamaica, however, is a much larger island; the slaves therefore had a much greater opportunity to leave the plantations after Emancipation and live life on their own terms as peasant farmers. A pattern developed there in which there is considerable correlation of denomination and social status within a very plural religious situation. So, although the Church of England in Jamaica was dis-established in 1870, it continued to be identified with colonial rule, and its membership remains predominantly though not wholly upper and middle class. It should be noted, however, that the challenge of dis-establishment and the consequent loss of state funding was faced energetically: between 1870 and 1890 Anglican Church membership doubled, the education system was developed, local ministerial training introduced and the autonomous Province of the West Indies was established with the Bishop of Jamaica, Enos Nuttall (1880–1916) as its first Archbishop. A Caribbean church history describes this period as the heyday of colonialism both for church and state, and names the period, in honour of one of the churches' 'most distinguished representatives', 'the age of Enos Nuttall'.[38]

So, as part of the process of Emancipation, the Anglican Church came to accept the spiritual equality of Black people and this development marked, for the Church, the transition from slavery to colonialism, from plantocracy to rule from London. It was, however, a gradual process, which had begun before Emancipation, and was not completed until long afterwards when, in the wake of the Morant Bay Rebellion of 1866 (see p. 73) and the outcry which followed its brutal suppression, the Colonial Office forced the political sub-mission of the old plantocracy, and abolished the planters' Assemblies. Colonialism did not, however, solve the question of *identity*; the Church continued to treat Black people as culturally inferior, as children to be cared for perhaps, but to be kept in their place. Although they were now admitted to have souls, their cultural tradition, which is the vessel of a people's humanity, was as invisible as ever. Noel Erskine describes the enthusiasm with which Black people looked to the churches to re-order society after Emancipation, but continues:

The Anglican Church, which was favoured by the establishment, saw their task as a slow process of civilizing black people. It adopted a cautious approach to giving any responsibility to black people . . . who were allowed to 'rise to the humbler positions of lay readers, catechists and, of course, school masters'.[39]

Education was used to bridge the gap between Africa and Europe, but did it in such a way that 'education became the guarantee that society would not change'. The Church aimed by education to produce a Black person reconciled to the plantation system, whereas 'the challenge confronting Black people was how their new-won freedom could become the means whereby they could regain their human dignity'.[40]

It should not be inferred from these words of Erskine that under slavery Black people had surrendered and abandoned their struggle. The story of resistance to slavery is one of persistent refusal to accept the White definition of Black existence. Black people sustained within themselves an alternative consciousness rooted in Africa and a perennial longing for freedom which continued to inspire the struggle against slavery, whether in the form of passive resistance, escape into 'marronage', or outright rebellion (see p. 43). Similarly, in the colonial period which followed, the struggle continued beneath the *Pax Britannica*, and issued forth from time to time in the form of Afro-Christian religious creativity, in Black nationalism, in rebellion and eventually in the independence movements.

However, in the process of resistance, both under slavery and colonialism, the Black community underwent profound changes. Not only were most of the outward, tangible aspects of African culture, such as language, religion and family and tribal structures substantially eroded, but the values and culture of the colonial power were deeply internalised by individuals and society. After Emancipation, when the British Empire must have seemed invincible, a cultural accommodation with the dominant culture was inevitable.

Even today, the struggle for a de-colonised consciousness is far from complete in the Caribbean, in Britain and even in the United States, as ample Black evidence testifies. The Black American 'womanist' writer Alice Walker, for example, writes of 'the Black community's dirty little secret', of a deep seated preference for so-called 'good' (i.e. straight) hair and a marriage partner of lighter skin.[41] This is but an illustration of the need to liberate consciousness. It is a need of which Bob Marley sang, in the celebrated lines from perhaps the best known of all his songs:

Emancipate yourselves from mental slavery,
None but ourselves can free our minds.[42]

The most thorough treatment of this theme has come from the
French-speaking Caribbean, in Frantz Fanon's passionate study
Black Skin, White Masks, in which he seeks to analyze the psychological predicament of 'millions of men who have been skilfully
injected with fear, inferiority complexes, trepidation, servility,
despair, abasement' in its all religious, sexual and cultural dimensions.[43]

A parallel theme is found in the writings of Caribbean theologians.
Thus Kortright Davis speaks of the 'perversion of values' that
plantation society engendered and describes the 'cultural alienation'
which has resulted:

> Under a dominant policy which stressed their natural inferiority
> and the inconsequential nature of their basic cultural heritage,
> Caribbean people became mutually contemptuous. They began to
> assume that anything foreign and white was good, whereas that
> which was local and non-white was not good enough. People
> became institutionally and systematically alienated from their own
> inherent characteristics and their own natural cultural endow-
> ments (race, color, language, belief systems, relationships, pre-
> ferences, entertainment and leisure, work schedules, family mores,
> aspirations), and also from their rightful access to the corridors of
> power, social mobility, and participatory citizenship.[44]

Ashley Smith writes of the implications of the colonial legacy for
education, for theology and for the church. In a recent paper he
describes the role of the Church in establishing the colonial education
system and comments:

> It is understandable that with the raising of the consciousness of
> the more enlightened of the majority who are victims of the
> system, the church has been identified in the minds of those who
> articulate the new political consciousness, as part of the system which
> condemns the majority to an existence of poverty, powerlessness and
> dependency.[45]

This is the legacy of a history in which Britain has been the source
of political, cultural and religious norms for all who wished or needed
to have any identification with the powerful in colonial society.
Moreover, they identified with the culture of the colonial power not
only out of expediency or necessity; it was clear to the liberated slaves

and their descendants that colonialism was preferable to slavery. Emancipation had not been the gift of the planters, but had been granted against the planters' will by the British Government. Thus a strong British patriotism became a feature of West Indian life, and is one reason for the service West Indian troops were willing to give in both world wars. 'Winston' became one of the most popular West Indian boys' names. When the large scale migration to Britain took place after the Second World War the deeper Black, African consciousness and identity were overlaid with, and, it may be said, infiltrated by the ambiguities of a colonial consciousness and identity. Many who made the journey to Britain believed they were coming to the 'Mother Country' and the 'Mother Church'.

REJECTION BY TWO 'MOTHERS'

On June 22 1948, the post- war emigration of colonial subjects from the Caribbean to the 'Mother Country' began with the arrival of 492 Jamaicans at Tilbury in the *Empire Windrush*.[46] These Black settlers, and the thousands who followed them in the next two decades, came often at the direct invitation of British industries and the Government,[47] to fill the labour shortage in the British economy. Thinking of themselves primarily as British citizens, patriotic colonial subjects travelling on British passports, they were quite unprepared for the degree of hostility and racism which they encountered. The rights and security symbolized by the passport were largely not honoured, a 'shattering of illusion' which Rex and Moore uncovered in interviews conducted with West Indians in the 1960's. Of one couple they wrote:

> A central theme was the brain-washing of West Indians at home about Britain. They had been told about the Queen and Parliament, but no-one had told them there was a colour bar. They had thought they could get a flat where they chose and that Frank could get a job like any other carpenter.[48]

Black people encountered British racism in three forms. First there was the residue of the racist doctrines surveyed earlier in this chapter. Most Whites believed in the inferiority of Blacks,[49] and many did not hesitate to express their convictions in public insults and anti-social behaviour. Secondly, they encountered racism as they were pushed to the bottom of the social ladder, discriminated against in jobs and housing, subjected to police harassment, disadvantaged in education and by the social services. Detailed presentation of the development of Black disadvantage in modern Britain is beyond the scope of this thesis, but material is well known and easily available.[50] Thirdly, they encountered racism in the enactment of openly discriminatory immigration and nationality legislation.[51]

Increasing hostility to Black people, exacerbated in key areas by the activities of racialist and Fascist groups, led eventually to the 1958 Notting Hill riots, in which large gangs of White youths attacked isolated Black settlers. Black people found themselves blamed for being thus victimized: their very presence was its cause; the solution therefore must be the reduction of their numbers as much as possible.[52] Unrestricted entry of Commonwealth citizens was terminated in 1962, and controls were tightened in 1968. These two Acts were racist in intention and effect, even if not in the strict letter of the law. The 1971 Immigration Act, with its notorious patriality clause, abandoned even this fig-leaf of decency, whilst the 1981 Nationality Act and subsequent immigration controls have undermined the security of all who have not submitted to the indignity of the expensive re-purchase of British citizenship.[53]

One of the most disabling consequences of racism for Black people is that they are rarely perceived, *as Black*, in a positive light. As has often been noted, a successful Black athlete will be accorded the title 'British'; a criminal is either 'Black, or 'West Indian'. Black as an identity equals threat; positive activity remains 'invisible'. A tragic illustration of this predicament occurred in the *New Cross Fire* (or 'New Cross Massacre' as it is regarded by many Black people). Thirteen young people attending a birthday party in a house in New Cross in South-East London in January 1981 died when the house caught fire. The event was interpreted by many Whites and in the media through the negative stereotype of Black people as perpetrators of noisy anti-social parties; in consequence the parents of the dead received unsolicited 'hate mail' rather than condolences. At the same time, the 'invisibility' of Black people was illustrated in two ways. Firstly, the government failed to send any message to New Cross for many weeks. Secondly, the news media ignored almost totally the subsequent action of thousands of Black people who, in peaceful and eloquent silence, walked through Central London in March 1981 to protest against this and other racist attacks. The 1981 Brixton Uprising took place a month later.

'Mother Church' in Britain, Anglican or otherwise, has had little to say in her theological writings about race and oppression. An early noted exception, however, is J.H. Oldham's book, *Christianity and*

The Race Problem (1924),[54] in which features of British imperial life in Kenya are described: racism, exploitation, forced labour, and the annihilation of cultural values. For these 'problems' of race Oldham proposed the classic liberal colonial solution of *education*. Time would expose the frailty of this response to issues of identity and 'visibility', but the book was a considerable achievement for its day, particularly in making clear that racism is not an individual, personal problem, but is ingrained in structures. *Race: A Christian Symposium*[55] is a more recent work, an ecumenical collection of useful articles on race and social justice, including the testimonies of three 'immigrants'. Again, however, the issue of identity is not really faced.

A parallel situation obtains in specifically Anglican writing. It is difficult to trace any impact the presence of Black Anglicans had on the theology, liturgy, government or identity of the Church before the establishment of the Committee for Black Affairs in 1986. My own counting in 1983 of Black and White baptisms, confirmations and marriages over thirty years in three inner-city Birmingham parishes may be the first statistics ever produced on Black Anglicanism in England. Renate Wilkinson's *A Chance to Change* is certainly the first comprehensive survey. One searches in vain Paul Welsby's 1983 publication *A History of the Church of England, 1945–80* for any mention of Black Anglicans, whilst John Tiller's *A Strategy for the Church's Ministry* (also 1983) mentions Black people only as 'losers in the urban race' and as Pentecostals. This is despite the fact that Tiller acknowledges the extent to which the Church is viewed as the guardian of civil religion, polarizing the 'true Britisher' from the 'alien'. The Church, he says, must free itself from its Anglo-centrism, yet he ignores the group whose very presence constitutes the most eloquent challenge to the Church's life and faith.

One practical response to the arrival of Black Anglicans was the establishment in Birmingham of a 'Chaplain to Overseas People,' Paul Burrough, who for seven years welcomed and ministered to Black Anglicans, and helped them to settle into Church life (see p. 25). The intensity of affection with which he is remembered (together with other rare examples of a welcoming attitude or action) shows how exceptional it was. Of the normal experience one example must suffice:

> On my first Sunday in Birmingham my friends and I, we put on our best suits and went to church. But after the service the vicar told us not to come again. His congregation wouldn't like it, he said.[56]

A Chance to Change surveys the position of Black Anglicans in the Diocese of Birmingham. The report sets the statistical reality against an 'ideal type' of the Church, taken from the British Council of Churches' 1976 publication *The New Black Presence in Britain: A Christian Scrutiny:*

> The Church when it is most true to its foundation is not a powerful body giving of its wealth to the powerless. The Church (in its foundation documents) is most characteristically the poor and powerless themselves discovering what it means to die with Christ and to be raised with Christ, and therefore to claim types of power, freedom, autonomy and humanness which differ fundamentally from the assumptions of the powerful.[57]

It finds that the immigrants came at a time of 'denominational-ization' for the Church of England, a decline of the 'folk' customs of baptism and marriage out of all proportion to decline in congregational life. Moreover, they encountered the church at its weakest points:

> White people in inner city congregations were often insecure and defensive because their institution was in decline; black Anglicans were bewildered and disillusioned because English church life was very different from what they had expected.[58]

Nevertheless, the Birmingham Diocese had (1983) a sizeable number of Black adults among its members and regular attenders, 1023 or 10%,[59] a membership figure which is comparable with at least one major Black-led denomination and shows that the 'staying power' of Black people in society is evident in the Church also. However, though Black people participate at least in proportion to their numbers in the 'spiritual' activities of worship, prayer, Bible study and altar serving, the disadvantage they suffer in society is mirrored in their serious under-representation in the structures and ministry of the Church.

A Tree God Planted, Heather Walton's 1985 survey of the Methodist Church in England and Wales shows that at least 5.2% of regular attenders are Black, rising to over 10% in inner city areas, (although it should be noted that 35% of all Black Methodists are in suburban churches).[60] Black Methodists endured similar patterns of rejection and acceptance to Anglicans, and are seriously under-represented among church officers, in leadership, and above all in ministry. Like the Anglican Church, Methodism has spoken out on issues of social justice, but neglected its own Black membership. Heather Walton writes:

Whilst there has been recognition of the fact that Methodism has a mission within our plural society, there is less consciousness that we are a plural community ourselves . . . there is a saying in the Caribbean, 'Baptise your own baby first![61]

The two surveys suggest that very similar patterns of racism and 'invisibility' as well as opportunities for reconciliation and transformation exist in all the 'mainstream' churches in Britain.

4

Black Christianity Before Emancipation

Black Christianity, the name of my third story, was born the first time a captured African slave called on the name of Jesus. As a term used by theologians, however, 'Black Christianity' has come into general use only since the late 1960's, since the publication of James Cone's *Black Theology and Black Power* heralded the arrival of the modern North American school of Black Theology[1]. Cone and his fellow scholars made it clear at that time that it was not their intention to write a speculative or 'new' theology as a White scholar might, but to 'write up' in their context the orally transmitted theology of three hundred years of Black Christian existence. For Cone, the need to write came from a crisis experience, from the discovery at the beginning of his ministry that classical White theology did not engage with the situation of Black people in the Deep South. As he writes, 'I encountered head on the *contradictions* of my seminary education as I attempted to inform Black students about the significance of theological discourse'.[2] The students simply refused to accept his 'prefabricated' theology, based as it was on the European tradition. White theology was 'bankrupt' in the face of Black experience. Cone was driven back to the songs, hymns, prayers and preaching tradition of Black Christians for the sense of his faith, and recovered from that source a theology authentically his own.

AFRICA IN THE NEW WORLD

The precise origins of Black Christianity in North America and the Caribbean are necessarily obscure. Written data do not exist, since the first Black slave Christians could not write and gathered together only in secret and at great personal risk. However, it is no longer possible to regard the religion of Black Christians as simply a 'folk' variant of White Protestantism. The definitive works of W.E.B. Dubois and Melville Herskovits[3], however much criticized in detail, have established that what Gayraud Wilmore calls the 'creative residuum of the African religions' was an essential ingredient in the formation of Black Christianity[4]. Wilmore writes:

> What many Europeans and Americans once regarded as a lower form of animism and pagan superstition in Africa is now recognized as highly involved ontological and ethical systems. This is partly because African scholars began to examine their own religions without the deferential accession to imported norms and values. On their part Afro-American scholars have become more appreciative of their own African past and now generally hold that the slaves who were imported to the New World were not completely divested of their belief systems.[5]

Although slaves were captured from a wide variety of tribes, religions and cultures in West and Central Africa, and included some who were Moslems (though often of an 'indigenised' African variety) and even some who had had contact with Christianity, we are nonetheless able to speak of the common African religious heritage of the slaves. This is for two reasons. Firstly, the different religions of Africa had much in common: a shared heritage of similar religions, principles, modes of perception and patterns of ritual. Secondly, the brutal separation of slaves from their kinship ties inevitably eroded local and tribal differences. No one local African religion or culture could remain intact in America. Slaves had to build new societies, 'in part from their diverse backgrounds in different African societies, and in part from the experience of enslavement in a new environment'.[6]

This common African religious heritage of slaves can be summarized under three headings. Firstly, there was the recognition, both by individuals and the community, of the *pervasive reality of the spirit world*. Over all was the 'High God', the Supreme Creator of the world and everything in it. Between him and human beings were the many spirits and lesser gods, including the spirits of ancestors who dwelt in and 'possessed' natural phenomena as well as endowing living humans with spiritual gifts – gifts of making mischief as well as of healing. The workers of 'good magic' were the 'medicine men' whom John Mbiti calls the 'doctors and pastors of the community', at once the source of spiritual ministrations, herbal and other remedies for sickness, and counsel and advice.[7] There were also the conjurers or witch-doctors who practised 'bad magic' for anti-social purposes of harming or taking revenge on others.[8] In such a structure of belief therewas a unity of experience; little demarcation was made between the sacred and the secular.

Secondly, there were the *common ritual characteristics and customs*, a common heritage of the use of instruments, dance, shouting and rhythmic beat, patterns of motor behaviour, of call and response in singing and preaching, of ecstatic experience, of importance attached to dreams, healing rituals and magical charms.

Thirdly, there was the *common heritage of a corporate style of leadership, polity and social organisation* including the position of women and the authority and charismatic power of the leader. The African religious heritage is more clearly and overtly visible in some parts of the Americas than others. Especially in Latin America certain African gods live on in the beliefs and rituals of the slaves' descendants: *candomblé* in Brazil, *santeria* in Cuba, *Shango* in Trinidad and *voudun* in Haiti. In Jamaica, home of the majority of Caribbean settlers in Britain, *mayalism*, the tribal religion and 'good magic' of the Ashantis, provided the African roots and impetus for the Great Revival of 1860–61, from which have come the Afro-Christian Revivalist cults of modern Jamaica, *Pukkumina*[9] and *Zion*, as well as folk customs such as the Nine-Day Wake following bereavement. The anti-social *obeah* magic is still practised. In the United States overt retentions are fewer. The African heritage, the 'creative residuum', lives by being adapted to influence more generally the worship and folk beliefs of Afro-Americans in an explicitly Christian context.[10]

In all slave societies in the New World, the African religious heritage is not to be regarded as simply a list of static 'Africanisms', archaic 'retentions' which occur more in some areas than others. Its importance lies in the persistence everywhere, even where it is relatively invisible, of a 'subterranean stream'. It is a dynamic, living and changing tradition, adaptable and always capable of transformation. When no longer overtly acknowledged, even when apparently deliberately rejected, it has remained the living repository of Black identity, the source of consolation, of strength to survive, and of power to resist the oppressive condition of bondage.

CATECHESIS

We have already noted that both Church and King intended that slaves in the British Colonies of North America and the Caribbean should be baptized and instructed in the Christian faith, but that, even after S.P.G. had begun its work in 1701, instruction (*catechesis*) was subject to severe limitations as a method of evangelisation. As applied to slaves in the British colonies, it was a highly racist principle of evangelization, in a context where the propriety of evangelizing Black people was grudgingly admitted, if at all.

The importance of the period of catechesis is that it introduced Black people to the elements of Christianity, making available a common religious language through which the first conceptual trans-actions between people of the two cultures, White European slave-owner and Black African slave, could take place. It produced the raw material, so to speak, with which the African subterranean stream would interact in the 'crucible' from which the Black Christian Tradition first emerged. Slaves were exposed to Christian ritual and to basic Christian beliefs and, for their response to catechesis to be more than mere parroting, they had to invest the ritual and the teachings with some kind of *meaning*. This work of translating and interpreting was the birth struggle of Black Christianity; like the first-century journey of Christianity from Hebraic to Greek thought, it was a critical moment of inter-cultural theology. For Christian ritual and belief could only 'mean' something to the slaves in terms of their cultural past and their present oppression. Hence the meaning the missionaries sought to give and the meaning the slaves created were not the same.

Meaning was thus no longer the exclusive possession of each side, but was being created through a dialectical process of 'negating', 'preserving' and 'transforming'. The African critique of slave-owning Christianity *negated* the appropriation of the Gospel by Whites to oppress Black people. It *preserved* the African inheritance through areas of continuity of meaning. Raboteau lists several of these: the basic African belief in God would obviously be carried over, the Trinity would be understood as a limited pantheon, the after-life with rewards and punishments would be familiar, whilst prayer would be an unquestioned obligation for Africans to whom 'the essence of piety consisted in propitiating gods and ancestors'.[11] However, a religion without drumming, dancing, sacrifice and spirit possession would be strange to Africans. Although missionaries would for some time to come report concern at the 'inaccuracy' of the slaves' translation of Christianity, White and African religious streams were nonetheless being *transformed* into a new form of the Christian religion.

Historical evidence from this 'crucible' period of Black Christianity is inevitably sparse.[12] Outwardly slaves remained totally under their masters' control, and most early missionaries presented Christianity as a means to strengthen that subservience. Francis Le Jau, a priest in South Carolina, wrote in 1710, 'slaves do better for their Masters' profit than formerly, for they are taught to serve out of Christian Love and Duty'.[13] Underneath, however, the Afro-Christian stream of faith and its 'invisible institution' (the 'Steal Away to Jesus' church) were being born. The Black Church and Black Theology began with the first sermons preached secretly in the swamps or forests of a plantation (the 'catacombs' of the Black Church), together with the first stories of healing and the first articulations of the longing for freedom.[14] Slavemaster Christianity said that the God of the Bible had created Black people 'to make a crop'. The slaves however, had known a different God in Africa, a divine power who sustained life and could not possibly have willed their life of suffering and meaninglessness. This fundamental aspect of their religious tradition became a critical principle by which to interpret the Bible, where they discovered a God who liberated the oppressed, identified with his people, and triumphed over evil.

THE EVANGELICAL REVIVAL

The Evangelical Revival was a major feature of eighteenth century Protestant Christianity in Britain and Europe as well as in the New World. (There were also parallel developments within Catholicism.) The varied fruits of this widespread revival included at least three movements important for the emergence of Black Christianity as well as for the emancipation struggle in Britain, the Caribbean and the United States.

First came the Moravians. The reconstitution of the Moravian Church had taken place in 1727 at the village of Herrnhut in Saxony, the result of the fusion of two streams of Protestant faith – one springing from the migration of refugees of the Moravian Brethren, the other from German Lutheran Pietism. This powerful spiritual awakening resulted in an amazing worldwide upsurge that firmly planted evangelical Christianity in the Caribbean, and the Moravian Church as an important element in West Indian life.[15] Next came the Methodist movement, which Wesley's itinerant preaching brought into existence; it also soon established a presence in North America and the Caribbean.[16] Thirdly, the Evangelical Revival took root in the Church of England in the second half of the eighteenth century. Though its adherents were generally political conservatives, they brought a strong moral sense to social issues, as supremely exemplified in Wilberforce's leadership of the movement to abolish slavery. In all denominations the Evangelical revival led to an intensification of overseas mission.

In North America the 'dawning of the new day' in the history of the conversion of the slaves came with the fervour of revival which swept across the American colonies in the First Great Awakening of the 1740's, and returned to the young Republic in the Second Great Awakening at the turn of the century.[17] For Black and White alike, *catechesis* was no match for evangelical zeal. The message of conviction, conversion and regeneration elicited a response from all classes of people, including poor Whites, the young and slaves. Some planters were also converted, and, as part of their new Christian conviction, began to allow slaves to go to camp meetings. There, many went through the conversion process in which a sense of their own sinfulness, perhaps a vision of damnation, and often a considerable period of sadness and loneliness on the 'mourners' bench' would precede a dramatic experience of being made new, and commissioned to live a holy life and preach the Gospel.

The mass of new Black Christians was found among Methodists and Baptists, denominations markedly more egalitarian in tendency than the Church of England. Not only did their fervent message communicate itself well, but the structures of both denominations more easily allowed for Black participation. Qualification for ministry as a preacher was charismatic rather than institutional; a converted heart and a gifted tongue, not theological training, were the main qualifications. Here Black preachers could qualify as readily as Whites; especially, no doubt, those already noted for their spiritual ministry. Baptists, with their congregational polity, were even more open than Methodists for the springing up of Black congregations. By the 1790's official Methodist and Baptist membership in America was about one quarter Black.[18]

At first this led to mixed but segregated congregations, although always under White control. In towns where Black membership became too numerous, some separate services and even separate congregations resulted, though always under the supervision of White ministers. Eventually some Black churches arose spontaneously.

In the West Indies the Moravian mission met with great success, firstly in the Danish colony of St. Thomas (1732), later in St. Elizabeth parish in Jamaica (1756), in Antigua (1760) – where four missionaries in a few years brought into being a community of over seven thousand Moravians – and finally in Barbados (1765) and St. Kitt's (1779).[19] West Indian Methodism began in Antigua when, in the 1760's, a Methodist slaveowner, Nathaniel Gilbert, began to preach to his own slaves and a church was formed. For four years after Gilbert's death Antiguan Methodism was led by two Black women, Sophia Campbell and Mary Alley. Methodism was firmly planted in other islands as a result of the four missionary voyages of Thomas Coke (1787, 1788–89, 1790–91, 1792–93), notably in St. Kitt's, Jamaica and the newly ceded Windward Islands. In the Dutch island of St. Eustatius he found his hearers already roused by a lay preacher from North America, the Black slave known as 'Black Harry'. Coke defended Harry's right to preach, and he left the church in his care. By 1804 there were 14,376 members of the Methodist church of whom only 112 were White.[20]

Baptist work had even stronger Black roots. In 1783, George Liele, a Black Baptist preacher from Georgia, was brought to Jamaica by his master who wished to continue living under British rule after the American Revolution. Liele established the first Baptist chapel in Jamaica and was for a while imprisoned for his preaching. By the time the first English missionary arrived at his invitation in 1814 there were over 8,000 Baptists on the island.[21] Even in the Anglican Church, as noted earlier, new currents began to flow in the decade before Emancipation. As the Abolitionist campaign entered its final phase, the Colonial Office sought increasing control over the plantocracy, and as part of this process established a West Indian episcopate in 1824. The new bishops supervised a programme of church development and the establishment of schools to reach the slaves, and tried to generate attitudes in the Church more appropriate to a 'free' society. What had been the planters' church gradually became the Church of England in the West Indies. Thus at Emancipation in 1834 a large Black membership was already established in the various churches, substantially the fruit, directly or indirectly, of the Evangelical Revival.

In the American states and the Caribbean alike, Black religion was superficially like that of the respective White parent denominations, after whose creeds and church order it was patterned. However, it was noted by many to have a different *style*, which aroused White hostility. The difference in style is accounted for by the African 'subterranean stream', which was there not simply as isolated cultural survivals, but as the spiritual repository of Black identity and humanity. In the earliest period Morgan Godwyn had condemned 'idolatrous dances and revels' as 'barbarous and contrary to Christianity'.[22] Later evangelists were alarmed by the religious behaviour of slaves at the camp meetings; in Philadelphia in 1819 John Watson complained that Black people 'get together and sing for hours, short scraps of disjointed affirmations, pledges or prayers lengthened out with long repetitious choruses' – this and the accompanying dancing is 'an evil only occasionally condemned' and was even imitated by some Whites.[23] As late as 1878 a Black church leader, A.M.E. Bishop

Daniel Alexander Payne was condemning the 'ridiculous and heathenish' ring shout.[24]

CHRISTIAN REBELLION?

The most important and, to Whites, alarming manifestation of the Black Christian Tradition was the interaction of the Christian story with the Black tradition of resistance and armed revolt. From the first days of captivity, and on the slaveships, slaves had rebelled, and resistance was an established tradition long before slaves had any serious involvement with Christianity. It is necessary first to survey this tradition in order to understand the later radical development of rebellion led by Christians.

The story of Black resistance to slavery is a complex one: like all stories of oppressed people it includes treachery and accommodation (real or feigned), passive resistance and violent rebellion. It is a difficult story for historians to recover since, inevitably, documentary evidence comes almost entirely from White observers who rarely penetrated the psychic and communal life of slaves.[25] But it is nonetheless amply clear that Blacks did not conform to White racist stereotypes such as the common image of 'unruly children, characterised by unformed intelligence and fitful moods, alternately manic and depressed, craven and rebellious'.[26] Michael Craton summarises his study of resistance to slavery in the British Caribbean in these words:

> The one growing certainty was that there was no such creature as a genuinely docile slave.[27]

REBELLION IN THE CARIBBEAN

In the Caribbean we note three forms of resistance, namely passive resistance, marronage and rebellion. By *passive resistance* is meant the ways in which slaves developed their own life, their own culture and their own traditions so as to shape, modify, but not of course overcome, the system in which they were trapped. Craton calls this 'the most fundamental form of resistance', and outlines the extent to which it drew on African skills, cultural legacies and above all on traditional religion which for all except the plantation elite, 'sustained their inner lives'. Craton writes:

As time went on and [slaves] came to belong, and to understand their indispensability, they were able to impose their own pace upon economic operations and to introduce their own cultural values into a creole mix . . . The majority of slaves discovered a pattern of behaviour that, by fulfilling the white man's image of the African, progressively lowered the masters' expectation whilst providing room for maneuver by the slaves. In a climate of barely suppressed violence and frequent truculence, no white man could resist the wiles of a slave who appeared to acquiesce . . . [28]

Marronage, the establishment of independent self-sustaining communities of runaways, was attempted in almost all the Caribbean colonies where plantations were established, including small islands offering but meagre natural protection such as St. Kitt's, Barbados and Antigua. Such communities were unable to secure safe locations for settled agriculture, and none lasted more than a generation. Communities in other territories survived longer because they were able to forge alliances with the native Caribs or other Amerindians. These include the Seminoles of Florida,[29] the Trio tribe in Surinam, the Miskitos of Honduras, and, above all, the Black Caribs of St. Vincent.[30]

The best known and most successful example of marronage is that of the Jamaican Maroons.[31] The Windward Maroons based in the Blue Mountains, originated in the attempt of Spanish slaves, perhaps with the remnants of the original Arawak inhabitants, to seize the chance of freedom when the English invaded Jamaica in 1655. The Leeward Maroons based in the Cockpit Country of St. James and Trelawny parishes were formed by Coromantee runaways from plantations, particularly those who escaped during the uprisings of the period 1673 to 1690. The most famous Leeward Maroon leader, Cudjoe, having amalgamated various groups during the 1720's, was able to hold the authorities to a stalemate. In February 1739 he negotiated a treaty allowing him the freehold of 1,500 acres of land and the right to raise crops and stock and to sell produce, in exchange for a promise to return future runaways and to serve the Crown against foreign invaders and rebels. The Windward Maroons under their leader Quao signed a similar treaty later the same year.

Marronage, unlike passive resistance, was not an option open to many. But for those who were successful runaways it gave a large measure of freedom, sometimes resulting in such a measure of agreement with the imperial power as to give the political security of a state within a state. Of course Maroons have been much criticised for their agreements with the colonizers, particularly for their 'treachery' in hunting runaways and returning them to certain severe punishment. Yet it is hard to see what alternative they had; by such agreements they obtained space and secure boundaries for their communities. Even though this eventually provoked the resentment of the slaves, the very survival of Maroon communities remained a powerful symbol that White power was not absolute. Many Maroon communities disappeared in a few years; the Black Caribs survived only by deportation, whilst the Jamaican Maroons were much reduced, and the survivors lost much of their vigour and independence. Yet we must agree with Michael Craton that 'given the power and tireless duplicity of capitalist colonialism, the survival of any maroons at all was a remarkable and inspiring achievement'.[32]

In *Testing the Chains*, Michael Craton lists seventy-one separate instances of *slave rebellion* (excluding Carib and Maroon wars) in the British Caribbean before Emancipation in 1838. Most involved tens or at most hundreds of people, but on at least fourteen occasions revolts involved thousands of slaves and threatened the survival of the White plantocracy of the island in which the rebellion occurred. We examine these rebellions briefly under three headings.

Firstly there are the *revolts of the African phase*, where the majority of slaves involved were those born in Africa. These revolts were essentially African in character, plotted, planned and prepared in African style; the fighting methods used were little adapted to the new situation of the Caribbean. The most famous revolt took place in St. Mary's parish in Jamaica in 1760, under the leadership of the Coromantee slave Tacky. The planter historian Edward Long believed that the example of the Maroons inspired the conspirators, yet their aims went far beyond those of Cudjoe and Quao, and involved the overthrow of White government and its replacement by small African-style principalities.[33] Tacky's revolt is one of the major rebellions of British Imperial history, comparable in its shock to the imperial system to the Indian Mutiny of 1857. It cost the equivalent of many millions of pounds in modern money and was savagely punished by torture, executions and deportations.

A second period of crisis occurred at the time when English military power was distracted by major wars overseas, firstly during the American War of Independence (1776–83) and more significantly in the period of the French Revolution, especially after the Haitian Revolution of 1792. Revolts in this period were normally no longer mainly African-led but were the work of creolized slaves, including the creole elite of divers, craftsmen and domestics.[34]

European writers have attributed this period of uprising to the dissemination among the slaves of European liberal and revolutionary ideas. This view makes Black slaves the dependent beneficiaries of progressive White thought, a kind of intellectual colonialism. As we have seen, however, Blacks already possessed 'ideas', namely that their humanity resided in their African identity, that slavery was an unjust burden which could be modified by pragmatic struggle, and that their longing to be free could be fulfilled. It is better to see the rebellions of this period as continuing the traditional opportunistic and pragmatic approach to rebellion, but in a new situation. Struggles between European powers distracted White military power and made it possible for slaves to obtain rewards for participation.

The third main period of resistance is that which immediately preceded Emancipation. As the movement for abolition grew stronger in Britain, and as rumours that freedom had been granted spread through the Caribbean, unrest and revolts occurred in most colonies. Three very large revolts must be particularly noted.

In 1816 the economy of Barbados was in recession, and this, together with the planters' complacency and the persistence of rumours of emancipation, proved fertile ground for slave discontent to be channelled into a revolt by a group of leading slaves and free coloureds. The thousands who participated in Bussa's Rebellion believed they had external allies, and that imperial troops would not come to the aid of the planters. Carefully planned for the Easter holidays, the rebellion was crushed within a few days and brutally punished. After executing over 200 rebels the astonished planters could still only blame 'dangerous doctrines which have been spread from abroad' for a rebellion which had involved half the island. In a sense they were correct, but they had failed to recognise the ever-present desire of the slaves to be free.[35]

Like Bussa's Rebellion, the Demerara Revolt of 1823 and the Jamaican Baptist War (1831–32) grew on the basis of rumours of emancipation and difficult local conditions. Additionally, however, and of first importance for our purposes, they were led by Christian slaves on the explicit basis of their church allegiance, with a degree of ambiguous involvement by non-conformist missionaries.

In 1823 John Smith's Bethel Chapel, six miles from Georgetown, Demerara, had a congregation of over a thousand adherents. The converts demonstrated a piety and diligence at work which contrasted with their former state; but they had also found in their Christian faith a repository for their African human dignity and longing for freedom, and in the Congregationalist chapel something of an alternative free society. Christian faith, African heritage and political aspirations together formed fertile soil for the seed of rebellion. In this case the slaves believed that freedom had already been granted by the King but was being withheld by the planters and could only be gained by force. On August 17, 1823 a group of slaves including the Bethel deacon Quamina took an oath of secrecy and commitment to an uprising. Quamina and his Christian associates ensured that a minimum of violence was used, and indeed only three Whites were killed in the entire revolt. The ill-equipped rebels were easily defeated; Quamina was tracked down and shot whilst other leaders and rebels were punished with extreme severity. Smith who, though he had been an implacable critic of slavery, had never supported armed rebellion, was also tried and sentenced to death, but with a recommendation of mercy to the King. Smith was reprieved and an order was made for his deportation, but before this news arrived in Demerara, he had died in prison. In Britain he became a hero of the abolitionist cause and he alone was acclaimed the 'Demerara Martyr', though 250 slaves including many deeply believing Christians had also perished at the hands of the planters.[36]

The last few years of slavery in Jamaica were characterized by a fertile mix of difficult economic conditions, rumours of emancipation, flourishing Non-conformity and the anxious resentment of the planters against Amelioration. The planters' paranoia that Ameliora-tion would lead to violence and emancipation fed the slaves' hope that the coming of freedom could be accelerated. In this situation a group of leading slaves from various estates in Western Jamaica met under the leadership of Samuel 'Daddy' Sharpe to plan the revolt now known as the Baptist War. Sharpe was the chief deacon in the Baptist Chapel in Montego Bay, where the English missionary Thomas Burchell was the minister. Several other conspirators were Baptist deacons. Sharpe was a charismatic and saintly character, a courageous leader and gifted speaker. He inspired his followers by his Christian conviction that slavery was evil and that human beings were equal in God's eyes and had the right to freedom. He was sure that 'the King' had determined on freedom, and that the planters and the Governor were withholding it. Bound by oath and prayer the conspirators determined not to work again, except for wages. Their intention was a non-violent strike-like campaign, again the fruit of their Christian conviction. In the event, as the rebellion spread, planters' houses, estates and crops were set on fire. The rebels were soon defeated in set-piece battles with the militia, whilst many who escaped were tracked down, partly because Maroon help again proved reliable to the authorities. There were few White casualties, but a horrific revenge was taken on the rebels, including the execution of no less than 344 slaves. Of the 440 indicted whose occupations are known no less than 142 had leading or skilled slave positions and a high proportion were Baptists, including many deacons. The leading missionaries, Burchell, Gardner and William Knibb were arrested and charged, but ultimately released. Though undoubted critics of slavery, they had also counselled obedience, not rebellion. They incurred the enmity of the planters, from whom they fled in 1832 in fear of their lives, but were unable to acknowledge that the greater heroes and martyrs were not themselves but the Baptist deacons and others who had claimed liberty as a God-given and Christian right, and had lost their lives in its service.[37]

In this final stage of slave resistance, planters' older explanations for slave unrest were no longer credible. They found an easy new target in the Anti-slavery movement in Britain and in its supposed agents in the colonies, the missionaries. In a sense they were correct, for Amelioration and Emancipation, when they came, were enactments of the British Parliament, the result of a long campaign asserting that slavery was, as Craton puts it, 'morally evil, economically inefficient and politically unwise'.[38] Yet, although it is important thus to recognise and respect the work of Wilberforce and the British abolitionists, this appraisal of their work must be subject to two vital qualifications.

Firstly, it was the unremitting struggle of the slaves, and especially the three final major rebellions of Bussa, Quamina and Sharpe, which indicated that slaves could not be ruled without repression, and would never be either contented or efficient under slavery. To sustain this struggle the slaves needed their own identity, their own strength to endure, their own vision and hope, and their own creativity. They needed a sense of their own createdness, and the possibility of deliverance and vindication. All this was, for the slaves, rooted in Africa, in the religious, cultural and communal resources they had brought with them in the Middle Passage. It is this that leads Michael Craton to describe the Middle Passage as a 'bridge between Africa and Afro-America' rather than a traumatic divide.[39] Slaves wanted to be free, and used all the resources at their command to bring about their freedom.

Secondly, the Abolitionists and the missionaries never really recognised or understood the human resources of the African captives for whom they worked. Nowhere is this clearer than in the way the slaves became Christians. The missionaries, whether they accepted or opposed the institution of slavery, saw their converts as culturally empty vessels in need of 'educating' and 'civilizing'. They failed to recognise the conversion of the slaves as a vital moment of inter-cultural theological 'collision' in which the Biblical story interacted with the story of Africa and the slaves' subsequent captivity.

They were unable to hear the new Christian story thus formed. For Christianity had rituals and talismans – the cross, bread and wine, the Holy Book – around which the religious sensibilities of Africa could re-gather. The solemn oath on the Bible which preceded the later revolts had its African equivalent. Conversion in the context of oppression signified both a quest for acceptance in the new society and also resistance and separation from its dehumanising aspects.

Moreover, the Church provided a new and alternative community, a sign of the liberated community that would one day be established. The more a church was under local Black control, as among the Congregationalists and Baptists, especially the Native Baptists of Jamaica, the more important these factors would be. They were particularly so in Jamaica where there was a whole generation of Black slave missionaries such as George Liele and Andrew Bryan whose congregations were founded not only against colonial and Anglican opposition, but often also in conflict with White missionaries of their own denomination from England. The Church gave freedom and structure to leadership among the slaves. Not surprisingly the slave elite were the ones who tended to become deacons, and of course leaders of rebellion. None of this should be understood as implying that they compromised their Christianity. Quamina and Sharpe both made it clear that they believed, and that, believing, they 'did theology'. That is to say they found in the Christian story, as discovered by Africans in the context of slavery, the grounds for the action they felt compelled to take. It also restrained them to use a minimum of force and, in conspicuous contrast to the White authorities, to abstain from vengeance. Their struggle and their death *was* their Christianity. Radical, liberationist, disciplined, and as restrained as circumstances allowed, they are touchstones of authenticity for the Black Christian story.

REBELLION IN NORTH AMERICA

In a briefer survey of developments in North America we note a parallel history of slave resistance and rebellion, though with a number of important differences of detail.

Firstly, although we can assume from the number of slave revolts and the well-documented fear of the slaveowners that passive resistance was practised, Marronage was not usually a possibility in the very different circumstances of North America.

Secondly, whereas in the Caribbean White opposition to slavery was centred four thousand miles away in the imperial capital, in the

United States it developed within the same country. Not only was there a powerful crusading Abolitionist movement, but Northern states actually abolished slavery at relatively early dates. This tension within the nation eventually became the major theme of the Civil War of 1861–65. Early opposition to slavery was voiced by some White church leaders, Quakers in the first place,[40] but – more significantly, because of their greater numbers – by Methodists, especially the great leaders Wesley, Asbury and Coke. In America the Methodist Conference actually called on members to free their slaves. But the charismatic freedom and egalitarianism of Methodists and other Evangelicals foundered on the rock of the intransigence of the institution of slavery.[41] The institutional White evangelical church quickly withdrew from its strong stance, though this did not prevent radical White preachers 'fanning the winds of prophecy'[42] among the slaves.

Thirdly, the relative freedom of the North enabled the growth of a new class of free Blacks who, many years before Emancipation in the British Caribbean, were producing a new kind of Black leader. Heirs to the Afro-American liberation tradition, they exercised their gifts not in an African style in the rural South, but with Western educational tools in the cities of the North. Here men like Richard Allen,[43] Robert Young and David Walker laid the foundations of the 'visible' Black Church, Black Radicalism and Black Theology.

Fourthly, substantial communities of Evangelical Christians emerged in the United States, including the South, earlier than in the Caribbean. This often led to severe restrictions being placed upon separate religious meetings or buildings for slaves, as happened in the colony of North Carolina as early as 1715. Rebellion and religion were associated in the minds of preachers, slaveowners and slaves alike. Religious gatherings, whether Sunday worship, holiday gatherings, or especially funerals, all provided opportunity both for release of religious emotion and for careful plotting. Wilmore writes:

> In the numerous slave revolts prior to 1800, religious factors were frequently present. Sometimes visionary whites, foreigners to their own society's values, were involved. At other times conjurers or witch doctors, who apparently were sometimes in the background, were called upon to provide inconspicuous supporting services. At still other times black preachers – unordained and illiterate men of extraordinary intelligence – kept the pot boiling by relating slavery to white immorality, and freedom to black salvation through Jesus Christ.[44]

Some Black Christian leaders and preachers emerged in the early nineteenth century as leaders of slave revolts which were well-planned, consciously political revolutionary uprisings. In 1800, Gabriel, slave of Thomas Prosser of Richmond, Virginia, believing that God had called him to deliver his people and inspired both by the Biblical example of Samson and the contemporary one of Toussaint L'Ouverture in Haiti, led a revolt of between one and six thousand slaves. He was prepared to kill Whites, but ordered that all Methodists and Quakers (church groups he believed to be on God's side against slavery) should be spared along with all French people (because their Government had recognized the independence of Haiti). The revolt was betrayed, however, and Gabriel was arrested and executed.

The Methodist preacher Denmark Vesey, of Charleston, South Carolina, was similarly inspired by Scripture, in this case the story of the Fall of Jericho. He was a freed Black of outstanding intellectual ability who had contact with radical Black groups outside the South. Vesey, despite the protests of some of his followers, thought it necessary to be even more ruthless with Whites than Gabriel, and planned a revolt in Charleston in 1822. It was similarly betrayed and, despite no White person having been, in the event, struck even a blow, ruthless punishment followed, including the execution of Vesey and thirty-six others.

Nat Turner was born a slave on the estate of a pious Methodist, Benjamin Turner. After his conversion he applied himself to the study of Scripture and developed an intense expectation of the return of Jesus to vindicate his oppressed people. In the pursuit of holiness he began to experience visions and signs, one of which, in 1828, he interpreted as a call to prepare for his great work, the final apocalyptic struggle with the 'serpent', the evil system of slavery. This time there was no betrayal, and in the thirty-six hours following Turner's Sunday night fellowship meal and preaching with his fellow conspirators, fifty-seven Whites were killed. The rebellion was nonetheless poorly armed and soon defeated. Turner made a full confession before his execution which is an important source for radical Black hermeneutic of the period. When asked after sentence if he did not now believe he was mistaken, he replied simply, 'Was not Christ crucified?'.

These three Christian leaders of rebellion, called by Wilmore 'Three Generals in the Lord's Army',[45] dominate the American struggle in the early nineteenth century. After each uprising, especially the last, slaveowners' hostility to the involvement of Black people with religion was renewed, whilst their suspicion of White strangers and preachers was reinforced. Black religious practice was subjected to increased surveillance, and the heart of Black religion remained concealed from White eyes.

5
Black Christianity: A Triple Inheritance

Although it is beyond the scope of this book to give a full history of Black Christianity, I complete the third story with an outline of the principal developments of the years since Emancipation, both in the United States and in the Caribbean.

THE AMERICAN INHERITANCE

In the United States, three developments must be noted: the emergence in the Black Christian Tradition of an institutional Black Church, Black Radicalism, and Black Theology. These three creations of Black faith, – a community, a vision and an 'interpretation' – are the resources with which the story of the Black encounter with God in the midst of adversity is 'preserved' and transmitted.

(i) The Black Church

The existence of separate mass Black denominations which are 'mainstream' rather than Pentecostal in polity and theology is one of the most obvious differences between the United States and Britain. They originated in the experience of racist segregation and discrimination in the South and North following the rise of Black Christianity in the eighteenth century.

We have already noted the beginning of separate Black congregations, albeit under White supervision. Black preachers were likely to prove popular with slaves, and, like Liele's convert, Andrew Bryan, attract hundreds each Sunday. Bryan, after a period of preaching to both races, was ordained by a White minister and became pastor of the *First African Baptist Church* in Savannah, Georgia. Inevitably Whites feared that the Black preachers would foment insurrection.

Bryan was twice imprisoned and whipped, declaring that he would 'freely suffer death for the sake of Jesus Christ' – until, as Raboteau puts it, 'the parallels to the Acts of the Apostles became too embarrassing to local officials', and permission for worship was restored, though only in daylight hours.[1] In such circumstances the first 'independent' Black churches came into existence in the South. Their preachers had to walk a theological tightrope to survive. They had to avoid arousing the wrath of Whites, which meant constant vigilance as meetings were infiltrated by spies and informers. On the other hand, they had to communicate to their congregations that they believed in a delivering God who would bring freedom, and that the White theological stance that slavery was ordained of God was a lie.

The origins of separate *Black Methodism* were in the relative freedom of the North. Black members faced two problems in church membership: firstly, there was no freedom to express either the African 'style' of worship or the liberation 'content' of theology which defined the Black tradition; and secondly, in worship they were actually segregated into separate 'African Corners' or 'Nigger Heavens'. Richard Allen (1760–1831) and Absolom Jones (1746– 1818), Black leaders at St. George's Methodist Episcopal Church in Philadelphia, felt both restrictions keenly. In 1786 Allen and Jones were ejected from the church by stewards as they knelt at prayer on the ground floor of the church among the Whites. They left to establish the Free African Society along Methodist lines, though not at first as a separate denomination. It provided Christian fellowship and teaching, social service and mutual aid, as well as being a place for racial solidarity. It became the classical pattern for the American Black Church. The movement spread rapidly in the urban centres of the north, coming together formally as the African Methodist Episcopal Church (A.M.E.) in 1816.[2] A similar movement in New York led to the A.M.E. (Zion) Church in 1820. Both churches were heavily involved in the struggle against slavery, including organizing the escape of slaves from the South (the 'Underground Railroad').

Black Episcopalians (Anglicans) and *Presbyterians* were far fewer in number. Their relatively formal worship was less attractive to Black people than that of the Methodists and Baptists. Increasingly though, as what Wilmore calls a 'hurricane of restlessness and rebellion' swept through the Black communities and churches of the North in the early nineteenth century, both Black Episcopalians and Presbyterians came to be in separate congregations.[3] (The first Black Episcopalian church was St. Thomas' Philadelphia, where Absolom Jones was ordained deacon in 1795). They never formed separate denominations, and remained in a state of dependence on the White institution with its discriminatory practices.

Although the ordinary church life of Black Episcopalians, Presbyterians and others in White-led churches was less independent and less overtly Black-orientated than that of Baptists and the A.M.E., as time went on it was precisely these churches which produced many of the famous Black Christian leaders of the nineteenth century, particularly the Presbyterian Henry Highland Garnet (1815–1882) and the Episcopalian Alexander Crummell (1819–1898). Both led the development of the *Convention Movement*, called by Wilmore the 'secular adjunct' of the Black Church which radicalized the abolition struggle before the Civil War. Garnet's 1843 *Address to the Slaves of the United States* was a bold and direct call to insurrection. It is interesting to ask why such talented Black leadership should arise in White-led churches. Wilmore believes that the mass Black churches were too busy evangelising and organizing themselves to produce highly trained clergy, whilst White-led denominations were too racist to use the highly-trained clergy they produced. He asks whether a similar combination of seminary education and racism were factors in the emergence of militant Black leaders from White-led churches in the 1960's in the U.S.A., an analysis which may also be relevant to the contemporary situation in Britain.[4]

Black Christians in White-led churches, as we have noted, have been chiefly in separate but dependent congregations and missions. By the late nineteenth century their leaders were organized into caucuses. The *Afro-American Presbyterian Council* was formed in Philadelphia in 1894; today's equivalent, renewed though the struggles of the 1960's, is *Black Presbyterians United*.[5]

The Episcopalian caucus, the *Conference of Church Workers Among the Colored People* was established in 1883. Despite a name which today sounds unbearably patronizing, it was in fact formed by Alexander Crummell as a 'Convocation of Colored Clergy' to oppose a Southern proposal to segregate all Black congregations into a 'missionary' district under a White bishop. In 1968 this was succeeded by the *Union of Black Episcopalians*, a national organization (with local diocesan 'chapters') for clergy and laity alike.[6]

The Episcopalian church now has a 'Black desk', the Office for Black Ministries, in its national headquarters to co-ordinate Black affairs in the church. Its magazine *Linkage* combines Black church news with features on Black Episcopalian history and leaders, and matters of common Black concern. The Episcopalian church has a hymn book, *Lift Every Voice and Sing*, which is a collection of spirituals, evangelical revival hymns and other songs precious to the

Black Christian tradition. Virtually all its contents would be familiar to Black Christians in Britain as recognizably of their tradition.[7] Other White churches have similar official Black departments. The Reformed Church's annual *Colloquium on Black Religion* has produced useful historical and theological texts; whilst Clarence Rivers of the *National Office of Black Catholics* has produced *Soulfull Worship* – a guide to Black liturgy in the Catholic tradition.[8]

Black *Pentecostals* are only a small part of the Black Church in the United States, an obvious contrast with the British situation. The modern *Pentecostal* movement is generally traced to the Azuza Street Revival which took place in Los Angeles in 1906 under the leadership of William Seymour. Seymour was a Black man, the son of emancipated slaves, an inheritor of the African 'subterranean stream' of Black religion including its experiential, Spirit-filled worship and its longing for freedom. The Azuza Street congregation formed by the Revival became a remarkable inter-racial fellowship which worshipped under a Black pastor on the basis of complete equality. Within a few years, however, a period of doctrinal controversy resulted in the emergence of White and Black churches. Iain MacRobert speaks of 'the degeneration of a united inter-racial body into one which mirrors the racial divisions of the older denominations in the United States'.[9] On a world scale, the Pentecostal movement has become a major force, in many cases outstripping historic denominations in membership and influence. In the United States, among Black people, it is at its strongest among the urban poor formed by the Great Migration from the rural South to the cities of the North. They challenged mainline Black churches by their sense of communal identity, and strong stand against the new pressures and immoralities of the urban ghetto. Certainly, as Wilmore comments, there was a greater obstacle to their mission in 'the misery and despair of the poor' than competition with mainline Black churches. Yet in the often desperate social conditions of urban Black America they have built major congregations, some with an outstanding social action ministry. So, despite the obvious difference that all the mainline churches in Britain are White-led, there are parallels between the circumstances in which Black Pentecostal churches have thrived in both countries.[10]

The Black Church in the United States covers a number of different denominations, which together contain 15–16 million Black people.[11] Most are in Black Baptist or Black Methodist denominations, which are the historic focus of Afro-American Christianity. Their life is characterized by the twin foci of free autonomous worship in the Afro-American tradition, and the solidarity and social welfare of the Black community. Much smaller but significant numbers are in White-led churches, whilst a relatively small but increasing number are in Black and White Pentecostal denominations. The whole Black Church is to be defined as *a body of people of African descent who have come together to follow Jesus Christ*; it is the community in which the Black Christian identity is grounded.

(ii) Black Radicalism

In the early nineteenth century a new class of mainly Northern free Black intellectuals in the United States began to articulate a radicalism to which all the various later developments of Black radical thought can be traced. Robert Alexander Young, a free Black from New York, published in 1829 his *Ethiopian Manifesto*.[12] Like so much Black preaching his hope for deliverance was grounded in the Old Testament deliverance of Israel. Like later Garveyites and Rastafarians, he believed in a Black Messiah, and like later Pan-Africanists he sought the liberation of all the people of Africa and of the African Diaspora.

Later the same year David Walker published his famous *Appeal to the Coloured Citizens of the World*.[13] In it he denounced American slavery as even more dehumanizing than that of the Israelites in Egypt and with blistering righteous indignation he exposed the falsity of White Christianity and prophesied its doom. He repudiated schemes for the Black colonization of Africa, being more concerned to see oppression ended in America. Incomparably militant, he was also ultimately hopeful, calling like Martin Luther King for America and White Christians generally to live up to the title deeds of their nation and faith. The theme of reconciliation on which he ended, however, always arose out of a recognition of the inevitability of judgement for Whites unless they underwent a thorough repentance and ended oppression and bondage forthwith.

Much Northern radicalism looked openly to Africa not only as a source of identity (as for example Richard Allen's naming of his Methodist church 'African' rather than 'Black' or 'coloured'), but as the homeland to which a physical return should be sought. The story of the American Colonization Society and the programme of repatriation is a complicated one, and, in the early period, a sometimes tragic interweaving of conflicting ideas and aims. Repatriation fulfilled not only the Black desire to return 'home', but also the desire of White racists to solve the 'problem' of the disturbing and anomalous presence of free Blacks in a slave-owning society, and the longing of zealous Christians from both races to bring 'civilization' and religious 'awakening' to Africa.

The religious basis of Black nationalism was the belief, expounded by Black preachers, that God would fulfil His purposes with Black people. They repudiated the view that he had forsaken them by permitting their enslavement, and searched the Bible and ancient history for evidence of the gifts of enlightenment and civilization that Africa and Ethiopia had given to the world. Repudiating racist attempts to demonstrate Black inferiority, they developed what have become recurring features of Black thought in America, namely an affirmation of the dignity of African humanity and culture, and an interpretation of Scripture rooted in Black experience and perceptions. In this interpretation one text, Psalm 68:31, is of especial importance. Countless sermons were preached on the words, 'Ethiopia shall soon stretch out her hands unto God'. All the great Black Christian thinkers expounded it, making it in Wilmore's words, 'the cornerstone of missionary emigrationism both in the United States and Africa'.[14] The A.M.E.Z. Bishop J.W. Hood, in his commentary on the text, expands a powerful vision of the role of the Black Church in the purposes of God:

> That this prophecy is now in the course of fulfilment the Negro Church stands forth as unquestionable evidence. It is the streak of morning light which betokens the day. It is the morning star which precedes the rising sun. It is the harbinger of the rising glory of the sons of Ham. It is the first fruit of the countless millions of that race who shall be found in the army with banners in the millennial glory of the Christian Church.[15]

In the early period, some Afro-American Christian leaders displayed an attitude to Africa which was as condescending and patronizing as any White missionary. *Daniel Coker*, a leading A.M.E. minister who sailed with the first American slaves to return to Sierra Leone in 1819, wrote:

> I expect to give my life to bleeding, groaning, dark benighted Africa.[16]

Others, like *Martin Delaney*, whilst believing that missionaries would bring a 'purer and higher civilization' to Africa, were keen to deny that Black people had been the object of divine punishment because of their immorality, which (as he acidly observed) was 'not half the wickedness . . . of the Whites.' He wanted missionaries who were one with the 'natural characteristics, claims, sentiments and sympathies' of the Africans, namely their American descendants. Delaney's vision of emigration included mission in the broadest sense, including the promotion by qualified Black people of agriculture, art, commerce, education and 'morality'. At the same time he sought precisely the same ends for Blacks in America, 'successful Elevation in this our native land'. He was also a leading Black in the Abolitionist movement. Underlying all these activities is his determination that Black people should be equipped to define their own reality and have jurisdiction over their own lives, not only spiritually but also morally and socially. He expected the Black Church to take a leading role in all these areas.[17]

Alexander Crummell, the Episcopalian priest and colleague of the Presbyterian Henry Highland Garnett, was an outstanding nineteenth century Christian advocate of Black pride and solidarity.[18] He not only supported missionary work in Africa, but laboured there himself for twenty years. His zeal for mass emigration waned, but his sense of Africa as the source of Black self-respect and pride did not. As Rector of St. Luke's Episcopal Church in Washington he had a platform from which to preach to able and influential Blacks his controversial message of Black racial solidarity, self-help and education. His teaching about the nature of Christian love is a particularly important contribution to Black theology: for Crummell the traditional obligation to love one's enemy is not enough, Black people must espouse self-love if they are to be truly free and equal with Whites. Delaney and Crummell's ideas are an extension of the concepts around which the first African societies were founded. They further define a corporate identity for Black Americans, and set out the means for a total emancipation.

Bishop Henry Turner brought Christian Black nationalism to its most developed form at the end of the nineteenth century. Wilmore writes of him:

> More than any other single individual, Turner not only made a black theology of liberation the core of his preaching and writing, but also helped to implant the spirit of revolutionary religion in the independent churches of Africa that were taking up the struggle against colonialism and racism in the last quarter of the century.

Turner explicitly affirmed God's Blackness as at least as valid an image of God as White depictions of Him. He worked increasingly for the mission of the Church in Africa and for the repatriation of Afro-Americans, whilst urging Blacks to attain their rights in America. His vision was of a 'highway made across the Atlantic, upon which regular social and economic intercourse between Black America and Africa could be carried on, and self-reliant energetic Black people could be permanently settled if they chose to do so'.[19] By the beginning of the twentieth century strong links were established with independent churches in various parts of Africa, especially with the 'Ethiopian Church' in South Africa, which actually became affiliated to the A.M.E. in 1898.

Of this whole stream of Black Christian thought and activity, Wilmore comments:

> The black church, as the primary institutional expression of black religion, erected the politico-theological foundation for black nationalism and Pan-Africanism . . . building blocks for the structure of Africa and Afro-American solidarity as it developed from the early Du Bois to Malcolm X.
>
> We owe something inestimable to them for what they taught that the church means in terms of self-respect, meaningful participation in the affairs of the world, and in terms of an institutional base for black enterprise and culture.[20]

The promise of nineteenth century Christian Black nationalism was not fulfilled in the period after the First World War – at least not within the Christian community. By this time the early failure of Reconstruction (the time of Black participation in political power in the South in the decade following Emancipation) had led to the rigid application of 'Jim Crow' laws of segregation throughout the South.

Whilst ordinary Black people suffered the extremes of 'lynch-law', or expressed resistance in the race riots which followed the return of Black soldiers from the War, Black preachers and church-sponsored self-help organisations espoused the accommodationist gradualism of Booker T. Washington.[21] As millions of the rural poor moved to the northern cities, the Church proved unable to grasp and interpret their experience. Whilst mainline churches became middle class and marginalized, those who left them went in two different directions.

On the one hand, new religious groupings emerged. The radical impulses of Black folk religion with its African subterranean basis, were grasped by an outstanding leader, the Jamaican *Marcus Garvey*.[22] His United Negro Improvement Association was grounded in his Catholic and Wesleyan roots, and had respectable White support. In America he met with opposition from the respectable mainline middle class church, from Black communist and other political radicals, and from many Whites. He provided worship, self-help and mutual support, education, soup kitchens and even temporary housing, but all in the context of a strong Black national-ism, Pan-Africanism and rejection of mixing with Whites. Garveyism was the most positive aspect of the bursting of Black religion beyond its mainline church bounds.

During this period a myriad of sects and independent congrega-tions arose, a 'plethora . . . no less baffling than the bewildering variety and colourful extravagance of the names'.[23] Wilmore speaks of Black people 'clustered in small congregations in response to highly stylized charismatic religious leadership'. But to the masses, even those who participated, it was a time of disillusion, deteriorating quality and irrelevance.

At the same time the stream, always present in the Afro-American community, of those who rejected religion grew. Intellectuals rejected the church, outstandingly Langston Hughes and the other 'New Negroes' of the Harlem Renaissance. They identified psycho-logically with the masses of the urban poor for whom the Church had become irrelevant, if not actually a 'racket' through which corrupt ministers earned an easy living from gullible and simple Black people. By the 1950's churches which were unresponsive to com-munity needs were being attacked and defaced.[24] Black Christianity would have no doubt lost its mass base had it not been for the emergence of a Southern Baptist preacher, one who was well immersed in the 'old-time religion' style and themes of Black folk Christianity, including the theme of Black liberation, but at the same time exceptionally able academically, well educated in theology and experienced in dealing with wider, White society. On December 1st 1955, in Montgomery, Alabama, Mrs. Rosa Parks refused to give up her bus seat to a White person. Her arrest formed the occasion for a bus boycott which lasted almost a year. The leader of this boycott was the young preacher, the Revd. Dr. Martin Luther King.[25]

Martin Luther King went to Montgomery not to organise protest but to join in a struggle that had already commenced. There he found himself thrust into leadership, for which internal resources of faith were needed. These King drew primarily from his Black Christian heritage, focusing in particular on the New Testament teaching about love, which he put into practice through the Gandhian method of non-violent resistance. The power of his campaign lay in his ability to tap the old-fashioned religion of the people, and draw out passion for justice latent within it, even though it was, as Wilmore says 'suppressed by years of subjugation, and domesticated by the prudence of a mute church'. The story of King's leadership of the

Civil Rights campaign needs no recounting here: his praise is in all the churches. But there is a paradox in his achievements. His starting point is conservative, even bourgeois: the faith of the southern Black Christian within the context of the American promise and the American dream. His methods were 'moderate' in that they were non-violent (although they were too much for many Black church leaders). But this non-violent struggle for incorporation into the American mainstream released contradictions that go far beyond a conservative or a political agenda. The struggle for civil rights was only one dimension of the deeper struggle for Black humanity. Martin Luther King's voice was not one of those openly advocating 'Black pride'; his concern was for equality, and for Whites to become free of their racism. Nevertheless, he incarnated Black pride and dignity. Black humanity unmasked the true basis of the supposed superiority of White people, revealing it to be extreme violence. Television screens around the world nightly carried those unforgettable pictures of Black courage, dignity and self-control, set against White terror, hatred and rage. So a despised and humiliated people became the vehicle of a new humanity. For Black people, the vision of the eschatological new society promised by Christian faith, the 'beloved community', began to be realised. For White people too it became clear that the Christian vision had remained alive among Black people, despite countless White betrayals.

King preached and lived out his vision, developing, especially in the last three years of his life, a radicalism into which many of his closest followers could not enter.[26] He discerned the injustice of economic structures both at home and in the world, and preached a revolution – a revolution against the evils of poverty, of unemployment and of American involvement in Vietnam. King wanted incorporation into the American promise, but he knew how radically that promise, once it was claimed by the downtrodden, would undermine features of American society, not only racism but all structures of injustice.

The very power of his impact was also the cause of King's failure to keep the 'movement' within a Black American-Christian framework. Even before the march on Washington, the unmasking of the crude violence of White power had provoked a response of Black violence. Through the 'long, hot summer' this grew, and with it came the revival of a strongly Black nationalism. As early as 1962 James Baldwin had asked the question, 'Do I really want to be integrated into a house that is burning?'[27] By 1966 the house was literally burning, and the anti-integrationists were not Christians. King's Southern Christian Leadership Conference (S.C.L.C.) gave way to

Stokely Carmichael's Student Non-Violent Co-ordinating Committee (S.N.C.C.) and its new cry of 'Black Power'. But although many of the new Black Power leaders were avowedly secular, the greatest Black nationalist took the Black religious tradition in a new direction. Malcolm Little, like King, was a preacher's son, though Little's father was an ardent disciple of Marcus Garvey. In prison he had been converted to Elijah Mohammed's *Nation of Islam*, popularly known as the 'Black Muslims', and had dropped his slavemaster surname to become 'Malcolm X'.[28] With powerful, irrefutable polemic he denounced White Christianity as the foundation of slavery and the tool of the oppressor. The Christianity of Black people was, for him, irredeemably tainted by that heritage; it had in effect collaborated with it, and was even now diverting resources and energy from the liberation struggle.[29]

Despite Malcolm X's rejection of Christianity, the strength of the Black Church, as well as the calibre of and commitment of its radical leaders such as Albert Cleage and Adam Clayton Powell, eventually forced him to restrain his attack on the Black Church and seek co-operation in the name of racial unity. Much of his message was in any case part of radical Black Christianity – the unmasking of White Christianity, and the prophetic message of the judgement of a righteous God on oppressive, unrepentant White society. Thousands joined Malcolm X; millions heard his words and knew that they were true. Gayraud Wilmore writes, 'the masses heard him and were purified and ennobled by his words'.

Paradoxically, Martin Luther King and Malcolm X belong together in bringing about the Black Revolution. Christian and Muslim, integrationist and nationalist, also Southern and Northern, they competed and co-operated, and established the terms in which the later debate has taken place. The nationalist critique that integration into a sick society is a foolish dream retains its power. Yet this dilemma can clearly no longer be resolved physically or spiritually by an actual return to Africa. The unwilling pilgrimage of Black people to America is an irreversible historical journey. Therefore, the 'integrationist' question remains, 'what place do Black people seek within a White-dominated society?' *Separation* is necessary for affirming cultural identity and developing political strategies that meet the ongoing experience of domination, yet *inclusion* is necessary if Black people are to obtain the political and economic fruits of what Louis-Charles Harvey calls their 'sweat equity', the labour invested in fighting wars and working in industry, for which full payment has yet to be made.[30]

(iii) Black Theology

Between the two poles of the 'rechristianized' radical vision of King's beloved community and the 'dechristianized' radical nationalism of Malcolm X, a new situation was created for the Black Church. As Gayraud Wilmore writes:

> The Church . . . was forced to acknowledge that its vision of an integrated non-violent America as the *telos* of powerless love had alienated large numbers of blacks irretrievably . . . The religio-political legacy of Malcolm X awakened the spirit of dissidence and rebellion in the black church, and Christianity will never again find easy acceptance among black peoples, without proving itself worthy of their respect.[31]

For this task, an articulated Black Theology was needed, one which entered the debate for the future of the Black Revolution and was not simply implicit in the general folk practice of Black Christians.[32]

The first theological response to Black Power came in 1966 from the National Committee of Negro Churchmen (N.C.N.C.), radical Black clergy from northern cities who saw that the coalition between King's Civil Rights movement and White liberals was breaking down. By 1967 Blacks were strong enough to force a National Council of Churches conference on 'The Urban Crisis' to meet in separate Black and White caucuses, a meeting at which Blacks defined the issues and the way forward, whilst Whites began to see their primary task as tackling racism in their own community rather than 'helping' Blacks. Black caucuses in the major White denominations were formed or renewed, as were self-help agencies for Black economic development. Out of these came the famous *Black Manifesto* (1969) which James Forman flung down before the startled congregation of the prestigious Riverside Church in New York.[33] The development programme laid out here was to be funded by 'reparations' totalling $500,000,000 demanded from the White churches and the synagogues of America.

The N.C.N.C. set up a theological working party which for the first time consciously set out to interpret Black faith both from its historic experience of oppression and struggle and in the contemporary context of White racism and of Black Power and Black Consciousness, the secular Black response to King's struggle. They rejected as starting points for Black Theology both Joseph Washington's negative assessment that the Black church had no authentic theology, and the non-violent redemptive suffering ethic of Dr. King. Black Theology was to come from the insight that Black Christianity is comprehensible only as a 'contextual' faith, one which discovers the Word of God in the midst of a necessary social and political struggle.

In 1969 James Cone published *Black Theology and Black Power*, a book of razor sharp polemic which showed how Black Power is a necessary expression of the Gospel in a particular situation of oppression. This book established Black Theology as a permanent contender in theology, and Cone as its leading exponent.[34] He rejected any form of 'theological integrationism', i.e. that Blacks too should sit down at the theological lunch counter! Rather he sought to re-orientate theology to the Black experience as the only possible location for authentic Christian reflection; because there, among the sufferings of the oppressed, the saving action of God had been revealed. The prime task of theology was to make clear what the story of Jesus had to do with liberation, and he concluded:

> Black power is the power to say No; it is the power of blacks to refuse to co-operate in their own dehumanization. If blacks can trust the message of Christ . . . this power to say No to white power and domination is derived from him.[35]

The raw material for Cone's theology was the Black Church, the faith community of his upbringing, with its spirituals and preaching tradition. He interpreted the categories of Biblical faith in that light. For example, both Black and White theologies speak of the 'Otherness' of God. But, whereas for White theologians this may be a theological metaphysic or a 'religious' experience of the numinous, for the Christocentric faith of the Black Church God's otherness is revealed in the sufferings of Jesus. He is a 'stranger' in a world of death and oppression and yet, for that very reason, a friend and ally with them in their struggle for life. ('Oh see my Jesus hangin' high'). James Cone signalled the emergence of Black theology as a liberation theology, one which, instead of approaching reality 'chiefly through thought about it'[36] as successive schools of European theology have done, seeks to answer the problem of the concrete historical existence of an oppressed community.[37]

Since 1969 Black Theology has come of age through a number of processes. Firstly, having broken into theological discourse by a polemical attack, it was necessary to explore the context of Black theological speech about Revelation, God, Humanity, Jesus, the Church, the World and Eschatology. Thus, in his fourth book, *God of the Oppressed*,[38] Cone shows how the God of the Bible story is encountered in Black experience, he reflects on liberation and suffering, and gives a Black Christology and ethic: in all of which the

Black story is made the starting point, the content and structure of Black theology.

Secondly, Black Theology was made to conduct a discussion with White theologians, some sympathetic, like Gollwitzer[39] and Lehmann,[40] others outraged. Discussion centred on the question of *ideology*, the charge that Black Theology confuses the project and aspirations of a particular people with the will of God. As a 'Black theologian who has experienced the dehumanizing effects of White theological reflection', Cone refuses to submit that issue to White judgement since, he says, it can only be answered from within the struggle. At the same time he insists that the biblical story is a check against ideological thinking because it 'has its own integrity and truth independent of our subjective states'.[41] The main achievement of the dialogue, however, was to 'unmask' the ideological nature of *White* theology. The 'interested' nature of supposedly disinterested, neutral theology was exposed. The insights of White theologians were shown to be limited by their privileged position, by the fact that, as Cone puts it, 'they have been only spectators and not victims of suffering'.[42] White theology's claims to universality were thus shown to be false. Black theology had therefore no obligation to seek authentication from White churches. The issue for Black theology is not its universal applicability, but rather, as Wilmore says, 'whether or not it could serve the needs of Blacks who were caught up in oppressive and dehumanizing structures'.[43] This remains the first obligation of Black Theology, in Britain as in America.

Thirdly, Black Theology worked through a number of discussions within itself. First among these was whether Cone's work was too dependent on White theology; despite the force of Cone's critique, was he still doing White theology with a Black veneer?[44] There is, after all, a great gulf between the intellectual world of White theological discourse in which Cone was schooled, and the world of Black culture and religion. This leads to a second question, namely the relationship of Black Theology to Black Christianity on the one hand, and to Black Religion and culture on the other. In other words, is Black Christianity to be understood primarily as a development of the Christian tradition, or primarily as one of the fruits of the journey of the African Diaspora? Wilmore stresses this latter culture-based emphasis. He writes:

It is possible to argue that . . . being black or identifiably 'Negroid' is a unique experience that has, since the contact of African peoples with the white Christian West, produced a unique religion – closely related to, but not exclusively bound by the classic Christian tradition. That, in fact, is the reason for the emergence of a *black* theology.

Having freed Black Theology from being necessarily bounded by classical Christianity, Wilmore pushes its boundaries further. James Cone, he says,

> opened up the possibility of a theology which was neither Protestant nor Catholic but the way black Christians think, feel and act about their liberation with the intensity of an ultimate concern.

Such a theology includes more than organised Black religion, it includes also the attempt of 'Black secular and non-Christian groups' to express and define their experience, in Africa as well as America and the Caribbean. It is rooted in 'ancestral African experience', and articulates 'liberation from every power or force that restrains the full, spontaneous release of the dynamism of body, mind and spirit'. It is, therefore, more than political and economic liberty, it is 'the freedom to be a human being'.[45]

This development will clearly be controversial among Black Christians, and not only with conservatives. Yet wrestling with it is surely vital to the Black theological enterprise, not least in Britain. Wilmore obliges us to return again and again to the actual experience of Black people. This involves the full spectrum of Black Religion including the 'underside' of the Black Church, that 'invisible' survival-oriented folk religion which Black church leaders usually reject, and which White evangelicalism has never fully domesticated. Wilmore instances the 'dreams, beliefs in ghosts, good luck charms and the efficacy of the hoodoo man' by which even 'converted' slaves survived; he includes the impassioned revivalism of storefront churches, and the expression of despair and bitterness.[46] In Britain we must add the powerful emergence of Rastafarians, and the prophetic interpretative role of their music.

Fourthly, Black Theology has developed a self-critical strain through wider dialogue not with classical White theology but with feminist, Latin American, African and Asian theologies. Dialogue with feminist theologians has shown up the remarkable silence of early Black Theology on the question of sexism, a silence which Black women theologians have pointedly compared to the silence of White theology about Black experience. It was James Cone who finally broke this silence, though not until 1976. Even in America there are as yet few Black women among either Black or feminist theologians.[47]

Dialogue with Latin American theologians has revealed the necessity for analysis of society including economic analysis. In this regard Martin Luther King and Malcolm X were developing towards the end of their lives insights which were far more radical than early Black Theology. Both realised it was not enough simply to attack White racism; its relationship to the capitalist organization of society needed exploration, as did the links between American domestic racism and overseas imperialism (at that time epitomised in the Vietnam war). The crucial questions here concern the usefulness of Marxist tools of analysis, so vital to Latin American understanding.[48] Can Marxist theory serve the Black struggle for liberation? Can it do justice to the liberating potential found within Black religion and culture, including Black Christianity? Or is Marxism so much a European product that it is inappropriate for the liberation of Black people? African and Asian theologians have been critical of Latin American rigidity, and failure to take into account indigenous cultures and traditional religions, and to address questions of racism and sexism. Cornel West, the Black American theologian, himself a Marxist, writes:

> When Marxists are preoccupied with an analysis that downplays or ignores the liberating aspects of degraded and oppressed cultures, it suggests that Marxists share the ethos – not of the degraded and oppressed minorities – but of the dominant European culture.[49]

In 1982 West published *Prophecy Deliverance*! in which he argues for an alliance between 'prophetic' (i.e. Afro-American) Christianity and 'progressive' Marxism. James Cone also has reached the conclusion that Marxist theory is indispensable for the analysis of capitalism and class relationships in the Black struggle.[50] This reckoning with class and economic structures is as vital for Black Theology as Wilmore's stress on the total cultural and religious experience of the African Diaspora. It raises just as urgently, however, the relationship of the debate to the institutional Black Church. In this 'religious bulwark', often conservative, other-worldly or bound up with its own internal issues, almost all Black Christians and the majority of the Black American community are to be found. In Britain the structures of the Black Church are different and the proportion of the community it contains is much less. But in both countries the Black theological enterprise has a crucial role, namely to articulate the experience of the Black community in the light of its religious faith whilst sifting both other theologies and secular tools of understanding so that the Black Church can, in Witvliet's phrase 'mobilize for a Messianic community'.[52]

THE CARIBBEAN INHERITANCE

The Afro-Caribbean inheritance is complex and varied – even when we limit our attention to former British colonies.[52] There are different histories of colonial occupation and different patterns of European missionary involvement. Another variable is size: some colonies were large enough for groups of rebel slaves to maintain their independence, and to support a rural free peasantry at Emancipation. In smaller islands where ex-slaves had to remain on the plantations as waged labourers, social uniformity and allegiance to mission churches is consequently greater.

Nevertheless, the variety of Afro-Caribbean Christianity results from the coming together of the same three forces as in North America, namely the original religions and culture of Africa, *the encounter with White Christianity*, and *the oppression of slavery*. So the observations above about an African 'subterranean stream' and the role of the Evangelical Revival are as applicable to the British Caribbean as to the colonies of North America; we have already noted the first efforts of Non-conformist missionaries and the slave rebellions.

The period before the Emancipation of the slaves in 1834 may be termed the period of *the Church against the people*. It was marked by Anglican subservience to the planters and their oppression of the slaves. Ministry even to the planters was half-hearted; there was little serious ministry to the slaves. The newer Non-conformist groups, as we have seen, took a different view, but their work was still conducted very largely within the confines of a slave society: even the most celebrated missionary heroes like Knibb and Smith were not prepared to support slave revolts. Nevertheless, Non conformist mission in the latter half of the eighteenth century pre-figured the post-Emancipation colonial era of *the Church for the people* (no longer 'against' but not yet 'of' the people), a period is only now coming to an end. In colonial times (as opposed to the era of slavery), the ruling powers of church and state recognised the humanity of Black people but regarded them as culturally 'empty vessels' who were to be 'civilized' into a society whose structure was determined in London. The question of *Black cultural identity* was not addressed.

The new mission church commitment had several positive results. Firstly, it helped to bring to an end the semi-autonomous rule of the plantocracy. Secondly, it eventually brought the Anglican Church into struggle against the plantocracy. The chief positive result, however, is the creation of large mission churches, including Anglican churches, with a mass Black membership. The Nonconformists had been growing in all islands in the period before emancipation; in the period immediately after they grew yet more. In Jamaica, Methodist numbers doubled from 1831 to 1841, whilst Baptist membership increased from 10,000 to 34,000 in the same period.[53] As Erskine makes clear, the slaves were not merely acknowledging what the missionaries had done for them; they were investing in the Church their hopes for social and not merely legal emancipation. The churches were, he says, 'an important key to understanding the experiment in freedom'.[54]

The churches had two particular services they could provide for the emancipated Blacks of Jamaica. The first was to provide *land*. The missionaries purchased large tracts of land and divided it between the various families. In just five years from Emancipation the Baptists formed nearly 200 villages totalling 100,000 acres. This movement from chattel to free peasant – from nobody to somebody with the help of the church – was fittingly celebrated by Baptism and church membership.

The second service was *education*. Teaching Black people to read and write was a dramatic lessening of the division between the planters and Black people, whilst giving the latter the opportunity to become deacons and preachers in the Free Churches, or in the Anglican Church, in due time, lay readers, catechists and village schoolmasters. It soon became clear, however, that the structure of the new society was to be determined from London, not by the emancipated Black people, and that the role of education was to bring *that* society into being, not one constructed from Black hopes and aspirations. Erskine writes:

> The Colonial Office wanted to see in the Caribbean a rising middle class made up of mulattoes and highly literate blacks. They wanted to see black people free, thrifty and industrious, but also respectful of the plantocracy and middle class. They did not want to see blacks acquiring political power.[55]

Black people soon discovered that the purpose of the new education was to keep them subordinate: colonialism had replaced slavery.

Here the fundamental theological failure of colonial Christianity must be underlined, for the process of 'decolonizing' theology is far from complete today, even in the Caribbean, let alone in Britain.

The Churches had responded to certain practical needs of the people (land and education) and they had struggled, in some cases most courageously, against obvious oppression. But they had failed to work out a theology for the context of the post-emancipation era. They had no programmes for social reorganization, no wider vision with which to engage their new members. They had not listened to the aspirations of the people; they had not recognised their *identity*. To the churches, Black people were culturally dependent children, empty vessels waiting to be filled. Any African vestiges were refuse to be destroyed; the church would 'civilize' Black people.

Chief among the signs of 'civilization' was the abandoning of African religion for Christianity. Missionaries therefore took the influx of Black people into the churches to mean a victory for Christianity over Black religion. But in fact Black religion continued, co-existing with Christianity. Black people in Jamaica as in the United States stood between their African heritage and White Christianity; they could not be assimilated into colonial Christianity, without sacrificing their identity and accepting the lowly status colonialism gave them.

As in America, the survival of a stream of African consciousness, focused in certain social and religious practices, was vital if Black people were to retain power to define their own identity over against colonialism. In Jamaica, and to a lesser extent in all of the British Caribbean, the stream is more overt, less 'subterranean' than in the United States. The *patois* or Creole language, for example, may be described as 'simply an African language structure in which a variety of European words have been introduced'.[56] Brer Rabbit and other animal stories are told, whilst many Jamaican proverbs are traceable to Ashanti or other originals. According to Barrett the African market with its religious, carnival, political and social atmosphere, is the source of the Jamaican market tradition.

African religious practices thrived, particularly *obeah*, the practice of witchcraft. This is the more anti-social side of African religion which was preserved and developed primarily as a form of resistance to slavery, a response to the 'white sorcery' by which many believed Whites held Black people in bondage. The Ashanti *obaye* ('he who takes away a child') is suggested as the etymological root of the word; the practice of obeah continues to be feared and punished. As Ivor Morrish writes, 'Obeah still seems to permeate the whole social scale in Jamaica, although it is strongly condemned in public, and its practice is a serious criminal offence'.[57]

Myalism, probably from the Ewe and Hausa *maya* (evil) and *le* (to grasp), is a form of 'good magic', grasping the evil magic (obeah)

71

and destroying it. Though myalism was the more positive form of West African religion, the fanatical zeal with which its practitioners sought to destroy obeah aroused an even greater condemnation from White people. This in turn helped the ascendancy of obeah which was the more secretive, malevolent and anti-White cult.

After Emancipation and the consequent influx of Black people into the mission churches, a period of disillusion with the churches and their schools set in. The seriousness of the missionaries' theological failure (described above) was demonstrated by Black people leaving the churches in considerable numbers, and by a series of Myalist revivals which began in 1842 and recurred at intervals over the next thirty years.

The focal point of Black religion was *Kumina*, the ritual worship of Myalism. Walter Hark, a nineteenth century Moravian, describes a service:

> As soon as darkness set in they assembled in large crowds in open pastures, most frequently under huge cotton trees, which they worshipped and counted sacred; and after sacrificing some fowls the leader began his song in a wild strain, which was answered in chorus; then followed the dance, growing wilder and wilder till those who participated were in a state of mad excitement. Some would perform incredible evolutions while in this state, until, utterly exhausted, they fell senseless to the ground, when every word they uttered was received as divine revelation.
>
> Drumming, blowing of the conches, dancing – Verily this more like Heathen Africa than Christian Jamaica.[58]

As we noted in chapter 4, the Great Revival came in 1860–61, a campaign actually launched by the mission churches against popular Black religion, which, however, as it proceeded became increasingly African, a mixture of Myalism and Christianity. This period gave shape to the spectrum of later Jamaican religious practice.

At one end was the *Church of England in Jamaica* allied to colonial rule and culture, the church of the upper and middle classes. It allowed Black people a lowly role as teachers and catechists in the task of conveying White Christianity, colonial culture and colonial social order to Black people. Then came the *various mission churches* which supported this basic colonial pattern, though in varying degrees. Among *Methodists* and *Baptists* Black people obtained higher office than among Anglicans, and exercised more independence of thought as class leaders.

Even so, discontent among Black Methodists at the lack of Black preachers occasioned a split, whilst the Baptists became divided into different factions. These Baptist divisions are of especial significance since the Baptist Church was *par excellence* the context in which in the immediate post-Emancipation era Black people could work out their relationship to the two worlds, missionary Christianity and African traditional religion. The '*Native Baptists*', in particular, being free of Baptist Missionary Society control, allowed considerable growth of Black religious practices. They also pursued issues of social justice such as fair wages, conditions of employment and land distribution, and even organised a political party for the elections of 1844. Such 'Africanisation' and pursuit of social justice produced phenomenal growth in numbers which the more colonial missions resented. Erskine comments:

> These divisions in Baptist and Methodist churches indicate that blackness had become an important point of departure for black people's understanding of their world. They had not surrendered their blackness nor had they abandoned African religious beliefs.[59]

(It should be noted that in the 1970 census, the Baptists were still the largest single Jamaican church with the allegiance of 17.8% of the population and are something of a norm of Jamaican church life by which other denominations can be measured).[60]

It was from the Baptists that the leadership for the *Morant Bay Rebellion (1865)* came. George Gordon was an upper class mulatto, who, as well as becoming a Native Baptist in the 1861 revival, also became a radical politician and champion of the dispossessed. He inspired Paul Bogle, a Native Baptist deacon, to lead the rebellion which led to the dismissal of Governor Eyre and the introduction of Crown Colony status for Jamaica, though only after the killing of over a thousand people in the brutal suppression of the revolt. Popular Afro-Christianity and political liberation were intertwined in the consciousness of the poor Black majority of Jamaican people.[61]

To the 'left' of the Native Baptists various Revival sects and traditions emerged, all fed by the general frustration which followed the crushing of the Morant Bay Rebellion. These include *Bedwardism*, followers of the self-styled Messiah Alexander Bedward; *Zionism*, and *Pukkumina*. All involve drumming, dancing, spirit possession, healing rituals and baptisms and washings. The same is true of the *Kumina* ceremonies, though, being a more direct descendent of Myalism, this has little specifically Christian content and involves the evoking of African tribal gods by name.[62]

Two later developments, of vital importance for understanding the development of Black Christianity in Britain, must be noted, namely Pentecostal churches and the Rastafarians. Iain MacRobert has traced the process by which the *Pentecostal* movement in the United States 'degenerated' from Seymour's original non-racial unity into three distinct streams: 'three-stage' and 'two-stage' according to their doctrine of sanctification, and 'Oneness' (churches who reject classical Trinitarian doctrine and baptise in the name of 'Jesus' only.)[63] American Pentecostalism became largely White and conformed itself to the racial divisions of the United States. The small number of Black people mostly went into the Oneness churches. In the period between the wars both the three-stage stream (Church of God) and the Oneness denominations (Apostolic) became established in Jamaica as the result of missionary activities. Since the Second World War their following has grown from 4% to 20% of the island's population.[64] They have also become established in the other islands of the British Caribbean.

Despite the fact that most Pentecostal denominations are mission churches dependent on a White conservative-evangelical parent body in the United States, three features about their Caribbean form must be noted. Firstly, the movement appeals primarily to the lower classes, those who in Jamaica were previously the constituency of the Native Baptist and Revivalist churches. Secondly, its expansion (as among Black people in the Northern United States) has accompanied an era of transformation from a rural-agrarian to an urban-industrial society. As MacRobert notes:

> Pentecostalism reflects values of modernity, and provides a sense of community and stability in an increasingly fragmented and anomic society.[65]

Thirdly Pentecostalism in the Caribbean, despite its White evangelical formulae, is indigenized under Black leadership and, like the earlier Afro-Christian sects, resonates with the tradition of Black Religion. Although most emigrants to Britain were members of the Anglican or other mission churches, among them was a small minority of Pentecostals whose closeness to the heart of the Afro-Christian religious stream was to prove vital to the future of Black Christianity in Britain.

The *Rastafarians* originated among followers of Marcus Garvey, whose work was mentioned above.[66] They saw in the 1930 coronation of Ras ('Duke') Tafari as Haile Selassie ('Might of the Trinity'), Negus ('Emperor') of Ethiopia a fulfilment of one of Garvey's prophecies and of Biblical revelation. Haile Selassie became for them the Black Messiah of African redemption, an identification which was confirmed when the Italians were finally expelled from Ethiopia in 1941. Until 1960 the various Rastafarian groups were seen as a threat to established order, and potentially seditious. Retreating into camps, they developed the community rituals and practices which now characterize the movement, including the famous 'dreadlocks' appearance, a symbol of their self-image as Ethiopian warriors. On several occasions their camps were raided by the authorities and destroyed.

In 1959 the Henry affair, a prophecy of a mass return to Africa, which led to ruin for hundreds and to civil disturbance when it failed, led to moves which marked the beginning of a more positive assessment of the Rastafarian movement. Sociologists and Rastafarians came together to produce a report in 1960 which made some positive proposals for social improvement and resulted in a Jamaican delegation, including Rastafarians, visiting various African countries. As most countries would only welcome emigrants with skills and qualifications, it brought little practical help for the dispossessed Jamaican poor from which Rastafarians came. The most important consequence of the 1960 report was much wider public recognition of Rastafarians as a repository of Black religion and identity.

The Rastafarians are a heterogeneous group, and it is not possible to summarize their beliefs and practices without oversimplification. However, the divinity of Haile Selassie is affirmed by most; he is the Black Messiah and focus of their hopes to return to Africa/Ethiopia. Jamaica, and thus yet more England, is Babylon, the land of exile where Black people are downtrodden and Rastafarians represent the most oppressed. Because the mind of all Jamaicans has been so polluted by colonialism, the use of ganja, the 'wisdom weed', is necessary to liberate a true consciousness of self, the universe and God. This happens in the 'reasoning' meetings or 'groundations' as well as times of worship and prayer. Rastafarians reverence the Bible, but use it as a collection of symbols to which they alone have the key. Jesus is revered, and the Hebrew Messianic expectations strongly affirmed, but the Christ of faith is not Jesus but Haile Selassie. Christianity is therefore regarded ambivalently. Some respect the churches; a few have joined the Ethiopian Orthodox Church. For most however, Christianity is the White man's religion and a tool of slavery. The Ethiopian Orthodox Church is respected, but most have found its relatively orthodox Christology alienating, as this necessary involves rejection of the divinity of Haile Selassie.[67]

The Rastafarian movement is messianic, but in its classical form escapist rather than revolutionary. It is also 'nativistic', that is an attempt by a de-cultured, oppressed people to reconstruct their culture with little regard to history including current developments in the Ethiopian 'homeland'. More recently Rastafarians have more publicly and more directly addressed the conditions of life in Jamaica. The criticism that the movement is 'dysfunctional in that although it opposes social ills and deprivation it does not seek to rectify those ills',[68] must be modified in the face of a new ideology, 'liberation before migration', stemming from the message believed to have been given to Rasta leaders by Haile Selassie during his visit to Jamaica in 1966.

The subsequent emergence of *reggae*, music developed in the slums of West Kingston which had from the beginning a strong Rastafarian content, has publicised the Rasta message to the world.[69] Through the famous Bob Marley and the *Wailers*, songs with a strong social critique and revolutionary flavour became some of the best known songs of western popular music. Along with praise of Ras Tafari and ganja the 'holy herb', the songs honour Jamaican heroes such as Marcus Garvey and Sam Sharp, and articulate the sorrows, troubles, sicknesses and longings of poor people, along with caustic social comment ('a hungry man is an angry man'), warnings to Babylon, and the longing for freedom.

Rastafari is in many ways a liberation movement, not because it has a clear political and economic programme but because it creates space within the existing system for mental and physical liberation from slavery and colonialism. (Even the language fashioned by Rastas forms part of the protective barrier against Babylon – 'I' instead of 'me' indicating that the Rasta is always subject of his own actions never the object of other peoples, 'I and I' instead of 'we' symbolizing individual freedom and the unity of the Rasta community based on unity with Jah (God). Rasta liberation is not grounded in class struggle as such, but in the deliberate reversal of a world in which a Black skin symbolizes inhumanity and bestiality. For the Rasta, freedom is grounded in humanity, and humanity is grounded in Jah, who is evoked in reggae and the reading of Rasta poetry with the aid of the 'holy weed'. Ultimately, 'Africa' can become a reality in Jamaica – or Britain – and could be open to White people who are prepared to become spiritually Black. In the spectrum of Black religion in Jamaica, Rastafari, like Kumina, is rooted in Africa and is mostly outside the widest definition of the Christian Church, but unlike Kumina it has become explicitly linked to a Messianic figure and is in the broad stream of Black nationalism.

Very few if any Rastafarians were among the Caribbean immigrants to Britain. At the end of the 1960's however, when many in Britain were responding to the Black Power and Black Consciousness movements in the United States, the Garveyite *United Black Improvement Association* was established in England, along with the *Ethiopian World Federation* (of which the Ethiopian Orthodox Church was the official religion). Continued contact with developments in Jamaica led to the first Rastas appearing on London streets in the late 1960's. Rastafari as a focal point for Black identity and humanity was to prove vital to the struggles of Black existence in Britain, especially of the second generation.[70]

The picture of Black religion in the British Caribbean given above is necessarily painted with a broad brush. It should not obscure the fact that for most immigrants to Britain in the 1950's and 1960's their primary conscious religious allegiance was to the Anglican or some other 'mainstream' denomination of missionary origin. Around the liturgies of these churches, within the colonial context, the Black Christian tradition was more or less successfully focused. Interviews with Jamaican and Leeward Islander members of St. James, Aston gave me a vivid picture of Anglican Church life in the late colonial period, with indications of the broader Black Christian tradition underlying it, as they described the norms of church life which shaped their expectations of life in the 'Mother Church' in England. These norms may be summarised as a high level of religious practice, thriving and organised church life, and space for 'unofficial' and personal religious devotion.

Those from *Jamaica* generally regarded the Anglican Church as mainly identified with upper class and English people, though having lower class members especially in the countryside. They respected other 'mainstream' denominations but regarded the Church of God as generally for poor people. Church members would attend church every Sunday, whilst in addition there was much visiting of other denominations within an overtly Christian cultural atmosphere. Confirmation took place at the age of eleven or twelve with thorough Catechism teaching as preparation. Confirmation was a great day; girls wore white dresses and a veil, the boys black suits.

In the *Leeward Islands* society was less religiously plural. Most people were Anglican or Methodist; both these churches respected each other, co-operated, and included all classes of society. Pentecostal churches were often looked down on as 'clap-hand' or 'sideways' churches, people who considered themselves 'more saved'. Church attendance each Sunday was again common, but with a more 'high church' liturgy than in Jamaica. There was a rigorous Communion discipline: people were expected to receive regularly, but only once a month; they would be challenged by the priest if they became irregular. The priest would usually be a well-known and respected figure in the community, a friend but also a figure of authority. The church was the focal point for the religious and social life of members.

In all the islands, religious life extended beyond church services into everyday life. Family prayers were common, people went to concerts, weeknight meetings and services in other churches, including Pentecostal congregations, where they would sing the well-known Sankey hymns. These hymns also accompanied funerals which were big occasions preceded by a wake. Despite criticism of the 'excesses' of the Pentecostals ('calling out', 'falling on the floor' or 'considering themselves the only true Christians') there was a clear area of continuity with the Black Christian tradition. Appreciation of the commanding voice of Black preachers, direct preaching from the Bible, 'feeling the Spirit' during loud corporate singing, the role of 'Sankey', familiarity with extempore prayer, funeral customs and a pervasiveness of spiritual things: all these constituted the outer signs of a deeper Black spirituality which underlay weekly participation in the liturgy of the Anglican Church. Along with their British passport Anglican settlers had brought their Bible, a Book of Common Prayer and a letter of commendation or Communicant or Membership card. Prayers had been part of everyone's farewell, along with tears.

THE BRITISH INHERITANCE

Just as the post-war settlers found that their British passport was not properly honoured in the 'mother country' in that the rights and security it symbolised for them were not really available to them, so the Communicant card was expected to function as a church 'passport' and was generally similarly dishonoured. One person I know well speaks for many:

> After the service I shook hands with the vicar, and gave him the letter of recommendation from my parish priest at home. We chatted for a while. When I came back the next Sunday he completely ignored me, and never spoke to me again. I stopped going soon after.[71]

It was a great shock to meet British Christianity in decay, particularly in the hard-pressed and insecure inner-city congregations where (with rare exceptions) Black Christians were greeted with such humiliating rejection.

(i) 'Black-led' Churches

In the decade following 1952 a major event in British Christian history took place, largely unnoticed by White Christians: *Black Christianity found a new and more explicit focus in the Pentecostal and Holiness Traditions.* As we have seen, 4% of Jamaicans were already 'Church of God' at the end of the Second World War. These were the churches of poorer people, and their tradition, under indigenized leadership, was closer to the heart of Afro-Christianity. Pentecostal leaders – with whom for our purposes must be linked the Holiness tradition – were among the first immigrants and gradually grouped around them disaffected members of other churches. Ira Brooks, himself an ex-Anglican alienated by a 'chilling' reception in a Gloucester church, tells the story of the New Testament Church of God:

> Even those who had entrusted themselves into the fellowship of the established religious institutions of the country began to sense an environment of growing coldness. With the natural human desire for fellowship and acceptance, most of the immigrants discarded their old religious differences, and in their need for consolidation, accepted the pentecostal gospel message.[72]

Obviously the rise of the new Black-led churches was prompted by racism in the historic churches. But racism in churches is not the only factor, even when we include the racism of White Pentecostals.[73] Entry into British churches, even friendly ones if such could be found, involved the automatic loss of contact with the wider oral-communal tradition of Black Christianity. In the Caribbean, the link between mission church allegiance and the deeper Black Christian tradition, with its capacity for sustaining survival and its implicit liberation theology, had been strong enough to sustain mass Black membership of the mission churches. The link was broken in England, a context where the need to survive and be free was now even more pressing. The encounter with British churches was part of a wider experience of loss, the loss of the Afro-Caribbean social context. Paul Burrough has described this as:

> four things of infinite value: a real community that upheld you, a wide united family not bereft of the wisdom of old people . . . a religion which was part of a living culture, and a climate which was loving and undemanding.[74]

The Pentecostal church fellowship made up for some of this loss in the way that a White-dominated congregation could not.

Black Christianity has always been, and in Britain today still is, much more than a response to loss and a reaction to racism. It is created through the continual interaction of positive historical, cultural and spiritual forces, many of which are rooted in Africa, with the difficulties of the present time. It retains the potential to blossom with creativity in each new stage of the Diaspora. The Black-led churches in Britain are such a blossoming.

Their development may be outlined by reference to five stages listed by Roswith Gerloff.[75] First came the period of *early mission*, mainly in the early 1950's. This was the time of rejection by the established churches and the emergence of house meetings fellowships, together with less successful attempts at open evangelism to the White community. Next was the period of *denominationalization*, in which the emerging church communities established links with parent bodies overseas, particularly in the United States. This was a period of great growth, but the American link raised serious questions for the future. As Roswith Gerloff says:

> Britain became an American mission-field. On one hand this gave support and recognition to people alienated from British church life and society. On the other hand it was a development which denominationalized an inter-denominational mission . . . and worked to the disadvantage of Black unity, comparable to the 'divide-and-rule' principle of colonial rule.

Thirdly, the period of *proliferation*, dating from about 1961, saw many new denominations formed because of personality conflicts, doctrinal difficulties, resentment at permanent White American oversight or the island of origin of members. The first African independent churches were also formed during this period. Fourthly, the period of *stabilization* may be dated from the early 1970's. In this period church government structures were firmly established, and strict doctrinal statements and moral discipline adopted. Smaller churches developed patterns of mutual support, whilst larger churches had considerable strength both in membership and financial viability, all, as Gerloff says, 'tested in twenty or thirty years of mutual support'. Some leaders were able to develop a wider community ministry, addressing the social problems, racism and alienation experienced in particular by young people. But the respect such ministers achieved was insufficient to prevent blocked communication between the leadership and younger people within the church. Many young people were radicalized, usually away from the church, and in many cases towards Rastafari.

Lastly Gerloff defines the current period as the period of *Inter-denominational, Interracial and Intercultural Fellowship*. From the early 1970's the Black-led churches have become better organised to respond to their people's problems. Several all-Black inter-church councils have been formed, such as the West Indian United Council of Churches, as well as interdenominational community service projects such as the United Evangelical Project in Birmingham. The churches established centres of theological education, outstandingly the Central Bible Institute in Birmingham and Overstone College, Northampton. At the same time co-operation with concerned White Christians developed, particularly around issues of social justice and theological education.[76] As well as informal links, two notable institutions have emerged: the Zebra Project at the Bow Mission in East London, and the Centre for Black and White Christian Partnership, Selly Oak, Birmingham.

Louis-Charles Harvey, on the basis of his recent research in Britain, adds a sixth stage, the *period of Radicalization* dating from the late 1970's. With a background of continuing co-operation between Black and White Christians, this period is characterized by the emergence of an explicitly radical voice in the Black-led churches, a 'small cadre of black Christians who are calling upon the country and the church to change'.[77] The promise of this 'cadre' and the problems they face are a key element for our examination later of the theological legacy of the Black Church in Britain.

As we have noted, the Black Church in Britain is divided denominationally, partly as a result of American mission, and partly as a result of later fragmentation. Gerloff defines nine traditions as follows:[78]

1) *African Methodist Episcopal*, with only a small presence in Britain.

2) *The Sabbatarian movement*, including the Seventh Day Adventists, one of the oldest English non-conformist groups now revitalized and expanded by its new Black embership. Tension in the 1970's between the existing White leadership of the church and the new membership who were much more community orientated, resulted in the emergence of a much freer, Black style of worship, as well as Adventist Gospel groups and choirs who have made a major contribution to Black Christian music in Britain.

3) A number of smaller groups related historically to the *Native Baptists and Revivalists* of Jamaica.

4) *The Holiness Movement*, a nineteenth century movement which traces its heritage back to Wesley's doctrine of sanctification. Its main representative is the Wesleyan Holiness Church, a church which

separated from American Methodism over the abolition of slavery, the emancipation of women, commitment to the poor, and non-hierarchical church structures. Its worship in Britain is clearly in the Black tradition though its parent body is White. The denomination is strongly aware of its Methodist heritage.

5) *The Trinitarian Pentecostals* represented by two large White American-based sister churches, the New Testament Church of God and the Church of God of Prophecy, and some offshoots. As the outspoken New Testament Church of God pastor Ira Brooks has pointed out, indigenization, both in appointment of senior leadership and in a more general freedom to address the British context and 'name' their Black Christian tradition, is a major issue for both churches.[79] The Calvary Church of God in Christ, loosely related to the North American C.O.G.I.C. may be linked with this group. Roswith Gerloff describes them as 'a rich ground for comparative studies in African retentions'.

6) The *Oneness Pentecostals*, about a third of Black Pentecostals. Malachi Ramsey's Shiloh United Church of Christ is the largest indigenous Black-led church in Britain, and is markedly dynamic in its pursuit of social change, and ecumenical links with other Christians.

7) *The Pentecostal Healing* movement, a smaller group of churches, strongly influenced by American healing evangelists.

8) The *African Independent Churches*, notably the Aladura International Church in London and the Cherubim and Seraphim Church in Birmingham. Though of West African origin, they have two features of particular interest for this study. Firstly, they are a yardstick of African cultural continuity in Caribbean churches, since their worship has several features, such as healings, dancing, shouting and speaking in tongues, in common with Afro-Christianity from the New World. Secondly, unlike the North American or Caribbean Pentecostal churches, the 'White' element in their origins and worship is usually Roman Catholic or High Church Anglican.

9) The *Ethiopian Orthodox Church*. Its recent history in Britain has been complicated by uncertainty as to how to respond both to Rastafarian interest and to developments in post-revolutionary Ethiopia. Rastafarians have been drawn to each of two factions of the Church, one linked with the Church in Ethiopia and the other not, but faced at times by the requirement that dreadlocks be cut off, they have remained small in number.

(ii) 'Mainstream' Churches

In the period following 1952 another important event in British Christian history took place, namely, the *consolidation of Black Christians in 'mainstream' denominations*. This tenth part of the Black Church in Britain, Black Roman Catholics, Anglicans, Methodists, Reformed and Baptists, remained 'invisible' to the White church, whilst Black Pentecostals, in most case only recently liberated from 'cold', 'nominal' White denominations have not often been able to reflect positively on the situation of their Black brothers and sisters.

Patterns of involvement vary. 2.1% of the 'Methodist community' (members and 'adherents') in England and Wales are Black, though many of these are concentrated in certain inner-city and other urban areas where they form a much higher proportion of the Church. In the second chapter of *A Tree God Planted*, Heather Walton outlines the different situations in which Black Methodists live their church life. Where Black people are a small minority they may be a passive but accepted group, or they may still be unwelcome. Where they are in a substantial minority or a majority this is the result either of the commitment of the minister, or of some struggle in the history of the church. In the former situation one minister fears 'what has taken six years to establish would disappear in less than six months if someone who was not flexible or not in sympathy with the people were to be given pastoral charge'. In other cases a strong and confident mainly Black church has resulted, one whose life is substantially determined by the needs and the future of the Black community. Even here, however, the question of what kind of future ministry the Methodist Church can provide will have to be faced. Black people are seriously under-represented in ordained ministry and in all offices and decision-making bodies of the Methodist Church when compared with White people.[80]

The Church of England has not produced any definitive study; such work as exists is the result of diocesan initiative or the concern of individuals. However, *A Chance to Change*, Renate Wilkinson's study of the Diocese of Birmingham, shows similar patterns of church membership. Over half the churches have some Black people attending regularly, although they are less likely than Whites to be on the Electoral Roll (the adult membership list). Nevertheless, as we have seen, in a Diocese which includes one rural and several suburban areas where few Black people live, Blacks make up 10% of electoral rolls, but are seriously under-represented in the ordained ministry, and in all offices and decision-making bodies of the church.[81]

A rather different study, *With You in Spirit?*, has been produced for the Roman Catholic Archdiocese of Westminster by the Cardinal's Advisory Group on the Catholic Church's commitment to the Black Community. It is produced by a mainly Black group rather than individual White researchers. It does not include statistics but delineates sharply patterns of racism implicit and explicit in Catholic church life and education. It confirms and complements the findings of the Anglican and Methodist studies.

(iii) Rastafarians

This picture of the British inheritance would be incomplete without mention of *Rastafari* in Britain. The 'Rasta Renaissance' in Britain took place in the 1970's, especially from 1973 onwards. Rastafari provided an explanation of experience and a new identity for the British-born generation of Afro-Caribbean people. Their consciousness as Black people developed, and their understanding of the racism they were subjected to grew, as they saw their parents' expectations of life in Britain disappointed. So the new Rasta religious style and concepts fed into and interpreted a pressing awareness of social context and identity. As this happened, whole sections of the community were touched by an experience of cultural rebirth, what one Rasta called 'the revival of our true self and the discovery of our history'.[82]

Once this had begun to happen the legitimacy of the existing moral and social order was undermined, and revealed as colonial and oppressive, a 'Babylon conspiracy'. Rastafarian order or 'God's law' was, by contrast, legitimated. Thus a gulf was formed not only between young Blacks and White society (including schools, social services and the police), but between young Blacks and their parents. Parents were suddenly shut out of their children's world view, and the peer group 'reasoning' sessions become all important. In this process not only White-led churches but also Black-led Pentecostal churches were seen as corrupted by colonialism.

Cashmore writes:

> The links between their parents' deprivation and their membership of a Christian church was a powerful one in the mind of the Rastas.[83]

In more recent years the practice of Rastafari has declined, though it is still strong. Its greatest importance will probably prove to be the permanent effect it has had on consciousness. Even older people are now 'de-colonized' to the extent that they are willing to affirm their African roots. Wilmore's concern that Black theology must proceed on the basis of the broad Black religious experience and cannot be restricted to 'Christianity' as normally conceived (see above, p. 67) receives powerful support. The challenge to the Black church to identity itself with the poorest and most dispossessed, and to affirm its Blackness as over against White allegiances (including Pentecostal ones) is powerfully articulated by Rastafari, and crucial to the future of the Black church.

As Rastafari grew in strength, most older Black Christians were horrified at their children's involvement. Their inability to affirm the new generation's search for authentic humanity, whilst understandable, was the source of much pain and estrangement. Parents did, however, rightly perceive that Rastafari, like earlier Black nationalism, fails to answer the necessary question of how Black people can survive and be liberated *within* Babylon, – within Britain, – as the dream of a literal return to Africa fades. Of investing in Babylon, of even seeking the welfare of that city (Jeremiah 29:[7]) without 'whoring' after false colonial gods, a radical Black Church may yet have much to say.

I have attempted above to trace the roots and outline the story of Black Christianity in Britain. It remains to note the importance for the Black Church of *developing a theology arising out of and relevant to the British context*. As Louis-Charles Harvey concludes in his research:

> The Black Church in Britain is in the process of developing a relevant theology which embraces their dual heritage as people of African descent and as Christians.[84]

This theology will be one that has the liberation of the poor at its centre, and derives its stance from reflection on the oppression of Black people in a racist society. It will, according to Harvey, be a movement parallel to that which developed in the USA from 1966 onwards, and Harvey challenges Black Christians here to produce an appropriate theological statement. Their main obstacle will, he says, be a deficient theological legacy in two areas: Holy Spirit and Eschatology. Clearly the Holy Spirit is of first importance in Pentecostal experience, and yet in Harvey's view, 'most do not see possession of the Holy Spirit as empowering them to fight the evil racist system which oppresses them'.[86] He finds the reason for this in traditional Pentecostal eschatology, where eyes are set mainly on the world to come, with consequent indifference to political and social problem. Harvey calls this 'living (only) on the Hallelujah side', a fatal separation of body and soul in which the oppressed unwittingly collude in their own oppression. This is not part of the African religious legacy, where religion pervades all of life, nor is it consistent with the Black Christian Tradition where faith in God is the means of survival and the source of hope for liberation. However, Harvey finds hope in the 'cadre' of radical Black Christian leaders who, significantly, include Black Christians from 'mainstream' churches, as well as Ira Brooks, Malachi Ramsey and those involved in setting up the Afro-West Indian Council of Churches. Harvey concludes:

The Black Church in Britain should rush to embrace the Biblical heritage of the Exodus, the liberating ministry of Jesus, the power of Pentecost and the continuing witness of God to the oppressed, and transmit this through its preaching and its ministry to succeeding generations.

6
Comprehensiveness and Black Christianity

So the three stories are told: my own, that of my church and that of Black Christianity. I have found myself priest and pastor at a point where the Black 'underside' of Christian history has 'collided' with White history. But this 'collision' has changed both parties, an interaction which gives rise to a new self-understanding for the historically White institution and for its Black members. In this chapter I will outline what I consider this self-understanding should be; in the next chapter I will record the articulated self-understanding of a number of Black members of the Church of England; and in chapter 8 I will outline and reflect on some key areas of new building for a truly Black and White church. The general shape of the argument, if not all the details, may illumine the experience of other 'mainstream' denominations.

THE CHALLENGE TO THE CHURCH

To speak of Black Christianity in the Church of England is to jolt the theological and conceptual framework of many Christians. Although the worldwide Anglican Communion has a Black-majority membership, and despite thousands among the post-war Caribbean settlers being Anglicans, Black Anglicans in England have been a forgotten and 'invisible' people. 'Invisible People' is, in fact, the title of a paper written by a Black priest.[1] It is a significant self-naming: by choosing a clearly unacceptable 'victim' designation for his community of faith, the author thereby makes a dialectical challenge to the structures and dominant consciousness of the Church. By asserting 'invisibility' he begins the process of becoming 'visible', and raises the question: what will the Church be like when that which is invisible becomes visible? To pursue that question we look first at an

Anglican understanding of what the New Testament says about the Church, and then at a self-understanding which coheres with that model.

THE NEW TESTAMENT

What, in the providence of God, is the Church? To arrive at a working answer to this huge question we begin by turning to the New Testament, the text which, in the Anglican as in other Christian traditions, is accepted as authoritative.[2] Alan Richardson, a modern Anglican theologian who stands in the mainstream of the Church's theological tradition, is our guide as to how Anglicans may understand the nature and purpose of the Church.[3]

According to the Biblical story, the Fall into sin has disrupted God's original harmony of things but it is His purpose to restore that harmony through Christ's redeeming work. Christ's work is God's forgiving judgement on history. In our salvation we are not returning to a golden age of lost innocence. We can never be as if sin had not been – Black and White can never be as if slavery had not been – but God sets the redemptive initiative of Christ over against sin, and through Christ's judgement and forgiveness we can become a New Creation. This New Creation will not be the rescue of a remnant from the fury of destruction as in the days of Noah, but a cosmic universal redemption, uniting all things in Christ (Eph.1^{10}).

We can appreciate how earlier generations even rejoiced over the Fall, because it leads to so great a salvation. '*Felix Culpa*', they called it, a 'happy fault'. As the medieval carol *Adam lay Ybounden* puts it:

Ne had the apple taken been,
The apple taken been,
Ne had never Our Lady
A-been heavenè queen.

Blessd be the time
That apple taken was.
Therefore we moun singen
Deo Gracias![4]

So we no longer have to make do merely with Eden, but can look forward to 'what eye has not seen, nor ear heard, nor the heart of man conceived' (1 Cor. 2^9), God's purpose firmly decreed for us 'before the ages', 'for our glory' (2^7). At the end of time the process will be complete, but Christians already taste and experience it within history in the Church. It follows that the Church is *the first-fruits of the New Creation*.

The New Testament further defines the Church through a series of images which are unfailingly organic and holistic. They do not allow of division, separation or denominationalism; they insist that all the people of God live together in one organism where there is neither Jew nor Greek, slave nor free, male nor female. The New Testament is so radical and so extreme in its teaching in this regard, that anyone coming to it for the first time knowing only the myriad of groupings which today call themselves 'church' would be amazed. Biblical teaching is reflected in the Nicene Creed: the Church of Jesus Christ is 'One, Holy, Catholic [=Universal] and Apostolic Church'. The Church is much more than a voluntary society, an interest group, or a useful alliance of individual believers for mutual support or the furtherance of common aims.

The most familiar term, *ecclesia* (assembly) is perhaps the least obviously organic. Yet it is the 'designation of a people, the citizens' meeting of God', and is chosen in preference to less organic terms.[5] A more organic image is that of *oikos* (household or family). Of this community God is Father; Father of Jesus Christ and our Father because of our new relationship to Him through Christ. Christ is 'over God's house as a son' (Hebrews 3^6), in contrast to Moses the servant (3^5), a status now belonging to Paul, his fellow workers, and by extension all Christians. Yet we are more than this, we become fellow sons and daughters with Christ, and by adoption are therefore heirs of all the inheritance of the household.

Similarly the Church is the *laos* (people) of God, into which Christians are born again, just as they are necessarily naturally born into a nation. They are a pilgrim people journeying towards the fullness of the New Creation, the 'city which is to come' (Heb. 13^{14}). On the journey they suffer experiences of hardship through which their discipleship is purified.[6] This people is named the (new) *Israel of God* (Gal. 6^{16}) an eschatological people born to fulfil his purposes. They are neither a mere continuance of the old Israel, nor an unconnected new creation, but the first fruits of the redemptive act by which the Christian Church, a community of Jews and Gentiles, was made the heir of God's promise.[7]

It is not surprising, therefore, that the New Testament uses Old Testament images to portray the inalienable, corporate unity of the Church. It is related to Christ like *branches and vine*; indeed Christ *is* the vine (John 15, cf. Is. 5).[8] Christ is the *bridegroom* and the Church the *bride* (Eph. 5, cf. Is. 54^{5-7}) and their unity is even described as *one flesh* (Eph. 4, 5^{22-23}).[9] So the Church is not just a community of those who follow a leader, they actually *become* Christ. Only once does the New Testament dare to use the expression *partakers of the divine nature* (2 Peter 1[4]), but the Church's total identification with Christ is expressed in the term *soma* (body) of Christ, into which people of diverse cultural and social groups are baptised (I Cor. 12[12–13]). The inescapable, corporate participation in sin, expressed through Adam who is at once an individual and a collective personality ('Everyman'), is reversed by the new or second Adam, Jesus Christ, in whom are all believers. 'For as in Adam all die, so also in Christ shall all be made alive' (I Cor. 15[22]).[10]

It follows that the *Church cannot be divided*. There are no 'denominations', for which the only New Testament words available are *schismata* (divisions or wounds, I Cor. 1[10], 12[25]), or *haireseis* (heresies, more accurately self-chosen opinions). Nor is the unity of the Church only an invisible unity, which as Richardson puts it, would 'imply a kind of "Christian Science" view of the *schismata* of the body of Christ, treating them (as Paul did not) as if they were figments of the imagination'.[11] The new commandment of love concerns actual visible relations of the disciples of Christ with one another, for 'by this all will know that you are my disciples' (Jn. 13[34]). There can be 'churches' only in the sense of the local church (e.g. 'the *ecclesia* of God which is at Corinth,' I Cor. 1[2]); it is the Church of Jesus Christ in that place. One may have the Church of Corinth, or Thessalonica, – or of Geneva or England, but not of Apollos, Cephas, Calvin or Wesley. 'The contradiction of universality is not locality but denominationalism'.[12] 'The total Church exists before local churches do'.[13]

This people of startling organic inter-dependence and unity exists, however, in a paradoxical situation, namely that what it is has not yet fully come to be. There is a *no longer* about being in Christ ('no longer under a custodian' Gal. 3[35]), but there is also a *not yet* – ('it does not yet appear what we shall be' I Jn. 3[2]). For all the indicatives about the Church (we are the body of Christ, purified, sanctified etc.) the New Testament abounds in imperatives. Col. 3[5] and 3[9] place the two startlingly close together 'Put to death what is earthly in you . . . seeing that you have put off the old nature'.[14] The fullness of the Christian vision is not thereby reduced; we cannot settle for less because the fullness is not yet realised. We must acknowledge that the present experience is less than the summing up of all things, just as we acknowledge that a child is less than an adult – but not in the way that half an adult is less than an adult! The child *is* an adult *in hope*. We, the Church, 'are what we are in hope'.[15] We rejoice in our hope of sharing the glory of God . . . and hope does not disappoint us' (Rom. $5^{2,5}$). So the Church is indivisible, but this is not a given, static reality, enforced by a powerful ruler or structure of authority. Rather it is a dynamic, eschatological reality, constantly being born through pain and struggle and guaranteed only by God's promise of his future.

THE CHURCH OF ENGLAND

The Church, which is a foretaste of God's purpose to unite all things in Christ, must necessarily seek to include 'all things' in it. It belongs to the nature of the Church to be catholic (universal) and therefore to be diverse and plural. The relationship between the diverse parts of the Body is to be sustained in love and unity of purpose, and it is the Apostolic task (in the Anglican tradition focused upon the Bishop) to guard and maintain that unity in diversity through love. Anglican writers often present their church as striving for New Testament inclusiveness by pointing to the very tension that exists between various theological and spiritual streams within Anglicanism.[16] Michael Ramsay, for example, wrote in 1936:

> (The Anglican Church's) credentials are its incompleteness, with tension and travail in its soul. It is clumsy and untidy, it baffles neatness and logic. For it is sent not to commend itself as 'the best type of Christianity' but by its very brokenness to point to the universal Church wherein all have died.[17]

More recently John Whale has made a similar claim:

> (Anglican) comprehensiveness . . . seems to me more than merely sensible. It is Christian. It is in line with some of the most self-authenticating things in the record of what Jesus said. 'Come unto me, all ye that labour and are heavy laden . . . '. It is a small paradigm of the mercy of God.[18]

William Wolf, an American Episcopalian theologian, speaks of *'comprehensiveness for the sake of truth.'* Anglicanism is for him a 'Christian archetype', a *'pastorally and liturgically oriented dialogue between four partners: catholics, evangelicals, and the advocates of reason and experience.'*[19] This model is used as the basis of our examination of Anglicanism.

Dialogue is, in Wolf's understanding, the dynamic of the Spirit by which the Church's unity is constantly created. It is not dependent on an external authority, and is constantly at risk (for example of being taken hostage by extremists) for the sake of God's future. Wolf is quite clear that the dialogue is *dialectical*, 'no mere juxtaposition of different views'.[20] Out of the struggle of conflict comes a new future, one well expressed by Charles Gore a century ago:

> It is the vocation of the English Church to realize and to offer to mankind a Catholicism which is scriptural, and represents the whole of Scripture, which is historical, and can know itself free in the face of historical and critical solace; which is rational and constitutional in its claims of authority, free at once from lawlessness and imperialism.[21]

The use of this last word is particularly prophetic for our purposes.

Catholics, the first partner in the Anglican dialogue, affirm that the Anglican Church is in continuity with the ancient English Church and rooted in the primitive, catholic and (as Anglicans have somewhat unhistorically called it) 'undivided' church. In Anglicanism the bishop, as we have noted, is the focus of succession to the authority of the apostles, and the Church affirms the Holy Scriptures, the Catholic Creeds and Dominical Sacraments. The Reformation is regarded as an event in the history of the English Church, a cleansing of an existing body, not the founding of a new one.

Yet within the Catholic framework is a theology which owes more to Luther, Calvin and Zwingli. To *evangelicals* Scripture is the touchstone by which all tradition is judged. The Creeds themselves are acceptable because they are 'proved by Scripture'. The Reformation restored the Bible to the people, and in their own language. Believers are 'justified by grace through faith' and clergy are servants and pastors, not mediators of a sacramental system between God and human beings. Nothing can be required as an article of saving belief which is not 'proved' by Scripture.[22]

Anglicanism has always recognised *reason* as a partner in the dialogue. For Richard Hooker (1554–1600), the systematic apologist for the Elizabethan Settlement, it was the human but God-given faculty whereby he delineated the Anglican *via media* between the excesses of Rome and Geneva. 'In defect of proof infallible,' he wrote, 'the mind doth rather follow probable persuasions'. 'Such as the evidence is . . . such is the heart's assent thereto'.[23] Reason affirms learning and culture, the fruits of the human spirit as uncovered and developed, for example, by the Renaissance humanists in Hooker's day. Reason requires critical enquiry; it led later bishops to found the Royal Association for the Advancement of Science. The

Cambridge Platonist Benjamin Whichcote (1609–1683) gave a forceful and celebrated answer to Puritan Calvinism:

> 'To go against reason is to go against God: it is the self-same thing, and to do that which the reason of the case doth require and that which God Himself doth appoint. Reason is the Divine governor of a man's life. It is the very voice of God.[24]

Experience is also a human faculty but at the opposite pole from reason, which it often perceives as a life-denying enemy. Experience is a free spirit which allows awareness of God and of human feelings which are outside the confines of Scripture and Church Tradition, and not bound by reason. This includes mysticism; it includes the Anglican John Wesley feeling his heart 'strangely warmed' at a meeting in Aldersgate Street.[25] Anglican comprehensiveness has been least at ease with this partner in its dialogue, however, as the eventual emergence of Methodism as a separate denomination indicates.

Anglicanism is a *liturgical and pastoral tradition* which in its attempt to be faithful to New Testament teaching and the historical reality of the Catholic church, tried to embrace the whole of the English Christian community at prayer. So the 'dialogue' has been historically expressed in a particular liturgical form, a particular way of being 'comprehensive for the sake of truth', which was crystallised in the *Book of Common Prayer*. This book, together with the Bible, historically contains all that is necessary for Anglican public worship, and more than any other book it is a private devotional manual as well. It has shaped the heart and mind of much of the English nation, its phraseology has passed into the language.[26]

If Anglicanism is a *dialogue*, the Anglican *via media* cannot be static achievement. There can be no agreement on the degree of loyalty to be given to each element in the dialogue, and they will often conflict. Dialogue is a dynamic process, one which is never finished and can therefore respond to the developments of human history, but which takes place within a 'common prayer', a shared liturgical life. Hence Anglicanism's most contentious issues are usually those which come closest to the liturgical heart of Anglican identity such as liturgical reform and the ordination of women. John Habgood has described how this liturgical heart, like the *via media*, cannot be static. Its development however must be slow, responding gradually to cultural change so as to continue to perform its historic unifying function for the Church:

A written liturgy can express the mind of a Church more subtly and more flexibly and hence more permanently than a doctrinal formulation. Christians are what they pray. And in so far as what they pray is the distillation of centuries of experience, then the Christian life can have a depth and security which transcends changes of intellectual exploration. A liturgy which is to exert this kind of stabilising effect must inevitably have a traditional air.[27]

Technically, Dr. Habgood notes, to use more than the approved liturgy is not lawful. But he recognises that in reality an experimental 'spearheading' function of liturgy is necessary. This is *ad hoc* and should be left to personal initiative. His ideal is the attractive one of 'a stable centre with adventurousness at the edges'.[28]

A FIFTH VOICE

An organically inclusive and indivisible Church, which is a dynamic and eschatological reality fashioned out of the tensions of the different groups within it, is a New Testament model of the Church. It seems, at first, to be fully reflected in the Anglican self-understanding of a liturgically and pastorally-orientated dialogue, the source of whose dynamic is the creative tension and dialectic of the interchange between four partners. However, this traditional Anglican inclusiveness has not been incarnated into the 'flesh' of social and political reality; it makes no reference to a pluralism of *culture*, no reference to issues of power and wealth; it is limited to the ecclesial and theological sphere. And where little is said about society, about culture and about socio-political existence, much is assumed.

Anglicanism began as a creation of the state, as under the Elizabethan Settlement the Church of England was made to hold together two sharply opposed forms of Christianity, one looking to authority and tradition, the other to personal judgement and Scripture. It has through the centuries legitimated monarchy, empire, slavery and colonialism as well as class and ethnic loyalties within Britain. It has not, for example, sustained the political aspirations of the mass of Irish or Welsh people, nor of the entrepreneurs of the English Industrial Revolution, still less those of the industrial working class. Anglicanism abroad is also bound by its history, by what the Ghanaian Anglican, John Pobee, in a recent article has called its 'Anglo-Saxon captivity'. Pobee writes:

Non-Anglo-Saxon dioceses have the English albatross around their necks and they need to free themselves of it . . . in freeing themselves of the English albatross they will be helping free the Church of England.[29]

Pobee's article is in *The Study of Anglicanism,* a symposium of articles by thirty-one contributors - all of whom except Pobee are British, Irish or North American! Moreover even his concern for the liberation of African Anglicanism is primarily 'cultural'; only in one paragraph does he allude to colonialism by mentioning the 'poverty and pain, suffering and degradation of Africa', and makes the following momentous demand almost incidentally:

> *Ecclesia Anglicana* in Africa cannot but affirm the preferential option for the poor and work out its practical implications. The model of the Church there cannot be the prestigious rich Solomonian temple, but a tent.[30]

Anglicanism has been an imperial religion; the demand to move from the temple to the tent strikes at the heart of its traditional socio-political role. It is a demand for conversion, for which the model of Anglican comprehensiveness outlined above is quite unprepared.

Habgood's model of 'adventurousness at the edges' would be utterly inadequate for this conversion. Though an appropriate model for gradual adaptation to general cultural change in England and perhaps useful even in contexts of more demanding cultural change abroad, as a response to Black Christianity it would be merely patronizing. For it would make Black people an adventurous extra, an exotic appendage to the Church's existing spiritual life, one which would scarcely, if at all, affect the core. It may be that this is precisely how Black Anglicans in England have been regarded.

Wolf's model of partners in a 'dialogue' nonetheless offers a way forward. Through Black Anglicans, Black Christianity becomes *a fifth partner in the conversation*, a fifth representative taking a full seat at the table of theological discourse at the heart, not the edge of the Church's life. It represents there the 'poverty and pain, suffering and degradation' that have been the underside of the Church of England's life, and will engage in a converting dialectic by presenting the face of the victim to the oppressor.

Black participation in the Anglican dialogue changes the dialogue almost beyond recognition. For Black Christianity is grounded in the historical relationship of Black people to White; it is their response to oppression. White Christians cannot converse with the Black

Christian Tradition without their oppressive identity being revealed. Black Christianity has a dialectical function which does not conduct dialogue in a discarnate ecclesial sphere but brings explicitly into the dialogue the story of a relationship of oppressor and victim. Its task is first to *negate*; to lacerate the polluted core of Anglicanism, as the beginning of a process of *transformation*. The Black American theologian Cornel West, describes this process (he is writing of course of White Christianity in general, not particularly of Anglicans):

> Black theologians have, for the most part, been compelled to adopt a dialectical methodology. They have refused to accept what has been given to them by White theologians: they have claimed that all reflection about God by Whites must be digested, decoded and deciphered . . . Since its inception, Black theologians have been forced to reduce White deception and distortion of the Gospel and make the Christian story meaningful in light of their oppressive conditions.
>
> Black theological reflection begins by *negating* White interpretations of the gospel, continues by *preserving* its own perceived truths of the biblical texts, and ends by *transforming* past understandings of the Gospel into new and novel ones. These three steps embody an awareness of the social context of theologizing, the need to accent the historical experience of Black people and the insights of the Bible, and the ever-evolving task of recovering, regaining and repeating the Gospel.[31]

Black Christianity poses this dialectical challenge to each partner in the four-way Anglican dialogue. It challenges the *Catholic* claim to be universal by exposing the extent to which that universality has depended upon imperial power. It negates the imperialism bound up with historic Catholicism. It forces us to re-examine the traditional symbols of the 'universal' church: the identification with Rome,[32] centre of a conquering, colonizing, enslaving empire; or the Bishop of Rome who, though 'successor' of the poor fisherman Peter, lives in a royal palace and is a prince among princes. It compels us to ask how in the Liturgy the Lord's death can be proclaimed when vessels of gold, silver and priceless jewels are used, or how bread can be His Body when it is bought with the sweat of the poor.[33] How can a privileged functionary of the ruling class be the 'representative of Christ' in celebrating Mass, and how has the dusty cloak of the poor man of Nazareth been transformed into alb, stole and chasuble, liturgical forms of Roman imperial dress.[34]

Nor is this only a matter of outward symbols; the whole of

'catholic' history will have to be re-examined from the 'underside' of Christian history, including even those struggles in the so-called 'undivided' Church which the Catholic Tradition takes as bastions of orthodoxy. For example, it will lead us to examine to what extent hostility to the Donatists of North-West Africa in the fourth century[35] and the 'Monophysites' of North-East Africa in the Coptic and Ethiopian Orthodox Churches in the fifth century[36] was an assertion of Roman, European, imperialism.[37]

In negating imperial Catholicism, both in Roman and English forms, Black Christianity seeks to preserve its own Biblical vision, experienced from the 'underside', of the universal people of God. In this vision, God's oppressed people, the 'humble and meek' of the Magnificat (Luke 1^{52}), are journeying towards the promised land, travelling to freedom with all who are in solidarity with them because, however 'mighty' in the past, they now 'consider abuse suffered for Christ greater wealth than all the treasures of Egypt' (Heb. 11^{26}). This vision transforms the Catholic tradition into a true non-imperial pluralism.

The challenge to the *Evangelical* claim to stand upon the Word of God and justification by faith alone is similarly sharp. Of course Black Christianity takes much of its language and its hymnody from the Evangelical tradition,[38] and can make 'conservative' statements about the literal verbal inspiration of Scripture. What is at issue, however, is whether the Word of God is heard as a liberating word to the oppressed, or whether, as in slavery times, it is in Babylonian captivity to the oppressors. Even when White and Black Christians use the same 'conservative' terminology the messages of their respective gospels can be in opposition to each other. Black Christianity bases itself on the Bible in order to negate White uses of Scripture which are oppressive, whether they be the conservative-evangelical identification with western capitalism and racism,[39] or the 'liberal' preoccupation with de-contextualized scholarly exegesis.[40] It seeks to preserve its own Biblical vision of the God of history, the liberator of the oppressed from bondage, whom Black people experience in their captivity in 'Egypt'.[41]

Modern White conservative fundamentalism is, as Bishop Lesslie Newbigin notes, an 'Enlightenment' approach, the autonomous reason dealing with 'objective' facts from the past, in which Genesis and Darwinian science are made into statements of the same kind, so that a choice has to be made between the two:

This kind of fundamentalism is a product of modern culture and its representatives find it easy to be at home in the modern world, and to prosper on the terms which the modern world offers.[42]

The Black preacher reflects the experience of a community which does *not* prosper on the terms which the modern world offers, and cannot accept White prescriptions of which facts are true, even in Scripture. Thus James Cone maintains that 'The Word is more than *words* about God, God's Word is a poetic happening, an evocation of indescribable reality in the lives of people'. So he recalls the preacher who began his sermon, 'Brothers and sisters this morning – I intend to explain the unexplainable – find out the undefinable – ponder over the imponderable – and unscrew the inscrutable'. Here, he says, 'the preacher is affirming not only his freedom in relation to the text; he is also making a sharp distinction between the *words* of the text and the *Word* disclosed in the text'.[43] And the Word is always a message of liberation for the poor. Black use of Scripture is not bound by White definitions of what must be true; it is not speculative or academic, but 'tells the story' of the God who acts to save and liberate in history.

Reason is similarly subjected to the Black dialectical challenge. The negating thrust of Black theology attacks the liberal concepts of detachment and autonomy which are necessary for the processes of rational enquiry, and liberal theological scholarship, as well as for discerning the Anglican '*via media*', the 'mean between two extremes'.[44] Here Black theology shares with other Liberation theologies the perception that the scholar is also a child of history; scholarly reason is culturally and socially conditioned, partial and subjective, and can be the tool of European domination.[45] Autonomy is an illusion; reason is, like all human activity, subject to the judgement of God.

James Cone has looked at studies of the relationship between faith and history in White American theology and searched almost in vain for examination – or even mention – of the White oppression of Black people:

the importance of the [problem of faith and history], as defined by white theologians, is limited to their social interests. The character [of the faith-history problem in American theology] was shaped by those who, sharing the consciousness of the Enlightenment, failed to question the consequences of the so-called Enlightened view as reflected in the colonization and slavery of that period.[46]

Cone's argument runs for several pages and is a most important indictment of White reason, a passionate testimony to Black astonishment and hurt at the way White theologians have ignored the suffering and even the existence of Black people:

> It was not uncommon for Anglicans, Presbyterians, Congrega-tionalists, Baptists, Methodists and other assorted denominational theologians to do theology as if slavery did not exist. For example, Jonathan Edwards, often called America's most outstanding theologian, could preach and write theological features on total depravity, unconditional election, limited atonement, irresistible grace, and the perseverance of the saints without the slightest hint of how these issues related to human bondage.[47]

Black theological reflection, however, begins from precisely that predicament, from Black suffering and need. Cone quotes Ernst Bloch's *dictum*, 'need is the mother of thought', and shows that Black slaves had neither need of, nor time for, White philosophical theology. Black theological reasoning preserves a different social starting point (a *sociological* negating of White reason), and therefore a different starting point for speaking of God (a *theological* negating). The question the slaves asked was whether or not God was with them in their struggle for liberation. Cone concludes:

> Black people did not devise various philosophical arguments for God's existence, because the God of Black experience was not a metaphysical idea. He was the God of history, the Liberator of the oppressed from bondage.[48]

So Black *experience* of God subjects White statements of experience to dialectical challenge. Black theology emerges out of the content of Black experience. It preserves the story, and gives an account of the journey, says 'how we got over', recalls the Spirit of Jesus going behind and before in the Exodus in battle against Pharaoh, and leading his people to victory.

All White statements of spiritual experience, including Catholic, Evangelical, Liberal and Charismatic traditions of worship and piety, will be scrutinized from this point of view. White testimony to the converting and sanctifying presence of the Spirit, will be negated if it is not testimony to the Spirit of the liberating God. Barney Pityana, speaking from the South African situation has a relevant word about charismatic renewal among White people:

There are some charismatic Churchmen in South Africa who have come to believe that apartheid will be abolished when individual white Christians are 'born again'. To the victims of racism that is surely a counsel for despair.[49]

The God who liberates the oppressed, does not at the same time comfort and uphold the oppressor; he judges and transforms. To be authentic, the historically White Church has to become obedient to the God of Black experience.

7
Naming Black as Black

The tension in the Anglican 'dialogue' between the Black story and the White is one which most White Anglicans have yet to face. But for Black members it is an urgent issue of their daily life in the Church. We now hear how a number of Black Anglicans have experienced the 'collision' from their side, how they describe the cost and the promise of being Black in a 'White-led' church.

Black people in the Church of England have, as we saw earlier, been described as an 'invisible' people. It follows that they can also be described as a 'silent' people. The suppression of their voice in slavery times was brutal and violent; in colonial times it took the subtler form of cultural domination, not least through the Church-run education system. Only recently have they begun to challenge this colonialism. A letter from a former Bishop of London to James Evans, a Black American theologian, indicates the need for the challenge:

> I think I should point out that there are no black Anglican churches as such in this Diocese. There are, of course, many churches with a preponderance of black congregations. The concept of black churches would be very difficult to fit with the role of the Anglican parish.[1]

Evans is not suggesting that the Bishop is any less sensitive to the issue of Black people in the Church of England than his colleagues, but he infers from the letter that, in a Church where one habitually speaks of catholic, evangelical, liberal or charismatic parishes, one cannot speak of Black Anglicans as 'constituting a viable worshipping community on the basis of a common history of oppression and affirmation of faith, but are in the church only to the degree that they conform to the dominant image of Anglicanism'.[2] That subordination of Black identity to White is a continuance of colonial church practice.

The Black challenge to the suppression of their identity should be seen as a work of the Spirit. For at Pentecost the first gift of the Spirit was the power of *speech*, the power of communication between different named cultural identities,[3] where the representatives of 'every nation under heaven' (Acts 2[5]) repented, were baptised, shared the New Common Life of the Church, and distributed possessions according to need (Acts 2[42–45]. The *naming and delineating of Black identity* is the only basis on which the New Common Life of the Church today can be fashioned between Black and White and possessions distributed according to need.

Black Anglicans insist that naming and delineating identity is *their* task, not that of White researchers who can be presumptuous in seeking to 'define' and 'authenticate' Black experience, exploitative by using Black people to further their careers, and inaccurate because they cannot share the heart of Black experience. In the 'Living Faith Project',[4] a series of extended conversations with groups of Black Anglicans, I tried to avoid these pitfalls. I felt it right to undertake the research, for three reasons. Firstly, the need was urgent; there being then no 'mainstream' church facilities for Black Christians in Britain to study theology on the basis of a Black identity.[5] Secondly, I was conscious of the need to exercise responsibly what Sybil Phoenix (a prominent Black Methodist) has called the 'gatekeeper' role of White people in church structures, occupying positions which give access to resources.[6] Thirdly, I realised that *naming* has to be a mutual task, and that to name myself, I must have at least a provisional image of the identity of those with whom I am in relationship. So I set out to record what I heard.

In the Project I met Black church members and clergy from four Birmingham congregations, selected to cover different strengths of Black congregational membership (the highest 85%, the lowest 11%) and a variety of social contexts. The Black members met in two separate groups, one of older people brought up in the West Indies, the other of young people brought up mainly or wholly in Britain. A Black priest, Rolston Deson, worked with me with the former group; a younger Black woman, Sadie Kenway, with the latter. I sought to discover: (i) whether Black members of the Church of England accept that there is a 'Black Christian Tradition', (ii) how they would define it, and (iii) whether they understand themselves *as Anglicans* to be part of it? I included White clergy in order to investigate how their perceptions of Black Christian Tradition among their Black church members corresponded to what the Black members would say.

I began with two doubts: would Black members be willing to describe their own spiritual heritage to a White stranger? And would my categories be meaningful to them? In the event, all members seemed to speak willingly, openly and eagerly; indeed it was often difficult to bring meetings to an end! At the same time I hoped the Project would be more than a source of data. I hoped it would be a creative event: for Black members an event of solidarity and clarification of consciousness, and for all an event of Christian intercultural interchange which through the grace of God in repentance and forgiveness would help to create the New Common Life of the Church. In the following sections the findings of the Project are presented, using the actual words of participants as much as possible.

ORIGIN AND TRANSMISSION OF BLACK CHRISTIANITY

The Black Christian inheritance has not been transmitted through books, since these have been until recently largely a White monopoly, nor has it been transmitted through the colonial church or its liturgy, for there a White identity has been the norm. Project members were aware that their Black Christianity was an *oral* tradition, a tradition powerful enough for all of them to recall its origins in slavery. As one member remarked:

> The Black Christian tradition is all from slavery. There weren't many missionaries in those days. Our deep-rooted Christianity comes out of adversity: there was nothing to fall back on.

It was not dependent, therefore, on White people or their ecclesiastical institutions:

> People think we got our Christianity from the missionary, but we had religion before the missionary came . . . The Black man will always break off and do his thing, even if allowed into a White church . . . it's a matter of roots, culture and origin, not the Church of England.

Black Christianity is not an opiate, facilitating the acceptance of oppression with the promise of heavenly compensation. It ensures *survival in oppression*, and nurtures the *hope of liberation*. The key to this understanding is the Cross. Black Christianity identifies with Christ's role as Suffering Servant as an effective means of salvation.

As a tradition it is sustained and developed in response to contemporary oppression which is in continuity with the historic forms of the past. These motifs featured clearly in the following remarkable Older Group dialogue, which arose out of a conversation about Black singing of hymns:

It all comes from slavery times, it comes to bring people out of bondage, praying to God to deliver them. It's the only way to get through. (Everyone agreed).

We have to sing here too, with some of the things Black people go through. We still say we in slavery here – only thing we short of is cow-skin!*

Oh it's bad, but it's not that bad.

(Others said how bad it could be, especially at work).

They take the chains off us, but the subtlety of it is still there. (This drew the response of the Cross from everyone:)

It's not on me, I'm looking straight to heaven.

Christ bear more than what they doing us.
But Christ's suffering does not alleviate the sufferings that we endure; we need the strength of Christ to *bear* them.

If He didn't do it, who would shield us?

Still He say, 'Forgive them'. My great-granddad told us how they used to pray that in slavery times. Black people still say, 'Forgive them.'

You must to forgive.

Right now we got a Man in heaven who got mark in His hand.

LITURGICAL MARKS

Black Christianity has a distinctive style of worship, again existing independently of written tradition or White institutions. The White colonial church has suppressed it with varying degrees of subtlety and conscious intent, and Black people have sometimes responded by repressing it within themselves. Project members readily agreed to the existence of such a distinctive style surviving 'in, around and

* a reference to the cow-skin whip used in slavery times.

104

under' White liturgy and church practice. They described its characteristics, namely a determination to be free, a longing to encounter
the presence of the Spirit of God in an emotional, existential
experience, and a desire for authenticity. The following are the
features which were important to this group of Black Anglicans:

MUSIC

Black Christian Music originated in slavery, and songs which speak
of survival, liberation, and the Cross in response to that oppression
or oppression now are the most loved:

> Christians are called upon to suffer and to endure. Black people
> have been in that situation most of the time. Their own resources
> were not sufficient, they had to look for Someone Else to pull
> them through. Whether as slaves or when they came to England,
> they had to suffer and endure. It's natural therefore to sing songs
> related to that theme. They identify with them, they relate to what
> is true for them.

> Some of the hymns, like *Rock of Ages*, *Amazing Grace* and
> some Spirituals, they sound more powerful. Those are the hymns
> associated with slavery. People would sing them every week if you
> let them.

Some hymns originating in the White church have become vehicles
for Black Christian expression, most of them from evangelical,
revival sources. As an Older Group member put it:

> Most people have a Sankey book, and everyone knows those
> hymns. We didn't use the book in the Anglican Church, but
> different churches bring in their own books, and we visit them and
> learn their songs.

Sankey may be less important to the younger generation, but the
testimony to Gospel music among the Younger Group was strong
and unanimous:

> Younger Blacks to some extent are losing their cultural heritage . . .
> but they really like Gospel music. They would welcome it at our
> church. I *love* gospel music, especially 'gospel soul'. I love singing.

The accompaniment offered in the White church, even when of a
good standard, is often unhelpful, for it is not from the same

tradition. One priest described a prayer meeting in which the Black tradition had vividly surfaced both in prayer and music:

> After singing several choruses to a [white person's] piano accompaniment, one woman said, 'Don't play this time, I'll sing it my way'. What she did without the White accompaniment shows how much more there is to be discovered.

Several people spoke of the importance of the feeling and the 'natural' voice in Black worship through music:

> Yes, the Black choirs, they really sing with their natural voices . . . It feels heavenly, it touches you . . . you can really *feel* God in the midst of it all.

Black Christian music should not, therefore, be understood as a corpus of songs composed by Black Christians. It is rather an experience, for which (as we have seen) White sources can be appropriated. Project members showed Black Christian music 'happens' when the words resonate with Black experience and the Black Christian Tradition, which can normally take place only within a group which is alive to that tradition. As one young person said bluntly: 'Billy Graham songs are one thing at *Mission England*, but quite another at *Young, Gifted and Black*!' [a vocational weekend for young Black Anglicans].

> Our music opens up for the soul a direct link with God. You feel the Spirit moving within you through the music. Once it happened in our church . . . you feel a bond, you feel it swelling . . . if only every week were like this in church . . . It's not just the music; you're deep and intense through 'spiritual' music with God at the core of your being.

PRAYER

Prayer within the Black Christian Tradition is free and spontaneous. It is a tradition distinct from White free prayer since the latter is not moulded by the same historical experience of God in oppression. It has been transmitted orally, through each generation learning it from their elders. In White-led churches it has not usually been sustained by the liturgy, but in smaller gatherings such as prayer meetings. Praying is a skill and art as well as a gift: 'She can pray well'; 'I love to hear him pray'.

Yes there is a distinct style. I wish I could get up [in church] and pray. Some people just get up and say what they want to say. I wish I could do that. Black people like to do it, but I personally couldn't . . . well, in the Lent course, in a smaller group, I could do it.

Black people pray in their own words, they don't believe so much in written prayer.

Prayer is likely to be a regular experience and practice even for those who feel unable to speak in the larger gathering:

One thing I do is to pray. I *do* pray. I pray at home, and I pray at work.

Black prayer is articulate, detailed and conversational, and includes many Biblical phrases and insights, as well as, for Anglicans, words from the Liturgy. As one priest testified:

Black people in our church have great freedom in praying, they pour things out in prayer, they share so much. They really express their inner longings and feelings – far more by praying with me than by conversation with me. My own prayer is stilted in comparison. I just can't match it.

Space for free prayer in the Liturgy or in house groups was welcomed, even if the former has not yet developed into a secure practice in any of the churches represented in the Project. One older woman testifies:

Now at our church we have a Praise Service at 6 p.m. We sit and read the Psalms and use the new book [i.e. the Alternative Service Book, Order for Evening Prayer]. Then we have open prayer. That's good. We should pray more at Anglican churches, we're a bit too secret. We should pray out loud. It helps. Now House Communions, that's a night of prayer!
[This church has considerable use of free prayer in House Communion services].

PREACHING AND THE PREACHER

Black Preaching is at the heart of Black worship. Even more than the music it was described as the point at which something must 'happen'. It must be an existential experience challenging, uplifting or changing the hearer. This, rather than an analysis of its formal content, is the test of its validity:

> Black preachers in the West Indies tended to be more moving as preachers, with greater emphasis on quoting the Bible with the congregation latching onto particular statements they had made, and taking particular phrases. The sermons would stay with them rather than be a fleeting thing and then 'gone'. The delivery would be more powerful, the preaching more authoritative . . . Although the *format* [of worship] is the same here and in the West Indies, we experience a definite difference: the preaching is more personal, more directly related to the congregation and the locality.

One person bluntly contrasted the place of preaching with that of the Eucharist in the religion of Black people:

> Whereas Anglicans like the Sacrament, Black people like the *Word*; they like good preaching first and foremost. They like to feel free . . . Religion is *inbuilt* in them. A good Black preacher *taps* that. He ignites something in Black people and gets them going. It's not something you learn at college.

To some it was evident that this kind of experience *is* possible within the Anglican liturgy because they experience visiting Black preachers from the Anglican or other 'mainstream' traditions, as in the response of one person to Sybil Phoenix: 'She preached strong; it's good to have that kind of preaching back in the church'. Another described a similar situation. 'It was so sweet, so sad that it doesn't last long enough'.

Black preaching was described as 'relevant to the situation' of the congregation; it uses the Bible to describe the situation and to proclaim the appropriate Christian response. A good preacher is one who has that spiritual gift; hence Black suspicion of White institutional training, and a feeling that study, preparation and the use of notes are all signs of lack of ability or even of sincerity in the preacher:

> Now a successful preacher is not from university. You're born with it in you. It's natural talent. Some are better off without university. You have to understand the Bible. You have to call the words and explain them, like a shepherd. And if you're not a good shepherd, you have to be rebuked.

A Black preacher preaches not as a *job*, the way some White preachers do. They are just 'theological priests' – at the end of the service that's it.

I heard a man preach in a Baptist church. He preach the raw way, he spit it out, he just tell you till you cry. It was good preaching.

The important thing is that Black preachers interpret Black experience in terms of the Bible; they always find something in the Bible relevant to the situation in which they find themselves. Then the congregation will give a response!

Some certainly valued what they regarded as the more typically Anglican sermon, 'thoughtful and well prepared'. One younger person vividly described her need for what she saw as more than a traditional 'powerful' preaching of the Word:

You can get really powerful preaching from Black and White, sometimes with hell-fire and all, but I say, 'Bring me up to date, I want the meaning of Him for today'. Sometimes, now, yes, I want the Word preached to me. But at the end I also want an explanation of how I can have Him in my life, at school, every day, at home, with neighbours, friends. I want help and encouragement to put God and Jesus into everyday life. I have read a book of Martin Luther King's sermons, and had he lived I would have loved to hear him preach. I found him fascinating; such convictions and courage!

But it should be noted that most Group members found preaching the least satisfying aspect of the ministry of Anglican clergy.

BAPTISM AND EUCHARIST

Project members had a clear broad agreement about the place of music, prayer and preaching in Black Christianity. Attitudes to the sacraments were much less clear. There was difficulty about Baptism because of a variety and conflict of traditions. To some, 'Christening' was not Baptism; this Baptist approach being reinforced and confused by the insistent claims of some Black-led churches, and by the practice by some churches of rebaptism of adults even when they have already been baptised as adults by total immersion elsewhere. This makes it hard to accept the doctrine and practice of the 'mainstream' churches, both Catholic and Reformed, namely that there is 'one Baptism for the remission of sins' and that the 'Christening' of infants constitutes that unrepeatable act.

Most Project members accepted Anglican teaching intellectually, but with varying degrees of reluctance. As one minister put it 'I sense that many [Black] adults would like to undergo adult Baptism, but they have been Christened as children and can't'. Adult Baptism with total immersion is felt to express authenticity and strength of commitment.

There *is* a strong desire for the dedication to God of a new born child, and most Black parents who come to Anglican churches want this done 'properly' – they want 'real' Christening, i.e. with water. One priest notes, 'Compared with most Whites, Black people tend to understand about the seriousness of religious commitment'. But for many it does not really feel to be *Baptism*. This was the majority attitude in the Group. A minority accepted Anglican teaching and practice without reservation. Another minority – one which represents perhaps the majority belief in the wider Black community – definitely rejected Infant Baptism, and thought the Church of England was wrong in 'not baptising' people. These were the same people who saw the Church as a community set apart to endure the sufferings of the present time ('we are living in Revelations') and await the coming of the Lord.

It is significant that the Eucharist was rarely mentioned by the Black members except in connection with Communion of the Sick. The one Black clergyman, however said:

> I too have gone around [to other churches] but the thing that was missing elsewhere was . . . the Sacrament. That's what keeps me joyful in Church, the sacramental life.

Another person spoke of his *need* for Communion as a means of grace and forgiveness:

> Christ came to call sinners to repentance and sinners need Christ's Body more. Receive as often as you can, even every day. Say, 'Lord I am not worthy . . .'

Both these views are, I feel, untypical, and represent the experience of individuals who, in different ways, are very strongly committed as Anglicans. Other members, certainly spoke of the Eucharist with great respect, but despite my attempts to concentrate on the Sacrament itself, their main concern was with the depth of preparation necessary prior to receiving. One member stated bluntly:

Black people are different from White in that they have deep feeling. Black people will not go up every minute to receive Communion even though it's given free.

Anglican practice in the West Indies had usually been to communicate at most monthly and after rigorous preparation, which clearly fitted the Black insistence on 'real' religion. It was a point at which there could be no hypocrisy, no 'unworthy' behaviour. Someone who was not properly married, therefore, or had been drinking, or had attended a party the night before should not receive the Sacrament. 'It's not for everyone in the street; it's for the Lord's chosen people'. Moreover, White people were seen to have profaned the Sacrament in their hypocritical rejection of Black people in church: 'There may have been equality at the altar, but it's usually stopped there'.

DREAMS, ILLNESS AND FUNERALS

The Black Christian Tradition is characterized by the recognition of the unseen world of spirit as a pervasive reality. Several Project members described the importance of dreams, as well as belief in ghosts as characteristic of Black people. In my parish ministry I knew of several church members to whom dreams had pointed to or confirmed important moments of their lives, especially conversion, or assurance of faith. Most Project members, however, were careful to distance themselves to some extent from belief in dreams:

This really meant something to my mother; she'd say, 'It's a sign'. It might be about going to a wedding – or a dream about a funeral would be a sign of death. People do believe in these omens.

Such beliefs also relate more directly than anything yet considered to the wider Black religious tradition. This is also true of the customs and experiences around illness and death. There is a sense that the 'natural' suffering in illness and death is part of the general 'suffering of Black people' just as the 'man-made' oppression of slavery and racism is. It too can be related to the Cross, and is shared by the community. As one Project member said:

Black people's faith comes out strongly in adversity. When some-one is sick they'll rally round to pray with them. They're always there at death, at funerals, in hospital, and they'll give material

111

support. Even now it shines out in darkness, it really shines out when they're in trouble, a beacon in a dark room.

Another said:

I know from my Aunt's funeral and my sister's death the strength that comes out of Black families in suffering. When someone is sick people will gather in the house. They pray with them, and will often be visited by groups of people who also pray, read the Bible and bring gifts.

This ministry often crosses denominational boundaries, especially when different denominations are represented in one family. A priest arriving to give Communion to the sick may find his ministration forms part of a healing visit of a Pentecostal church. In hospital his prayers will join those of visitors from his own and other congregations:

When Dad was ill people from the 'clap-hand' [Pentecostal] churches came and prayed, one group from Mum's niece's church and one from a friend's church. Our Vicar gave Communion and anointed him with oil, and people came from our church. Black people believe in healing and it's good that we have that at our church.

At death the community support intensifies, in obviously marked contrast to White tradition: 'When anyone dies *they* like to be left alone, but with us the house will be crowded for two weeks'. Again the priest's prayers will join the ministry of others, usually during the 'Wake', as one White priest describes:

There's a much greater expectation of the priest. You are expected to pray. You're welcome to. There's no outward embarrassment. There is usually a religious dimension to life which is less apparent in most White people. And there is much more input from them, the 'wake', the whole mixture of the religious and the social, the women's prayers, the men's rum and dominoes, all the general hubbub.

The funeral itself is a major statement of the Black community's identity and faith – congregations usually are several hundred strong. In a White funeral the friends and relatives wait in church till the 'mourning party', the family, enter behind the coffin. At a Black [Anglican] funeral the whole community forms the mourning party, so all follow the coffin into church. The quality of singing is distinctively 'Black'; there is a tradition of hymns and songs more from 'Sankey' than the Anglican hymn books. Friends, relatives and ministers of Black-led churches may sing solos, lead prayers, preach or give testimony, and in most cases the coffin is opened to allow the congregation to file past and pay their last respects. This is often the most emotionally intense part of the service, and grief is expressed freely and openly. Even here, however, there is an understood 'liturgy of grief' – the less overtly distressed care for the others, and the service is ended in dignity with the singing of the final hymn. At the graveside, after the committal, the closest male relatives themselves fill in the grave whilst everyone else sings hymns and choruses – again from Sankey. Except for the filling of the grave the whole funeral service has taken place within the framework of the Anglican liturgy, and those who are Anglicans by upbringing in the West Indies will often request 'full rites', i.e. full and 'proper' church ceremonial. Funerals have usually been the services at which Black Christianity is most fully expressed within Anglican worship. The tradition is strong and well known, and people are relatively confident in making their expectations clear to the clergy.[7]

One Project member described the death of her sister in America. Although it did not actually in this case involve an Anglican Church it brings together many of the points made above:

I remember when she died, when we went over to America, we prayed with her, we held hands. I did feel that she would be healed. You could feel the moving of strength. In that hospital, it was a wonderful hospital, with Christian medical staff; we were always welcome. There would be prayer meetings in the room. The doctors, being Christians, cared. They saw the spiritual side as part of their work. The Church was praying too, the Church there, and the Church here. In their church there was free prayer and singing, sometimes tears; the service went on for three hours just like in a Black church, although it wasn't a Black church – though some Black people went to it. We had our self-expression, but with a format. We all held my sister, we held her together. We were all really close to each other, and close to God. Since she died we have all asked each other what it was that we went through together.

EXPERIENCING RACISM IN THE CHURCH

Black Anglicans in England who are Anglicans by upbringing in the West Indies remember their church at home with affection and loyalty. For all its colonial features it 'carried' the spiritual lives of many Black Christians. One Project member, in the Older Group but not yet forty, remembers:

> We're Anglicans, and I was confirmed when I was 13. I'm from St. Thomas, Lowlands [in Nevis]. The service was at 10.00 a.m., using the old Prayer Book [i.e. the 1662 Book of Common Prayer], and Hymns Ancient and Modern. The priest had to visit different churches, so it wasn't Communion every Sunday. A lay preacher took these other services. Sometimes our priest was English, sometimes West Indian. We had incense and servers – *that* was service! After service came Sunday School which I went to till I was fifteen or sixteen. Harvest, Palm Sunday, Good Friday and Easter, and the Confirmation – these were all important days. But most of all I love Christmas Eve. There was a different atmosphere, leaving you feeling nice. It was a beautiful service.

With this background the inevitable question arises, *why is it not the same here*? Partly this was for reasons of culture; Older Group members in England remembered their home countries as places with a strong Christian popular culture. There was a sense that, despite colonial features, denominational church life was upheld by this common base of orally transmitted Black Christianity: 'We all know the Sankey hymns; we had them at home – and Gospel records'. Church people visited each other's churches for concerts and anniversaries, and not a few Anglicans visited a 'sideways' church in the afternoon. There was an 'easier unity of churches in Jamaica than here'; contrasts between churches, especially between 'Black-led' and 'White-led' denominations had been 'sharpened by what has happened to us here'.

Racism and rejection here are undoubtedly an important reason why Black people left the Anglican Church. The ministry of the Revd. Paul Burrough, Bishop's Chaplain for Overseas People (1959–67) in the Birmingham Diocese was remembered with warm appreciation. 'He was the one who visited us in our homes,' said one member, whilst others remembered personal help received, and the simple caravan in which he lived whilst moving from parish to parish to discover new settlers from the Caribbean.[8] Individual acts of welcome were also remembered. But all this served only to highlight the appalling experience of most Black Anglicans when they attended their new parish Church:

> A lot of Black people were living in that area, but they didn't go to St. ____'s although it was across the road. [Our church] was the main church for Blacks; the other doors were closed.

English people didn't want to see Black people coming to their churches. Some were especially unwelcoming.

When we came to live in this house we went to [our church]. We went two Sundays in the morning. Each time the people we sat down by got up and moved to sit somewhere else. So we started to go at night; fewer people went at night so it was easier to find somewhere to sit alone. Often I think it's better to sit on the lavatory and pray there.

On my first Sunday in Birmingham my friends and I, we put on our best suits and went to church. But after the service the vicar told us not to come again. His congregation wouldn't like it, he said.

These churches are all inner-city churches, and when the settlers arrived they were already in decline. Fear of 'West Indian immigration' accelerated an already established pattern of flight to the new suburbs. Racism was less overt in newer or outer-ring churches; Project members from these congregations spoke warmly, but with reservations:

I was made very welcome at St . . . 's. [Our Rector] visited the West Indies and met my family. I helped to organise a dance to raise funds so that he could go. That visit meant a great deal to me . . . Some White members were unhappy about it. They said it would 'emphasize differences'.

We were made very welcome; we were treated like *citizens*. Mind you, for me racism has to be blatant. I *do not* look for it.

This, as Rolston Deson reflected, showed that whilst overt racist rejection may no longer be a serious problem, there are many situations which are 'OK on the surface only'. Disquiet about the visit, for example indicated that the White interest in Blacks is simply to 'have them on the outskirts of a White-dominated congregation', and that 'deep down people are not ready for the Black presence':

There is still prejudice in the Church. It's not hard-core blatant prejudice, but the prejudice of liberal Whites. They're a real problem because they are not dependable.

At the same time it was recognised that several churches had a harmonious relationship of understanding, especially between

115

younger people, or else were so strongly Black that racism as personal rejection did not arise:

> When I started to attend (my present) church there was no pressure to go. I like [this church] very much. The service is shorter, and I enjoy being involved in a lot of church activities – 'Young, Gifted and Black', 'Live, Learn and Share', retreats, as well as the weekly programme. Everything is well organised and the members do not have favourites. I grew up here into being a Christian.

BLACK WORSHIP IN A WHITE-LED CHURCH

What is the place of worship in the Black Christian Tradition within a White-led church? This is clearly a key issue if the deeper institutionalised racism of the Church is to be overcome and the colonial era ended through a process of repentance and forgiveness. The Tradition exists and, as we have seen, is recognised as such. Rolston Deson said:

> It often seems that a Black people are at their best, their highest, their most holy point, when persecuted. The divine within us surfaces more, and somehow we are able to be joyful, and within that joy to feel a kind of sorrow for what we consider to be the ignorance of the oppressor. It's like we, in the midst of our affliction, are always saying we stand ready to forgive and wanting to embrace. It's a strange feeling, that really cannot be put into words, but I don't think there is any bitterness to the point of wanting to destroy *anyone* . . .
>
> I long for the day when the Church of England will become truly Black and White. I don't believe that the present administration within the Church is able to bring it about. I believe Black people will do it for themselves, despite the reluctance and caution about accommodating in full the Black presence in the liturgical worship of the Church . . .
>
> We would never reach the depth of Black spirituality. It is so rich, so spontaneous, it has such variety that one is always amazing oneself at the heights to which one is being constantly lifted up.

What is people's actual experience in church nowadays? At its worst it can still be a very alienating experience. One meeting heard how a group of Black people had met in one church (not represented in the Group) to discuss their experience:

116

The Bible is not sufficiently expounded in the Mass. They have difficulty in raising a song, they feel emptier coming out of church than going in. This indicated the dryness they felt in certain totally set forms of worship.

Others in more sympathetic, even Black-majority situations still feel a distinct frustration at the formality of the liturgy and the control of the priest (who in all four congregations is White):

In worship things should not be predictable every week. In running the church and in leading the worship the person in authority should not seek dominance.

In the Anglican church it is so easy to become habitual and not take in what you are reading. We are not led by the Spirit, but rely too much on tradition. New Christians are not really nurtured, and there is little for younger people to identify with.

I don't know why it doesn't happen at our church [i.e. the sense of 'really worshipping']. There's a barrier between the minister and the congregation. The liturgy feels too rigid; we can't express ourselves in it.

The majority of Group members expressed both a basic satisfaction with their churches, and a strong sense of yearning for *something more*. This 'something more' is a sense of authentic worship, true faith, real commitment:

I value the order in [our church] but something is drastically wrong with me. I do not feel I am a Christian . . . I want to be pointed in the right direction . . . I don't want to be part of the noise and disorganisation of [Black-led churches] but I *do really want* their experience of faith.

The three important things in our kind of church are space, order and freedom. This provides a welcome relief after a 'rough experience' elsewhere. But after a time the breathing space has been sufficient, and young people start looking for something more. Then they find the Church lacks vitality and challenge.

At the moment, it seems a basically colonial situation prevails: clerical authority and liturgical practice suppress, fail to recognise, or at best allow limited space to the Black spiritual tradition. How is this tradition to be released within the Church? Is the liturgy a White liturgy or is it a liturgy capable of various cultural interpretations?

The answer to these questions is not to be found in superficial 'indigenization' but in the deeper struggle both in theology and in praxis for the New Common Life of the Church.[9]

Freedom for Black self-expression within the liturgy is essential; it was an insistent and oft-repeated demand of Project members. At one meeting, when I asked whether those present intended to remain in the Church of England, all replied that they were definitely Anglican at the moment; only a few might change in the future. But all agreed that freedom to make an emotional response was needed in worship, together with preaching that 'moves the heart'. As Rolston Deson put it:

> What makes people feel a part of, and wanting to burst forth in spontaneous prayer are hymns. The first step would be to sing hymns whereby people are caught up in the Spirit by the singing of certain hymns. Secondly, in Black worship, individuals who want to sing get a chance to do so. There is a spot given to such people who want to sing, who believe that their singing will help towards the gladdening and the lifting up of the heart. Young people will certainly have their equivalent. They have to have their spot. When children have their spot it makes them part of the worship, and it unites their parents with them. The Church of England has got to let black youth have self-expression within the Mass.
>
> The Church of England has got to find a spot within the liturgical setting for spontaneous prayer. I am not saying at all that there must be an 'altar call', but I believe that after the sermon a time could be given, probably about five minutes, for silent or spontaneous prayer.
>
> If people feel moved by the Spirit to pray out loud, then they should be free to do so in the context of the Mass. Time should be allowed. Then the formalized bidding prayer could be said, so that the minister can incorporate the spontaneous prayer into the structure of the prayer of the Mass. So the Black spirituality could add its portion to the liturgy of the Church of England.
>
> Black people want to express themselves, and they are not allowed to within the present setting of the Mass. They should be allowed to sing. They should be allowed to praise. They should be allowed to pray. That's why there needs to be more Black priests in the Church of England, people who feel and know the way the Black populace feel, and would encourage them to rekindle what the Church of England has dampened.

It will be evident that the liturgy as such is not rejected; the call was for it to be liberated so that Black speech can be heard within it, and Black culture and experience named as such. It was a call for transformation.

THE BOUNDARIES OF BLACK ANGLICANISM

The groups attempted to delineate the 'boundaries' of being both *Black* and *Anglican*, which define and shape Black Anglicanism, knowing that the White church usually thinks patronisingly of these boundaries, failing to do justice to the distinctive identity involved. One priest had heard a colleague say, 'Our few Blacks fit in very well, they wouldn't want things any different, and they like the old traditions'; seeing people as so Anglican that they cease to be really Black. The reverse danger, of seeing people as so Black that they cease to be really Anglican, was exemplified in a comment made to me by a colleague on another occasion, 'I'm sure they all take their religion really seriously, and I suppose you have really lively services'!

Black Anglicans are *Black*, not White Anglicans with a different skin colour and a few interesting cultural customs. They inevitably live the Black experience, and have the fullness of Black identity in a White-dominated racist society. As one project member put it:

> Blackness is not only the apparent externals of culture. It's also about the solidarity of constituting a community in a dominantly White society. It's a matter of consciousness.

At the same time Black Anglicans are *Anglican*, a tradition which we define here not in contrast to other White-led 'mainstream' denominations, but in contrast to Black alternatives, principally the Black-led Pentecostal and Holiness churches, but also the very different phenomenon of Rastafarianism.

BLACK SELF-DISCOVERY IN A RACIST SOCIETY

Several older Project members had experienced crude overt racism:

> When I got to the factory they told me 'no vacancy'. When I got back to the Labour Exchange they rang up the firm who said I'd turned down the job. That wasn't true. It was my first experience . . . Finally I got a job at I.M.I. There were five

other women, all White, in my section – milling. They were all welcoming in the morning, but in the afternoon all of them except one refused to work with me. That one woman was called Margaret; she was young and very upset at what had happened. She started crying.

At home all our preachers and schoolmasters and hospital matrons etc. used to be English . . . Why then they treat us like that when we come here? My next door neighbour she said, 'Why did you come to live here you black bastard? It was winter when we came, we had no coal but she wouldn't lend us even a bucketful . . . I'd have given her a bag back. Later I did her a favour, but she threw rubbish into our garden, and one day she hit me on the head with a broomstick! Yet now she has come to understand that we're all God's children.

The racism more typical of the present which determines the life of the younger generation also featured:

A friend of ours had an experience which shows why many blacks . . . give up trying. She was one of ten people, five White and five black who applied for a job with the Post Office. When they went for interview the five blacks were called to one side and sent away. The Whites were told to remain for interview.

But two people had had 'no experience of racism'; this was from younger members who were mainly speaking of happy and positive school experience. A third claimed 'no experience of racism', but added, after an extended pause, 'except the obvious' – which she then proceeded to describe at length, including this remarkable incident:

Sometimes I feel very sad. I came here when I was six, but I don't have a clear identity. It's not fair, White people *don't* accept me. They're always talking about 'you' and 'your people' and 'where you come from'. At work they asked me, 'Why do you let your people starve in Ethiopia? We've told you what to do to overcome famine, and still you don't do it'. With remarks like that you can't avoid an identity crisis! I'm not responsible for all black people, and I've no connection with Ethiopia.

One young woman holds a quite prestigious secretarial position and spoke of her experience and that of other Black people with 'good jobs':

If I'd had better experiences maybe I could feel British. I have a good job, but Black people with good jobs still feel they are not accepted. Among us, conversation always comes round to 'things are happening which we don't like and can't change'. I 'talk White' at work but I'm pretending, I'm always on guard. It's very, very hard to be normal and authentically myself.

Racism, therefore, is experienced not simply as crude abuse from a minority of hostile Whites, but as a subtler and far deeper poison, sapping and eroding personal identity and the possibility of being authentically oneself.

Several Project members described their strategies for survival. A primary resource is the Black Christian Tradition, but there is also the particular dignity of an individual's achievements in life, as well as the wider support of the cultural tradition of the Black community. One man's dignity and survival lay in his skill as a welder – a skill he had learned at home in the Caribbean – and in his 'socialist solidarity' with other workers:

For nine months I worked in the Austin factory at Longbridge . . . they say I was the first Black welder ever to work there. But I was treated just the same as the others and I got on well with the foreman. I had good solidarity with other strong socialists as well . . . In all these years I've certainly come across difficult individuals who have been racist. But I can shrug that off . . . I am carried through by the knowledge that I am capable of doing my job, my trade.

Another man had a justifiable pride in the strength of his family life which had survived all the difficulties of the earlier years:

We had nine children, and we had to clothe them and feed them. We denied ourselves to look after the kids . . . I'll say this: they always went very decent [i.e. well turned-out, presentable]. They got on OK at school, and everyone always talk well about them. At that time any decent person could get a job. All my children are in work and doing well – except the youngest. He's only eighteen and things are different now.

Most referred at some point, implicitly or explicitly, to the family of the Black community, which nourished their identity and gave them strength to go on. Their attitudes were not uncritical, but the strongest testimony is to that which, like family loyalties, hardly needs to be articulated because it is always there, the sense of being a part of the 'large family of the Black community'.

> In a West Indian house there are certain ways which are different from most White homes – the food, the discipline, the various chores you have to do (and you get beaten for misbehaving!) – but I feel these ways are the best. In church we like gospel-type music. We prefer reggae to 'pop'. If anyone is sick or dying, the other members of the church will look after you. If there's a funeral everyone visits the house. You have to go, even though you haven't been invited. I'd never want to lose that sense of being a part of the large family of the Black community.

The process of growing up within that family – like adolescence in our natural families – is complex and varies greatly for different individuals. One young woman who had 'never experienced racial disharmony' but understood about it from the experience of others, described her identity with conviction: 'I'm British, it's where I was born and I don't know any different. I certainly see myself as Black. I'm Black-British'. But others found it almost impossible to identify with Britain in any but the loosest way:

> In America I'm sure there's racism, but no-one doubts that Black Americans are Americans. They have no other home and they don't belong anywhere else. White people in England won't feel like that about us for many, many years.

Others again had insulated themselves from Black consciousness. A personal description of the way the 'layers of insulation' function, and how they were stripped off is particularly moving and perceptive, and perhaps supplies the key to understanding many of the positive and negative statements about Black identity and self-discovery in our racist society:

> In Britain, Black people turn in on themselves, they insulate themselves. But it comes out when they get together . . . I had seen myself as English. I had White and Black friends, and didn't especially identify with the Black group. It was very painful for me to admit the *racial* nature of attacks on me. I couldn't do it. Till one day, talking to my vicar [a Black priest], he asked me, 'Which side of the fence are you on? What are you? You tell me. Think what has happened to you, why won't you identify as Black?' Slowly I began to acknowledge the Black-ness of my

experience. I saw the racism behind remarks of colleagues at work (talk of being mugged and the like). It made me myself, though. I don't know why it doesn't happen more at church . . . often there's opposition from some older Black people. It's probably too late for them to admit in church their true identity. But not for me. I'm going to do it.

THE BLACK-LED CHURCHES

Black Anglicans in Britain have to acknowledge that Black-led churches are the main repository of the Black Christian Tradition. They are generally so strong, with a vital and lively fellowship, a good membership of young people and a style of music and worship closely related to classical Black Christianity, that Black Anglican perceptions of these churches are specially significant. *It should be born in mind, however, that we were attempting to uncover personal experience and the assumptions which had shaped attitudes, even if rooted in the past; we were not engaged in constructing a comprehensive, objective description of Black-led churches.* (Thus, for example, the social outreach ministries of several Black-led churches did not feature strongly in the consciousness of those interviewed.) The groups looked at four issues:

(i) What is a 'True' Christian?

It was generally clear that being a 'true Christian' implies a real, living personal commitment different from mere churchgoing or the conventional religion which some regarded as typical of White people. It certainly involves a clean upright life, though some (those most attached to a Baptist theology of Baptism) were more insistent than others in talking of a 'changed' or 'different' life. All were aware, however, that many Black-led Pentecostal Christians would look on them as less than 'true' Christians, 'nominal' rather than truly 'spiritual'. Responses to this varied from resenting it to almost accepting it.

Pentecostal churches were resented for proselytising:

> they're always getting people in from other churches, which isn't right because it's one Man you're going to serve. They try to tell us there is no God in the Church of England. But I tell them we serve just one God. Yet the same people are happy to keep their service in our church!

They were resented for seeming not to recognise the integrity of their brothers and sisters in 'mainstream' churches:

> I ignore those who look down on my church and its worship. I treat that with contempt. After all I *know* I love God, I *know* I am worshipping. How *can* they tell me otherwise?

The pain of divided witness was particularly acute in the workplace:

> Some of them think the Anglican Church is not properly Christian. For instance I work with Pentecostal friends. They call each other 'Sister'. One day, a man who works with us – he's Black, but not Pentecostal, though his wife is – he asked them why they don't say, 'Sister' to me. They all laughed. So he said, 'If you all are Christians why can't you say 'Sister' to all?

Some older Project members were less hurt and more bemused:

> I've always been in a church – but not in a clap-hand type. All this jump-up and noise, that's not for me. And it goes on for so long; those people stay in their church all day!

Most typical though was a combination of responses to different aspects of Black-led Pentecostal church life:

> My sister used to go to St . . . 's, but she's now in the Church of God of Prophecy. I went to her Baptism: it was lovely. I too have a lot to give, but I don't want to shout it out in that way. Mind you, my sister's church would say I'm not a proper Christian. I don't believe they are more Christian than me, but they do ask for more.

Here we have a combination of rejection of Pentecostal judgement on Anglicans, an affirmation that Pentecostal style is not the only way to worship God, and a clear admiration and respect for aspects of Pentecostal worship and challenge.

Sometimes rejection of Pentecostal exclusivism went hand-in-hand with a rejection of *all* exclusivism. Listening to the discussion one had the feeling that Pentecostal claims were considered a 'man-made' restriction of the free stream of the Black Christian Tradition. Perhaps there is a sense in which *all* denominational allegiance is an imposition upon the living stream of Black Christianity:

It's not denomination but *people* who matter. There is only one God; church [i.e. denomination] doesn't count. Some people tell you all the time that they are Christians and that theirs is the true Church. But the main thing is to let people *see* Christ in our lives.

This is not, however, to deny that there are many Black people, Anglican, Methodist and Pentecostal to whom denominational allegiance is important.

(ii) Worship and Ethics

Some Project members, who earlier had affirmed the liturgical marks of the Black Christian Tradition described above, drew a clear distinction between those Black universals and the Pentecostal expression of them. One member put it very clearly:

The Methodist Church in the West Indies was very enjoyable, you'd do some clapping . . . self expression is all right, but these Black churches . . . their rules and regulations . . . and their services, they go on and on! Once I visited one as a teenager. I was amazed at their hard and fast rules: it was the age of the mini-skirt, but they all had to wear longer skirts. And people kept falling about – it was a frightening experience. I felt, 'I'm Black and I ought to feel confident here – but all this falling down in the aisles!' *I found it alien, yet I felt that I shouldn't* (my emphasis).

Another interviewee said:

I was brought up in a Pentecostal church . . . and a lot of that is still in me, but I never really felt happy worshipping in the Pentecostal way . . . People in that Church couldn't understand that and they said I was less of a Christian. I even began to believe that too. My personality dictates a different way of worship. That doesn't mean I'm just White – there are different kinds of Black. I'm not Pentecostal but I am Black.

However, the main problems this group of Anglicans had with the Black-led Pentecostal churches they knew lay not in the worship but in *exclusivism* (described above) and in *ethics*. One young woman, still reacting against her Pentecostal upbringing, told how her decision to leave home had come to a head over her decision to attend a Christmas party at work:

125

> Our church had been very strict; no boyfriends, no pubs, no alcoholic drinks, no smoking, no jewellery – apart from wedding rings and watches. Divorce and re-marriage were forbidden. Women were not allowed to wear trousers or make-up. Now what has not wearing trousers got to do with following Jesus Christ?

Extensive discussion over areas of practical Christian living showed the most clear perceived division between Black Anglicans and Pentecostals. The idea of a list of ethical rules was rejected, the weight of moral example, guidelines, guidance and an indication of moral 'parameters' being preferred.

Essentially this was a plea for the discovery of an authentic Christian ethic by personal experience. This, it was freely admitted, meant running risks. One Project member – certainly one of the more conservative on this issue – nonetheless testified:

> Running risks is what life is about. Often I was advised against certain things . . . but I had to find out for myself. That is the way people are. Becoming a Christian doesn't destroy your humanity. You are still a person, still in this world. We Christians remain as human as the next person.

This was filled out by others in terms of 'moderation' and 'discretion'. Christians can go to parties – but not just any parties. They can drink alcohol, but not irresponsibly. A church may organise a dance or even have a bar, but it is important that no-one goes 'over the top'. It was recognised that this kind of looser moral guidance does not prevent everyone from going 'off the rails' – but the alternative of imposing strict rules has its own danger of provoking a strong reaction.

Similarly on sexual morality, whilst everyone thought casual sexual relationships and promiscuity to be wrong, and affirmed the traditional Christian marriage commitment of life-long voluntary union to the exclusion of all others, most accepted that divorce (not only for adultery) is permissible and in some cases necessary. In appropriate cases the Church should bless the re-marriage of such people. Sexual relations before marriage were felt to be acceptable if the relationship was long-lasting and stable. Clearly Project members, particularly younger ones, were describing their own standards of behaviour, for which the watchwords are 'responsibility', 'moderation', 'guidance not rules' and 'living as part of this world – not separate from it.'

(iii) The Anglican Church a Place of Refuge

For some the Anglican Church was a haven for 'refugees' from the Pentecostal churches, mainly individuals who reject the strict ethical code, but also those who cannot or will not respond to demands for a radical commitment of time and money. There were individuals who needed time and space to think, whose life experience just would not fit what were described as 'neat, packaged answers'. One Project member spoke vividly: 'My time in the Pentecostal Church I would call "spiritual harassment".'

In pastoral ministry I discovered thoughtful young people exploring a more liberal theology, individuals seeking to live, as Christians, a 'normal' life in the midst of this world, and those who rejected what thet had experienced as Pentecostal Church control over their private and social life, in some cases including approval of their marriage partner. Those who wished to re-marry after divorce knew that it would in certain cases be possible in the Church of England; unmarried mothers would probably not meet rejection on that account, and their children would be accepted for Baptism on the same basis as the children of married parents.

(iv) Missing Something

At the end of one discussion the Younger Group came to the following conclusions about their experience of Black-led Pentecostal Churches:

1) We know what we reject (their 'exclusivism', the sense of being 'true' Christians, the 'excesses' of their worship, the ethical codes).

2) We know what we value in our Church (space, order, freedom to think and make up our own minds).

3) We feel we are missing something which they have.

The yardstick for vitality and challenge, as well as for quality of fellowship and Christian music, is often that supplied by the Pentecostal Churches. Several Project members regularly visited Pentecostal Churches, partly as a spiritual complement to Anglican Church life, partly for particular needs such as healing services or conventions, and behind all this, to feed and nurture the Black Christian Tradition within them. Younger Group members were less likely to visit Pentecostal Churches, but all had access to the music and the tradition through friends. Several criticized the Anglican Church for its lack of evangelical challenge, whilst one person, very appreciative of some features of Anglicanism, spoke of her own intense spiritual hunger: 'I do really want their experience of faith.' The inadequacy of Anglican attempts really to teach, and really to help younger Christians to grow was mentioned in different ways by most people.

Black-led Churches will remain for the foreseeable future the main reference point for Black Christianity in Britain. Black Anglicans will draw encouragement from their numerical and spiritual strength and from their achievements, and will continue to visit them and refer to them as sources of Black spiritual nourishment. At the same time the clarification of a Black Anglican identity will surely generate a different ecclesiology and ethical teaching. It must also generate clear and systematic Christian teaching on the basis of a Black identity for Black Anglicans. Out of this will come the development of truly Black theology in an Anglican or 'mainstream' context.

THE RASTAFARIANS

The purpose of our discussions about Rastafarians was also to uncover subjective attitudes, not to undertake an objective analysis. Initially, the Group's response was hostile; 'misguided', 'pitiable', 'pathetic' were typical of adjectives used. 'They are terrible', said one older woman; another concentrated her hostility on the distinctive 'locks'. These responses came primarily from the more conservative older people, but some younger people shared their outlook.

It was generally known that Rastafarians had originated in Jamaica through the teaching of Marcus Garvey and that he had brought hope of re-patriation to Africa to poor Black people in Jamaica. It was known that the hopes of thousands of Black Jamaicans had been aroused by the coronation of Haile Selassie in 1930, and that these hopes were disappointed. The Jamaican middle class had rejected Rasta claims, and Rastafarianism had continued as a peaceful but eccentric 'drop-out' religion:

> When the S.S. Black Star didn't come to take them to Africa, the richer class people chased them out of Kingston. They retreated into the hills and 'went funny' by themselves.

Underlying this was often a respect for their adherence to Black roots: 'They knew their history; they wanted to go to Africa. Our foreparents came from Africa'. But at the everyday conscious level Rastas had been a highly marginal group in Jamaica, and everyone believed that there were no Rastas among the original immigrants to Britain.

However, the more radical older members, and perhaps the majority of younger members, had a different understanding. For one thing, there was a distinction to be drawn between 'true' Rastas – deeply religious, sincere and peaceful, living out their convictions in a radical life-style involving a strict diet and the smoking of marijuana for 'spiritual purposes' – and 'counterfeit' Rastas, members of a 'youth cult' in rebellion against their parents, 'oppressed kids going tough' who had adopted Rasta externals without the internal spirituality. At worst this group were 'just trying to avoid work' and hypocritical with it: 'they say they won't work for White people, yet they accept the government's money'.

Several members thoughtfully challenged the rest to ask why Rastafari had taken root in Britain. Instead of drawing a rigid distinction between 'true' Rastas and others, they saw more of a continuum, from the 'deeply religious' Ethiopian Orthodox Church members at one extreme to 'anti-social' youths wearing the 'colours' at the other. They were the ones who had the clearest analysis of the situation of Black people in Britain but were not simply resigned to wait 'until the Lord comes'. Rolston Deson described how, in his view, the particularly British form of Rastafari had arisen as a way for young Black people to give vent to their non-acceptance of injustice, suffering and inequality. 'They are barred from jobs and from education. The resentment builds up till it is so strong that they show it outwardly. I understand why they are Rastas, so I cannot hate them'.

One reason for the antipathy expressed at first was the perception that Rastas were often hostile to their parents and their values, a hostility which had found religious expression in the rejection of their parents' churches and by the strongly African iconography with which they had replaced the White religious pictures of the traditional Black home. Yet as an Older Group member understood:

> In the end, they often keep a relationship with their parents. They are not rejecting their parents – Black parents – as people, or even as parents. They are rejecting what they see as their parents' acquiescence in oppression. They would say, 'You came here and accepted bad treatment. We are born here and we aren't accepting what you did'.

The combination of admiration and resentment this arouses in parents who recognise that their children's criticism is correct and yet find it hard to face can be readily appreciated. So discussion uncovered in most people an understanding of Rastafari as one form of expression of resistance to the oppression of Black people – an oppression which they were conscious of sharing. But everyone still considered it to be an inappropriate or counter-productive form of protest. Some could see that their 'Africanism' bore little relation to the reality of modern Africa, and felt that their outlook, however sincere and religious, prevented the acquisition of skills and the development of strength necessary to effect a true liberation of Black people in Britain.

It is not clear how important Rastafarianism will be in the future, and to what extent its original eschatology – of waiting for a return to Africa – will be replaced by a 'realised' eschatology of finding liberation in Britain. Meanwhile Rasta music and iconography continue to be the most obvious distinctive cultural symbols developed by younger Black people in Britain.

ESCHATOLOGY: SURVIVAL AND LIBERATION

Towards the end of our time together, an important spirited interchange took place. One older member was unhappy with the direction the discussion had taken. It was, she said, about 'this racial business' rather than 'the Bible'. She agreed that Black people still suffer oppression, indeed knew it well from personal experience, and had therefore wrestled with the question: 'why does this happen?' Her answer was that it is part of the necessary suffering of God's people in this present time. The human predicament is bad and getting worse – but 'this is what's supposed to happen, . . . we are living in Revelation'.[10] She was quite clear about her duty: not to take action by, for example, demonstrating or overtly protesting, but to pray, to have Jesus in her heart, to remain faithful, to live a clean and upright life, a changed, redeemed life which would be shared with others in the fellowship of the Church. They would encourage one another to rely on God until He comes.

This 'survival' theology was in marked contrast to the general tenor of the discussion. Several of the most vocal members of both groups were keen to rouse Black Christians from any such social passivity. And despite the challenge that this attitude was 'race' not 'Bible,' their analysis was equally theological. The suffering of Black people was to be identified with the sufferings of Christ. Black people were exploited in society, as in attitudes like, 'you can only have the jobs not wanted by Whites,' or, 'we will use your service, but not allow you to sit around the table'. 'These two attitudes are the insults, the spittle, the thorns, the nails, the spear and finally the crucifixion of the Blacks', said Rolston Deson. A similar process was discernable in the Church, where Black experience was mediated to those who hold authority in the Church, if at all, only by White intermediaries:

> We don't want someone to go to the Bishop and say 'the Blacks need this or that'. Only Blacks know the interior of a Black person, how we feel, how we suffer. We need to represent our own selves. We don't want to hear it through the keyhole. We've got to sit round the table where decisions are being made. Come now, let us reason together.

The situation of crucifixion meant a cry was being raised, like Christ's on the Cross. 'There is a crying out for something to be done; it is of primary, paramount importance.' From it must follow two consequences. The first was the *repentance of White people*, a repentance that was not just 'feeling sorry' but an actual turning around and being different. Only this could bring about the healing society needs. Thankfully, signs of this repentance were already discernable. At last White Christians were beginning to ask questions like 'What is it you want us to do?' 'How can Black and White together work for the healing of the church and the nation?'

This development made the second consequence the more urgent and possible, namely to develop a *programme of action for the liberation of Black people in the church and in society*, and thus to rid both of the sin of racism. Not that sin could be eradicated by human effort, but it was our duty to work with God for the change He intends. Rolston Deson interpreted the task as follows:

> God wants us not only to pray, but to use the minds, strength and health that He has given us. In the particular situation of His arrest Jesus told Peter to put away his sword (Matthew 26[52]), but His instructions to the disciples about *their* future were quite different, 'Let him who has no sword sell his cloak and buy one' (Luke 22[36]). I do not interpret this to mean violence – I will always oppose the use of violence. But it does mean that we Black people should not simply accept what is done to us, but always struggle towards something better. There is a great division in the human family and our work to overcome this is a spiritual struggle.

From this analysis the Group developed a considerable liberation programme from young and old alike. Older members spoke of the need for Black people to be appointed to work with Whites at different levels in church and society (liaison officers, youth workers, hospital chaplains). Black people needed to be encouraged to come forward into the ministry, and to be given opportunity to sustain and develop their Black identity. Facilities for training Black Christians, not only ordinands, were needed; the existing ones 'stifle Black expression'. Moreover, Black people should not accept marginal or 'second best' facilities.

Younger Group members were particularly concerned about the quality of their participation in Church life. Fellowships of Black young people needed materials and guidelines, and more 'authentic communication' with their clergy. Worship should be more orientated to the needs of all ages, and expressive of the Black Christian Tradition. Existing patterns of meetings and decision-making hindered the real participation of young Black people. Black people should get together and organise their strength and let their voice and experience be heard. The Group rejected the role of 'pew fodder' and asked for their Black authenticity to be recognised: 'The Church must look beneath the skin.' At two levels, diocese and parish, it was necessary to identify who had the power and authority to change things, and to enter into dialogue with them. If that was ineffective, 'then Black Anglicans must really "hit the road", just as Martin Luther King did, and showed that Black people are no longer prepared to be pushed aside'.

8
Plumblines and New Building

What kind of action is required when the White church and the Black story 'collide'? What tasks and challenges face those who respond to the call to participate in what they believe to be God's building of a church which is truly Black and White?[1] In this chapter I try to answer these questions by examining five areas which are important for building the Household of God: (i) Black people claiming their Black Christian inheritance; (ii) White response to the new Black presence; (iii) changing the Church at national level; (iv) changing local church structures and (v) reforming theological education. They are tested against the five 'plumblines' of Black Christianity which were listed in chapter two: authentic Black Christianity (i) is rooted in Africa; (ii) involves encounter with the name of Jesus; (iii) is a religion of the Spirit; (iv) is a liberation faith; and (v) has a vision of the future. Some of this is the story of one particular church, the Church of England, whilst much of the rest uses the example of a particular organisation or college. All are chosen not because they are necessarily the most 'successful' or significant examples in terms of their impact on the Church, but because each illustrates a vital principle or issue. If the *method* is grasped, it can be used to guide 'building' in other churches or institutions.

CLAIMING THE INHERITANCE

One afternoon in 1988, an energetic discussion about contemporary Black life took place in a Black bookshop, during which the shop assistant was heard to say: 'I used to be a Christian, but that was too easy. It's not enough just to love everybody; we need to struggle for the freedom of our people'. The word 'love' no doubt carried for him a sense of submission, of meekness without dignity. Even so, the verdict 'too easy' is testimony to the extraordinary failure of churches, both 'Black-led' and 'mainstream', to communicate Black Christian faith as a resource for Black living today. Hence most younger people are without a yardstick for evaluating their tradition and for bringing it into dialectical encounter with the present oppressive context.

From its birth, Black Christian faith has been in dialectical tension with White theology and White structures in a context of oppression. White distortions of the Gospel are negated and the truth of Black faith preserved through encounters with the God of the Bible, transforming past understandings of the Gospel into new ones as a changing social context makes necessary. Just as the contemporary context is in continuity with its oppressive past, so the Black Christian tradition, though engaged in what Cornel West calls 'the ever-evolving task of recovering, regaining and repeating the Gospel',[2] is in continuity with the enduring and tested inheritance of its past.

How is this faith to be lived in Britain today? There exists as yet little writing on the subject; a 'manual for the struggle', a textbook of indigenous Black theology, is urgently needed.[3] As Louis-Charles Harvey writes, 'It can only be written by Black Christians who have been through the struggle and have triumphed'.[4] The struggle is taking place every day that Black people live in Britain; the triumph has come to those believers who, compelled by hard times, have responded to their situation and overcome. Their lives are the work of the Spirit; their testimony is the raw material out of which the 'manual' will be written. They are not isolated individuals, for they share the solidarity of the wider Black community, and of the new Black Church.[5] This Church already has its oral testimonies, and now increasingly, its written testimonies, in the form of papers prepared for meetings, minutes of grass-roots organisations and reports of conferences. The Birmingham-based group *Claiming the Inheritance* (C.T.I.) is one such organisation.

In 1986, C.T.I. held its first conference in order to bring together a large number of Black British Christians (mainly from 'mainstream' churches) and leaders who were identified as possessing the gift of 'telling the story'.[6] C.T.I.'s *methodology* was to identify the actual 'grass-roots' Black Church in 'mainstream' churches, and those who were recognized by the community as leaders. Since no such previous identification of the Black Church within 'mainstream' churches had taken place, the step was a crucial liberating break with an oppressive past of 'invisibility'. It involved a strategy, aided by sympathetic White clergy, of collecting names and addresses and identifying appropriate Black networks of communication.

Guidance came from two Black clergy. The first was Roderick

Hewitt, a Jamaican minister then in Birmingham on an international exchange programme, who had already shown prophetic leadership in his response to the Handsworth Uprising of 1985.[7] The second, David Moore, then a team vicar in St. Paul's, Bristol, had made an effective contribution to the first 'Young, Gifted and Black' conference organised for young Black Anglicans in 1984. Louis-Charles Harvey, an American Black theologian and a specialist in the study of Black Christianity in Britain led the conference which attracted over 300 people, mainly Black.

Harvey's starting point was the reiteration of the Black Christian story from its African-creation roots through the oppressive history of slavery and colonialism to post-war emigration from the Caribbean and the enactment of racist legislation in Britain. A constant in the oppression had been economic exploitation, supported by racist ideology. This history had a *positive legacy of protest*, in the tradition of Ottobah Cugoano (1757–1804), the first Black English writer to declare that enslaved Blacks had not only the right but also the duty to resist, and of Olaudah Equiano (c. 1750–1797),[8] the first political leader of Britain's Black community. There was also a positive legacy of *co-operation between Black and White* in the liberation struggle, especially that linked with the names of William Wilberforce, the most celebrated of the many Evangelicals and humanitarians who struggled for the abolition of slavery, and Granville Sharp, perhaps the leading name from a slightly earlier period.[9] This legacy was available to shape faith and struggle today.

But there was also a *negative legacy of Black disunity*, including '*islandism*', the belief that one island or language group in the Caribbean is superior to others, which continued to weaken the attempts at united action. Harvey was clear that this disunity was not rooted in Africa, but in the false identity imposed under British imperialism; forsaking their true identity, Black people had accepted from the oppressor a false identity which must now be exorcised.

In the process of recovering true identity, the important distinction between *cultural assimilation* and *economic inclusion* must be understood. Cultural assimilation led to loss of identity, obscuring the dignity of the divine gift of the African creation. But economic inclusion, was a right which had already been earned by 'sweat equity', the labour of Black people who had fought for Britain in wars and worked in British factories.

This history was the context in which the liberation faith had been kept and developed by the Black Church, including the Church in Britain. Black people had a faith rooted in the identification of God, who was originally revealed in the African creation, with the Father of Jesus Christ, the source of hope for liberation. The Spirit had sustained Black people from this time into the British stage of their Diaspora, enabling them to survive, maintain their human dignity and keep a vision of a new future. Again this story had a *positive legacy, the formation of the Black Church in Britain and the emergence of acknowledged leaders*. These leaders came from the new Black Church in Britain which, though predominantly Pentecostal, had also consolidated in 'mainstream' churches. The Black Church in Britain was an exciting place to be, full of 'joy, liveliness, warmth, and a pervasive sense that God is a living force with us'. And Harvey detected increasing radicalism and the emergence of new leadership.

But there was also a *negative legacy*, a *false theological conscious-ness* which was not true to either the African legacy of religion as all-encompassing, or the authentic Black Christian Tradition. Harvey called this 'living on the Hallelujah-Side', a term taken from a church chorus, which he defined as the belief that 'the Church should only be involved in saving souls, and not with the social, political and economic problems facing black people'. This false theology was a legacy of slavery times when masters had attempted to keep slaves docile by promising rewards in heaven. Against this view Harvey fashioned the term 'living on the Amen-side'.

> To say 'Amen' in a black worship service is to witness to the reality of God's presence in the Church, and his continuing presence in the world where Christians live and struggle. To live on the Amen-side is to see the Gospel as a Gospel of spiritual, social, political and economic freedom. It is to claim the Church's mission as one of struggle for the oppressed.

Such a church could take the lead in developing a new positive self-image of Black people. It was a church which gave hope there for a 'beloved community' of Black and White together, for Black Christian faith had the potential to transform White church life as well:

> Blacks in black or white churches have the responsibility to be the *leaven* in the churches to enable them to see that the true and liberating Gospel of Jesus Christ is one which relates faith to struggle.

On the 'Amen' Side' there was more than rejoicing; there was also freedom.[10]

The testimony to the accuracy of Harvey's analysis was in the 'happening' of the conference. The large assembly of Black Christians from (mainly) 'mainstream' churches, interacting in a 'positive image' environment of appropriate posters, literature, music, celebration and food gave a response which confirmed that he had 'told the story'. When amidst a celebration of Gospel songs Eve Pitts sang 'Steal Away to Jesus', and Patrick Rosheuvel led the singing of Bob Marley's 'Redemption Song' the same deep authentication was evident:

> Old pirates yes them rob I
> Sold I to the merchant ship
> Minutes after they took I
> From the bottomless Pit
>
> But my hands were made strong
> By the hand of the Almighty,
> And we forward in this generation
> Triumphantly! . . .
> All I ever had –
> Redemption song . . .
>
> Emancipate yourself from mental slavery,
> None but ourselves can free our minds . . .
>
> All I ever had –
> Redemption song.

Following the conference, *Claiming the Inheritance* became an organisation. It holds regular quarterly services with worship devised and led by its committee members who are almost all 'mainstream' church Black Christians. Preachers are chosen who, like Louis-Charles Harvey, have the gift of 'telling the story' of Black experience and the Gospel.

The second conference, *Celebrating the Black Family*, adopted a similar methodology to the first, but also looked to the wider Black community for a definitive presentation of its story in post-war Britain. In their production *When Two Shifts Meet*, the Black Theatre company *Third Dimension* portrayed the conflicts which a young Jamaican faced within himself and within his family, on settling in Britain after service as a British soldier in the Second World War. The play appealed to younger people, revealing to them the forces which shape their lives. As a C.T.I. member observed, 'It was wonderful to see so many of the audience caught up by the songs, games and music with which they identified.'

C.T.I. thus reiterated that Black faith and the Black Church have arisen in response to Black experience, and are part of it; that the community story has its own 'plumblines' which interact with the theological criteria. So the first main speaker Sybil Phoenix, the celebrated London community worker and Methodist local preacher, reflecting on 'The Black British Family in the Church', told the parallel story of the substantial rejection of Black people in 'mainstream' churches. Against this stood the Black *family* as an expression of God's creative will, rooted in Africa and shaped in response to later oppression; a model of 'family' based neither on the modern White 'nuclear family' nor on an unhistorical ideal type. That was the inheritance, proclaimed Phoenix; the challenge of the Gospel was to preserve and develop it so as to transform the future.

In this story, the emergence of the Black Church, most freely and fully in the Black-led churches but also against all difficulties in 'mainstream' churches, had sustained the Black family. It had been the community of faith which had developed the Black Christian Tradition, and from that strong foundation had been the main springboard to achieving Harvey's 'economic inclusion' in British society. Black people in the churches, therefore, had the need and the right to be separate from White Christians in order that, being strengthened, they may return and be together with them.[11]

Next, David Divine, Director of Social Services for the London Borough of Brent, reflected on 'The Black British Family in Society'. His starting point was the continuing Black experience of institutional racism, 'our daily companion (whose) influence will last our lifetime, no matter how successful we are'. Divine did not explicitly refer to Africa, but he was clear that positive human identity of Black people was the only way forward:

It is an illusion to think that by denying our blackness, our history, our daily experience, we will somehow become less threatening and thereby more acceptable to the majority culture . . . Ethnic identification . . . is the only route to our advancement.

It was necessary for Black people to have a strong Black consciousness. This would liberate them from 'mental shackles' which distort awareness. For instance, the Black family had until recently, even in the United States, been evaluated according to White criteria. This meant that researchers had begun with negative presuppositions (a 'pathological framework') and had ignored particular functions of the Black family, notably its function in socialising children to cope with the realities of the Black community, and deal with prejudice and discrimination. Black researchers, by contrast, without ignoring real problems, nonetheless had identified five basic strengths: strong kinship bonds, strong work orientation, adaptability of family roles, strong achievement orientation and a strong religious orientation. These were the basic strengths on which alone a future could be built. Divine suggested several ways in which Black people should develop consciousness. One was to strip themselves of the inheritance of slavery which gives inferior worth to Black skin colour and hair. Another was taking power wherever possible, within the existing system; whilst a third was to affirm Black heroes, who were defined not simply as those who achieve, but as those who achieve whilst remaining accountable to the Black community. For, as Divine memorably concluded:

> With my job, higher up the scale, I need to be even closer to my own people. For, at the end of the day, when 'push comes to shove', I'm not going to be supported by anyone other than my own people.[12]

C.T.I. has sponsored several events similarly designed to develop Black Christian consciousness, its vision of the future and thus its vitality and liberation faith. Worship, prayer and reflection on Scripture ensure that the development of consciousness and of strategies for action (for example in the field of education) are rooted in the Church. An address given by Dr. Rose Jackson, an Apostolic Church minister from Chicago, in September 1987 re-affirmed these roots. Drawing on the American experience she described the Black Church as 'the foundation of our racial solidarity', for when slavery and racism had torn apart even the Black family, only the Church had endured. The Church was free space, the only place for free expression, celebration and experience of a 'high and holy gladness'. The Black Church had three definitive burdens: the first was to 'heal the oppressed', by speaking out, by taking political action, and by being 'missionaries, visionaries of a new world order'. Included in this liberative definition was a survival element:

> The Black Church is a Rock in a weary land of oppression. It faces a mean world and says, 'We shall overcome'.

The second burden was to 'reveal Jesus' through its weakness, poverty, and the inferior status it was given by White Christians. The third burden was that of 'saving white religion' – the dialectical encounter by which 'white heresy' was expunged and White religion purified. The White heresy was the conviction that a person's Baptism and standing as a Christian did not affect their worldly status and that church allegiance could, therefore, co-exist with oppression. Simon of Cyrene was the icon of the Black Church, for without his 'burden', the pain of bearing Jesus' Cross, the completion of work of salvation would not have been possible.[13] Dr. Jackson's vision of the Black Church undergirds Professor Harvey's challenge to the 'Black-led' churches in Britain to free themselves from false theological consciousness. At the same time, it reminds Black Christians in 'mainstream' churches of their debt to 'Black-led' churches and encourages them to claim 'liberated space' within their own churches.

The story of *Claiming the Inheritance* is that of Black Christians seeking to interpret Black Christian Faith for living in Britain today. The texts produced by their conferences accord with the 'plumblines' of affirming an identity rooted in a primal African revelation of God, in the discovery of Jesus Christ the liberator, and in the power of the Holy Spirit who is sustaining the community in its struggle for freedom. This freedom can be claimed, and will be in a future in which White people who collaborate can also be included. But the Spirit must be allowed to divest Black and White of their negative legacy of false consciousness which had arisen out of a past injustice.

THE WHITE RESPONSE

The White response to the Black Christian tradition is to be evaluated by the extent to which the White Church 'hears' and 'names' the Black Christian Tradition and is prepared to acknowledge its own identity in relation to that tradition. The authentically Christian White response will be a repentant one; the encounter will be a converting ordinance. It will be one which recognises the victims not only as victim, but as mediators of the presence of Christ, in whom forgiveness, new life, and the 'exchange of gifts' are made possible. On this basis I now examine a representative number of White responses.

'INTEGRATION'

Through the two decades of primary settlement of Black people, 1948–68, the predominant White Christian response was to seek to achieve 'integration' and 'good race relations' and to exhort Church members to good neighbourliness. With British 'fair play' and 'decency' – still favourably compared with the injustices the Civil Rights Movement was revealing in the United States – the accommodation of the 'immigrants' to British society could be achieved, and the strains of unusual events such as the Notting Hill riots of 1958 or the Smethwick Election campaign of 1964 could be removed.[14]

This response rested on an inadequate understanding for two reasons. Firstly, failing to understand the structural, institutional and historic nature of racism, it saw race relations as merely one aspect of individual personal relations. Secondly, it implied that the 'problem' lay substantively with Black immigrants themselves, who were seen as lacking the skills, experience, qualities and even willingness to adapt to life in Britain. This 'problem' could be 'solved' by White Christian kindness and the benefits of British education.

The response is in continuity with the colonial attitudes which had regarded White culture and colonial society as the norm, and the emancipated slaves as 'empty vessels' waiting to be filled with White culture as a basis for integration. Little positive recognition was therefore given to the existence of a Black cultural inheritance, and virtually none to a distinctive inheritance of faith. Black people in 'mainstream' churches were not regarded as constituting a distinctive community of faith; the emergence of Black-led churches was simply deplored. But the 'colonial' project of integration through subservience was not even a possibility in Britain in this period, a period in which Black people were undergoing the trauma of being rejected by the society – and the churches – they had been taught to regard as 'Mother'.[15] Integration in this context clearly could not mean a 'hearing' of Black experience, or a 'naming' of the Black tradition of faith, but rather the suppression of identity.

'PARTNERSHIP'

At this time, which was also a period of daily struggle for the basic necessities of life for Black people, co-ordinated articulation of experience by Blacks themselves was necessarily small. By the 1970's, however, White Christians with the ears to hear were responding to a rising volume of Black speech which, through 'telling the story' of the experience of racism, rejection and disillusionment in Britain, began to affirm the Black inheritance of faith, liberation and vision of a new future. There were two major dimensions of the Black voice, to which White Christians responded, the new Black-led churches, and Black criticism of society.

Firstly, the *new churches*. By 1970 a large number of Black-led churches, some quite small but others with hundreds of members, had become firmly established in the areas of Black settlement. White churches had to accept that they were a fact of life, and in the new ecumenism of the inner city, were compelled to deal with issues such as sharing, letting and purchasing church buildings. Slowly clergy from both traditions started to meet each other – in Birmingham a monthly Black and White Pastors' meeting developed – and gradually hostility and suspicion on both sides gave way to mutual discovery and to the exploration of partnership.

The work of Roswith Gerloff, a Pastor from the German Protestant Church, and the consequent founding in 1978 of the *Centre for Black and White Christian Partnership* is an outstanding example of 'hearing' the 'Black-led' churches. Gerloff's early work involved visiting the young Pentecostal, Holiness and Adventist congregations at worship in school halls and sometimes still in private homes. In later research, she traced individual congregations to their Caribbean roots.[16] The Centre's first task was to meet the need of Black pastors for accredited theological education, but as Gerloff writes, much more than this was involved in the Centre:

> It was conceived as a turntable between the historic and the charismatic tradition, between the 'Third' and 'First' worlds on our doorstep, between the oral and the literary cultures, poor and rich, Black and White. It was envisaged as a partnership scheme on all levels to loosen the bonds of tradition and to break through discriminative and exploitative structures. And it developed into an alternative model of ecumenism which builds on relationships from the bottom up rather than from the top down. In this way we hoped we could equip ourselves, God's people from different directions, for a joint Christian mission in a segregated and disjointed society.[17]

There was no doubt that the Centre made outstanding progress with these aims. Nevertheless, it had, particularly in the early years, a number of limitations. There was for example less than complete support from the two largest Black-led denominations; some White voices in both the management of the Centre and its teaching programme were not necessarily attuned to Black experience or theology; 'mainstream' churches provided inadequate and random funding, whilst the Centre itself for many years gave little recognition to Black people in 'mainstream' churches. However, the Centre is an outstanding testimony of the emergence into White consciousness of the Black-led churches as communities of faith born of a distinctive experience. In so far as its life has been determined by their identity, inheritance and needs, it has been true to the 'plumblines' of the Black Christian tradition. It has made a real break with the colonial 'integration' model, and has offered instead the promise of equal partnership. But, despite the vision of its founder and the work of individuals, institutional White involvement has not journeyed into that area of dialectical interaction with Black Christianity where repentance and conversion make possible the New Common Life of the Church.

Secondly, the White response to *Black criticism of society*.[18] Reflection on their experience of settlement in Britain was leading many Blacks to realize that not only were Whites as individuals prejudiced, but that the very structures of society itself were racist. For Christians, a powerful impetus to this analysis had come from the World Council of Churches Consultation on Racism held at Notting Hill in 1969.

Subsequently, reflection in this perspective was pursued by the British Council of Churches who in April 1976 published *The New Black Presence in Britain: a Christian Scrutiny*. The heart of this report was an article by Gus John which combined testimony to the Black experience of alienation and discrimination with a socio-historical analysis of the racism which had produced it. Britain, said John, was guilty of ignoring history in its dealings with Black people (even though West Indians as a people were a British colonial creation), and therefore could not see how the oppression of the colonial era was still being perpetuated, albeit in a new 1970's form. Black people as 'second class production factors' were condemned to inferior conditions, for which, in a classic case of 'blaming the victims,' they were then held responsible. Lack of clear analysis meant that ameliorative agencies such as the Community Relations Commission were unable to engage meaningfully with institutional racism. Black people, especially younger ones, were therefore placed in an impossible dilemma. Society invited them to 'assimilate', whilst at the same time denying them any place but the bottom of the heap. 'To wish to integrate with that which alienates and destroys you, rendering you less than a person, is madness' wrote John, echoing James Baldwin. Hope for Black people lay not in 'remedies White society prescribes for us', but in their own struggle for freedom. That struggle was where the Church should be located, but if the Church failed in its evangelical witness, the Gospel – and the world-wide struggle of oppressed people for liberation – did not.[19]

The working party's reflections accepted the validity of the historical perspective. They affirmed the present uniquely oppressive

143

experience of Black people by rejecting 'assimilation' as either a desirable or a possible option, and by accurately identifying the role of institutional racism in excluding Black people. For in examining institutional racism, the point at issue was not the moral intention of the White individuals involved but whether in actual practice Black people were excluded or not. Of this the report was in no doubt:

> To [many] Black people, Church, School, Police and Social Services are seen to have linked against their entry into white society . . . the normal expectations and methods of operation of these institutions have the effect of maintaining a colour bar.[20]

The report asked whether Britain could change, or whether it must always have a group at the 'bottom of the heap'. It accepted that the Church was most truly itself in solidarity with the poor, and made up of the poor, rather than as the powerful, maintaining others in dependence.

The report concluded with a list of possibilities for action, an agenda which did, in fact, outline much of the way the White response actually developed during the next decade. Recognising the dangers of paternalism, it nonetheless challenged the Church to 'form its own programme to combat racism in this country . . . and discover theological and material resources for this enterprise'. Aid for self-help projects was advocated, as were intervention and witness in the struggle for justice, for instance over housing, education, employment and immigration procedures. A new ecumenism was also commended, consisting of sensitive closer relationships with and support for the Black-led churches which did not 'pauperise', co-opt or make dependent.

The Black statement in the report certainly arose from the identity, inheritance and needs of Black people and was therefore true to the 'plumblines' of the Black Christian tradition. It broke with the colonial 'integration' model, and offered instead the promise of equal partnership. The White response journeyed some way in the direction of repentant practice, though with some important limitations. For instance, the report still found it necessary to reassure its White readers that Black testimony was believable, and that the working party had not suspended their critical faculties when gathering it! Also, in his short preface, Harry Morton, the B.C.C.'s General Secretary declared, without giving reasons, that he actually rejected Gus John's 'prognosis about our society' on which the report was substantially based. And it is remarkable that nowhere in the report was there mention of the continuing presence of Black people in the very churches which constituted the B.C.C., and from which the working party was drawn. Penitence was briefly expressed for the rejection of earlier years, but a reader could be forgiven for assuming that Black Anglicans, Methodists and other 'mainstream' Christians had ceased to exist as communities of faith in British churches.

The Centre for Black and White Christian Partnership and *The New Black Presence* have been highlighted as marks of a decade in which there was a significant shift among concerned White Christians from the colonial-integration model to a 'partnership' model. They had been prompted by two kinds of new 'building' by Black people themselves, namely the formation of separate ecclesial institutions and the development of a critical social analysis of British society.

The African Diaspora had created *churches appropriate to the new British context* in which the 'plumblines' of African creation and the sustaining power of the Lord Jesus could be affirmed in the freedom of the Spirit. In these churches the language of liberation was often muted, and the future vision expressed in other-worldly imagery, but they were always more than a haven, as, like the Spirituals of slavery times, they carried a people's determination not to accept the imposed identity, but to affirm and develop their own. By the beginning of the 1980's the Black-led churches had found at least some White Christian leaders capable of 'hearing' and fashioning a response. No longer rivals who were 'dividing the church,' they were now recognised as potential partners in the Christian mission. Black-led churches were now inescapably part of responsible White ecumenism.

By the beginning of the 1980's, *Black social criticism* had likewise found at least some White Christian response. In particular, the B.C.C.'s Community and Race Relations Unit (CRRU) became a valued means for pursuing this response, as well as an important symbol of it. It developed structures which were flexible, involved the minimum of bureaucracy, and gave recipients of aid a sense of dignity and control over their destiny. It has been prepared to run the gauntlet of controversy and criticism to aid Black self-help groups, most notably in its 1981 grant to the *Liverpool 8 Defence Committee,* which may be considered part of the cost of repentant White discipleship. (The manner in which grants are made is always a crucial issue, since it is the touchstone of how 'un-colonial' White thinking actually is.)[21]

In the year following the publication of *The New Black Presence*, much White Christian response to racial injustice took the form of opposition to immigration law and practice which were, in the words of Ian Martin, Secretary of the Joint Council for the Welfare of Immigrants, 'not merely oppressive, (but) deeply imbued with racism'.[22] CRRU's detailed research and campaigning was given symbolic and prayerful expression in a Vigil for Justice sponsored not only by CRRU and other Christian Groups, but also by J.C.W.I., and held in the parish church of the House of Commons, St. Margaret's Westminster, from June 22nd to 24th 1980.

In 1977, the General Synod of the Church of England, also responding to *The New Black Presence*, affirmed that Britain is a multi-racial society and called for a programme to educate church and nation.[23] It also challenged the Church of England to contribute £100,000 annually for seven years to Black self-help projects. In November 1978, rejecting the idea of a separate Anglican fund, it decided to channel this money through CRRU.[24] Some dioceses made no response, some proved hesitant and half-hearted, but others not only fulfilled their contribution but developed responses of their own which (as in Birmingham) were to have far-reaching consequences. Meanwhile, ecumenical disquiet at the Nationality Act of 1981, already focused in a statement by bishops and other leading Anglicans after the 1979 General Election,[25] was channelled through bishops in the House of Lords, who, despite determined and widely reported opposition, were unable to prevent its passage into law.[26]

This response of some 'mainstream' Christians to 'Black-led' churches and Black social criticism was, of course, far from being a mass movement of church members. But it did involve some White Christian leaders in the corporate recognition of the real ecclesial and social experience of Black people. They were no longer seen as 'dividing the church' or 'the problem', but rather as victims of a corporate injustice, the roots of which went deep into history. So, the earlier exhortations to White Christians to be 'welcoming' and 'kind' were replaced, in some places at least, by positive action to achieve social justice. Racial justice had become one of the most prominent issues of Christian social responsibility.

Black people now featured on the *Ecumenical* and *Social Responsibility* agendas of the 'mainstream' churches. They did not, however, appear on the *domestic* agendas, such as Education, Ministry, Pastoral Organization or Finance. Mention of Black people might now call to mind meetings with (for example) a local Church of God pastor, or the struggle against the Nationality Act, but not the intimate table fellowship within the Methodist or Church of England 'family'. There, Black people remained 'invisible', leading one Black priest to ruminate with sad irony that local vicars (who ten years earlier had been accusing Black-led churches of 'splitting the Church') were now falling over themselves to have a Pentecostal congregation in their church hall, whilst not yet 'recognising' the Black people in their own congregations.

CHANGE AT THE NATIONAL LEVEL

Robinson Milwood's *Let's Journey Together*, published in 1980, marked the first written 'cry' of Black people in 'mainstream' churches to claim their rightful place. Introductory articles by George Mulrain, a Trinidadian Methodist minister and doctoral student at Birmingham University, by John Hick, Professor of Theology at Birmingham University, and by Sybil Phoenix, took up the theme of *The New Black Presence in Britain* by reminding the reader of the Black experience of racism in British churches and British society. They particularly reflected concern at the activities of the National Front and other fascist groups, then at the height of their influence.

Milwood broke new ground by taking this story as the basis of his critique of the Methodist Church. He called for the culture, history, identity and approach to worship of Black people to be made explicit in the Church, so that an equal fellowship could be developed with White people. The 'plumblines' of African-creation roots and the long story of the Black encounter with Christ became once more the basis for purifying White religion. Black people might appreciate the 'social responsibility' of enlightened Whites, but their basic cry, as Milwood articulated it, was not for help but for 'acceptance and participation; for space in which to cultivate self-reliance, self-determination, moral and social rectitude, despite all historical and modern stigmas'.[27] Black Christian self-assertion was not, however, for the 'verbal castigating' of contemporary White Methodists about the past, but the basis for the demand for equality and inclusion. So there was a future vision from which White people were not excluded.

By these criteria, Milwood found Methodism sadly wanting. Often Black people were openly insulted; where this did not happen, Black ministers were still only accepted if they conformed to White norms rather than expressing their true identity. Supposedly multi-racial congregations were not 'multi-racial in depth', but kept Black people in a lowly and dependent position. They thus failed to generate Black lay leadership and ordained ministry. To remedy this Milwood set out a detailed plan of action through which the Black Methodist community could express and affirm itself, and develop its own leadership. He outlined the qualities of character and commitment which would be necessary in such leaders.

Milwood thus formulated a strategy for liberation, with an inclusive future vision. This strategy draws on the 'plumblines' of the Black Christian Tradition to meet a specific oppressive situation and through it gives hope to Black and White together. His booklet marks a watershed in British Methodism.

The Church of England published its 'watershed' document the following year. *The Church of England and Racism* (the 'Leicester' Report), contained the recommendations of a Consultation held in Leicester in October 1981. Like Milwood's booklet it occupied a strangely marginal position in relation to the structure of the church, being published by an official Church body, but not authorised as expressing the convictions of that body. Unlike Milwood's booklet, however, it was the product of a basically White process, not the result of Black Christian reflection.

In July 1980 the General Synod of the Church of England had agreed to the appointment of a Race Relations Field Officer by the Board of Social Responsibility. This post had grown out of a series of Synod debates on *The New Black Presence*, and a subsequent B.S.R. report, *Britain as a Multi-racial and Multi-cultural Society*.[28] Kenneth Leech, the new officer, called together a wide cross-section of clergy, theologians and race relations workers. Of the fifty-one participants, only eleven (21%) were Black, including four Church of England clergy. Most of their report was concerned with issues of racial justice, from the functioning of law and the police in Britain to international racism, especially in southern Africa. The report was a 'watershed', however, because for the first time a critical look was taken at the structures of the Church of England itself, including Church schools, thus acknowledging that Black people, including clergy, existed within the Church. The injustice they experienced there was to be tackled by ensuring Black representation and participation, whilst the fostering of Black leadership and Black vocations to ordained ministry was recommended. At the same time White clergy were given guidelines for appropriate styles of ministry and patterns of theological education.

However, incredible though it seems a decade later, *The Church of England and Racism* contained no reflection on the meaning of Blackness, and failed even to mention the religious, cultural and historical resources of Black people. The report recognized the existence of black-skinned people in the Church, and that they are victims of injustice. But it did not proceed from 'creation', from the roots and historic identity of Black people. This, as we have seen, is a necessary condition for theological reflection within the Black Christian Tradition, as it is also for any truly post-colonial vision of the Church. Accordingly it is necessary to point out that this document, though progressive, did not burst out of the bounds of a White 'colonial' theological process. It failed to recognise Black Anglicans as a community of faith (contrast Milwood's reflections on Methodism) and was thus unable to 'name' the most powerful resources Black people have for fashioning their own liberation struggle, namely their identity, history, liturgical traditions and theology.

It was a member of Kenneth Leech's support group, David Moore, a Black priest from the Southwark Diocese, who remedied this deficiency in an unpublished discussion paper, *Invisible People: Black People in the Church of England,* prepared in 1984. Moore followed a methodology comparable to Milwood's which was true to the 'plumblines' of the Black Christian Tradition. He affirmed the identity of Black people, including Black Anglicans in particular, by 'telling the story'. He named the African homeland, and described the encounter with British imperial expansion and White Christianity, including the more recent experience in Britain. He described the development of Black-led churches as a place of refuge, self-affirmation and hope.

On this basis he outlined a liberative praxis, 'Reclaiming Zion', which began with an affirmation of equality and partnership:

> We black Anglicans have stayed within the Church of England because it is our church as well as a white church. It is our tradition and means of religious expression which we will not be deprived of . . .

As an established community of faith Black Anglicans should be producing their own leadership, including ordained ministry. This would not be achieved by importing clergy from the Caribbean, still less by appointing black-skinned people who lack a Black conscious-ness. 'Being black', Moore wrote, 'is not a state of colour but a state of consciousness'.[29] The Church of England must indeed examine its structures and policies, but the process of developing racial justice in the Church also involved the development of 'space' for Black people where their 'cultural perspective' could be affirmed. White clergy also needed to undergo a process of 'consciousness-raising' which would equip them to 'build and affirm the black presence'. Such a building from 'below' was the only way forward; without it, attempts at reform from above, even the appointment of a Black bishop, would be fruitless tokens.[30] If Moore's paper is judged true by the 'plumblines' of the Black Christian Tradition, it will be a useful standpoint from which to note two other important developments of the 1980's.

The first development is the formation in 1981 of the *Association of Black Clergy*. The Association is a focus for Black clergy in 'White-led' churches, not unlike the Black caucuses in 'White-led' churches, and indeed secular institutions, in the United States. Though ecumenical, its membership is predominantly Anglican. Its aims are (i) support for each other, (ii) identification of issues of social justice and theological reflection upon them, and (iii) action in community and Church which is a sign of commitment to 'Kingdom principles'.

Since 1983 the A.B.C. has sponsored annual *Young, Gifted and Black* weekends, initially with the aim of fostering vocations to the Anglican ordained ministry. This has developed into the Black Anglican Youth Association (BAYA), the first national youth caucus in Britain, which held its first conference, *Forward into Freedom* in September 1987. The Association's aims are still rooted in fostering participation in the life of the local congregation, but have been widened to include learning about Black culture and exploring contemporary social issues facing the Black community in England. Though small in number, the young people who attend BAYA weekends represent a crucial focus of concern for the future of Black Anglicanism. They differ from most of the clergy of the A.B.C. in three important if inevitable ways. Firstly, because they are young, they have nearly all been born, or at least substantially brought up, in Britain. Secondly they are, therefore, the 'product' of Church of England congregations, some from the relatively 'cosy' setting (as one participant has put it) of largely Black congregations, others relatively isolated individuals in largely White congregations. Thirdly, they are mostly from an Afro-Caribbean background. They are the young Black 'grass roots' of the Church. By developing their aims so as to work through issues of culture, history and identity rather than simply claim a place in existing structures, they have signalled to the Church their determination to be true to the plumblines of the living Black Christian Tradition which they have inherited.

All this makes for complexity in the relationship between young Black Anglicans and the clergy of the A.B.C. Black clergy in Britain come from many and varied backgrounds; most were born and educated overseas. Their relationship to the Black British community of faith in the Church of England, the majority of which has a common historical, cultural and theological background, is obviously not straightforward. As Sharon Palmer, a leading BAYA member, has said:

> Before we could think about ordained, or any other, ministry in the Church, we at first had to work through our own experience. We needed an organization 'owned' by us. For, unlike our parents and most Black clergy, our lives have been lived entirely in Britain; there is nowhere we can go to. The pain of our rejection in British society is greater than that of those who have come here from elsewhere.

This of course is not to overlook the rejection and racism from hierarchy and from congregations experienced by existing clergy, nor the importance of the A.B.C. in developing solidarity and confidence. As one priest writes:

> I have been quiet for twenty years. I was on my own. Belonging to the Association of Black Clergy has changed that. Through its corporateness I have gained confidence, and I speak up now.[31]

The A.B.C. has clearly been a means to a solution to what an American writer, James Evans, has described as the 'identity crisis of Black Anglicans'.[32] But the kind of way forward it should offer for the Black Anglican community of faith has been, at one point at least, sharply controversial, with David Moore a leading critic.[33] Writing in 1985, Evans noted that the A.B.C.'s current aims were concerned with claiming a rightful place for Black people in the leadership and ministry of the church. There were three particular objectives: the appointment of a Black bishop, the creation of an office of Black Ministries similar to that in the Episcopal Church of the United States, and a 'site and programme' for theological education of Black candidates for ordination. As we have already seen, Moore regarded the appointment of a Black bishop as a 'fruitless token'. Clearly the second A.B.C. objective, an office of Black Ministries, is primarily a 'top- down' process, though it has potential for being interpreted differently. The third objective, a theological centre, is in itself not one that Moore would oppose: indeed what is probably the earliest such proposal, *Pre-Theological College Training: a Discussion Paper*, comes from him. Such a centre would be a place where the new 'product' of Afro-Caribbean British congregations would meet the established Black clergy of the Church. It would have the potential to be either a 'top-down' or a 'bottom-up' institution.

The A.B.C. has been successful in all three of its objectives: The Rt. Revd. Wilfred Wood, a priest who came to England from Barbados in 1962, was consecrated Bishop of Croydon, a semi-autonomous episcopal area in the Diocese of Southwark, in 1985; whilst, as we shall see, Mrs. Glynne Gordon-Carter began work as Secretary to the Committee for Black Anglican Concerns in December 1987, and in September 1989 Dr. Sehon Goodridge took up his post as the first Principal of the Simon of Cyrene Theological Institute.

The second development is the publication in 1985 of *Faith in the City*, the report of the Archbishop of Canterbury's Commission on Urban Priority Areas (ACUPA). Four of the eighteen Commissioners (22%) were Black, including the Bishop of Croydon and two priests. It was regarded nationally as a Church critique of Government policy; it soon became a best-seller after publicity given to the (mistaken) view of an anonymous Government minister that the report was 'Marxist'. However, it also contained both analysis and proposals for the Church, and has since inspired much activity, from the £80 million Church Urban Fund to local parish audits and inter-parish 'twinning'.

Faith in the City, much praised for its detailed practical proposals, has also been strongly criticised for lack of theological undergirding.[34] Judged by the plumblines of the Black Christian Tradition its understanding of the position and experience of Black people in the Church was certainly inadequate. Of course it is significant in itself that almost a quarter of the Commissioners were Black – few comparable bodies in Church or State could claim this. Black-led churches, moreover, were fully recognised as partners in mission, even if the reasons for their growth were not fully investigated. And the hurts of Black people, not only in society but also in the Church, were acknowledged. Sometimes the language suggested a certain subjectivity about the experience ('black people *felt themselves* unwelcome in English Churches' – my italics), but at least at one point the Report mentioned the 'alienation, hurt and rejection experienced by many black people in relation to the Church of England'.

The report's most significant proposals concerned the alteration of central Church structures; a 'clear lead from the centre' being seen as the best response to discrimination, disadvantage and rejection. This lead was to consist of four actions:

(i)   the appointment of a full-time Race Relations Field Officer funded wholly by the Board of Social Responsibility of the General Synod;

(ii)   the setting up of a Standing Commission on Black Anglican Concerns with its own full-time worker;

(iii)   the appointment of a Selection Secretary with responsibility for Black Anglican vocations to the staff of the Advisory Council for the Church's Ministry (ACCM), together with the nomination of a senior black clergyman to the ACCM Council by the House of Bishops to promote 'the recruitment, training and deployment of Black Anglican priests.

(iv)   the development by Synod of a 'more appropriate system of representation' to remedy the disproportionately low level of Black representation in time for the General Synod elections of 1990.[35]

These four proposals together constituted one programme; each by itself would be inadequate. For example a Commission for Black Anglican Concerns could become 'just one more pressure group' if ACCM, Social Responsibility and Synods were left untouched. The Field Officer and the Commission would together spearhead a joint programme of education (presumably of the wider church) and empowerment ('more effective participation and leadership among Black Anglicans'). Later on the Report stressed the importance of local leadership, of educating clergy to facilitate local leadership and develop both theology and worship in response to 'local cultures'.[36]

The flaw in the analysis and proposals of *Faith In the City* for Black Anglicans was as serious as it is by now familiar: there was no reflection on Black identity, on the Black encounter with Christ, on the Black experience of the Spirit, or to Black liberative praxis and vision. There were indeed only the most oblique allusions to the spiritual and cultural resources of Black people. Black Anglicans were simply 'there'; the nature of their relationship to other partners at the table of Anglican comprehensiveness was not considered. For all its determination to do justice, *Faith in the City*'s testimony to Black Anglicans as a community of faith consisted mainly of silence.

This had a number of serious consequences. The first was practical. The Report assumed that considerable numbers of Black Anglicans were able and willing to take up positions of power in the structures of the Church. It was by no means clear that such people exist in any number; it is in any case first necessary to ask not only how many Black Anglicans possess the skills necessary for Commissions, committees and synods, but, more importantly, whether these are the needs that arise out of the liberation struggle of Black people. A movement into church structures which does not arise out of the praxis of the mass of Black Anglicans will inevitably lead to isolated Black members of committees struggling to find a role and being hurt by rejection of their identity.

This practical difficulty arises out of a second consideration. *Faith in the City* implicitly defined Black Anglicans by their relationship to a White, middle-class institution and its hierarchy, rather than by their own lives and experience. At times they were seen as one among a number of cultures which were 'strange' and new to most clergy and the wider Church; at other times they were a 'constituency' which, for reasons largely unexplained, had become victim to marginalization and was therefore in need of enfranchisement.

It followed, thirdly, that the way out of this victim status was not really something which Black people could create for themselves; it could only be received from 'above' or 'the centre': hence the emphasis on White-led reforms of church structures and developing the awareness of White clergy.

Fourthly, the Report implicitly regarded existing Black clergy as if they had been generated by the mass Black Anglican community in England, and therefore were unambiguously representative of that community. We noted above why this cannot be the case.

In the event, the 'centre' proved much less willing to give a clear signal to the Church than *Faith in the City* hoped. The three aims of the A.B.C., however much criticized by Moore, have nonetheless all been achieved. The *Faith in the City* programme has been much less successful. General Synod rejected the proposal for a Standing Commission.[37] Later it agreed to the establishment of a *Committee for Black Anglican Concerns* (C.B.A.C.), though sharing its secretary with the Board of Social Responsibility's Field Officer post. Glynne Gordon-Carter, was thus appointed to the unenviable task of combining in one job what were envisaged in *Faith in the City* as two separate full-time appointments and was accountable to two separate committees. In 1990, the BSR post was suspended and the C.B.A.C. work became full-time. Meanwhile, Margaret Sentamu was appointed an ACCM Selection Secretary whilst Dr. John Sentamu joined the ACCM Council.

In November 1988, General Synod overwhelmingly approved a motion calling for legislation to increase Black representation in Synod to be prepared. However, it narrowly rejected the actual legislation the following February.[38] This defeat, brought about against the advice of both archbishops, was the most painful and deeply felt rejection of Black people by the Church of England in recent years. The Bishop of Croydon was outspoken, as the *Church Times* of 10th February 1989 reported:

> The rejection of the measure showed, he said, that there were Synod members still trapped in what he called the 'Christian slave-owners' thinking . . . they wanted black people to be happy, but under conditions they provided, and without requiring any adjustment of their own comfortable state.

Another article testified to the 'scarcely-veiled racism' of some of the speeches in the Synod debate.

The pain of defeat, for Black and White supporters alike, was occasioned by more than the surprise of rejection. It led to heart searching as to whether the strategy pursued was the right one after all. For those who seek to bring about change from 'above' or the 'centre' are always limited by the bounds set by the White institution, and they can be left frighteningly isolated if not firmly grounded in the mass of Black people 'below'. There is a time, as David Divine had warned the previous summer, when 'push comes to shove', and Black leaders can then rely only on their own people.

Five years after the *'Leicester' Report*, Kenneth Leech convened another consultation at Balsall Heath in Birmingham. The event marked the end of Leech's period as Race Relations Field Officer and showed very considerable developments in approach. Of the 67 participants, 28 (41%) were Black, double the proportion at Leicester. Moreover there was a determined effort to include 'grass roots' Black Anglicans, including a small number of sixth formers. Ten participants, including the Bishop of Croydon and the visiting lecturer from the United States, the Revd. Sandra Wilson, were Black clergy, whilst seven were employed in Race Relations posts and three were from the Black-led churches. Wilson, a leading Black American priest, spoke on the title 'Towards a Black Theology of Liberation'; quoting from James Cone, she left the Consultation in no doubt about her starting point for understanding the struggle of White and Black in the Church, namely the history and identity of Black people from Africa onwards, and the identification of Christ with that history:

> Christ is to be found . . . where men are enslaved and trampled underfoot; Christ is found suffering with the suffering. Christ is in the ghetto – there also is his Church . . . (Christ is) fighting the racism of churchly white people.[39]

It was with physical and historical Blackness that Christ had identified in his incarnation, and this was to continue in the life of the Church:

> So it is the job of the Church to become Black with Christ, and to accept the shame which society has placed on Blacks. The Church knows that what is shame to the world is indeed holiness to God. Black is holy, that is: it is a symbol of God's presence in history on behalf of the oppressed person.

But where did the struggle for justice begin? What was the liberative praxis? Wilson made it clear that it began with the oppressed claiming their own freedom, on the basis of their history and inheritance. Freedom depended on loving oneself, on claiming one's identity, only then could it move out into a wider vision for humanity:

> The issue is Black independence in thought and action, and that cannot happen if what we think and do is dependent on those who have not shared our history of oppression. *For no oppressed people has ever had its freedom given as a gift or financed by its oppressors* . . . the new vision will need to include an emphasis on Black unity, through an affirmation of Black history and culture. To love our people will not mean hating whites. Indeed, we cannot love anybody unless we love who we are as Blacks: that is the culture and history that has sustained us through centuries of slavery and second class citizenship. The enduring message of Black Power has nothing to do with hate. Rather it teaches love. But it teaches that love, like charity, must begin at home. We must begin with ourselves, our beautiful selves. (my italics)

So much for a lead from the 'centre', or from 'above'!

Wilson ended with a reiteration of the universality of the Black vision. By beginning with Black history and identity, by being obedient to the Black Christ, and by developing their own liberation struggle, Black people would not end up merely vindicating their own interests at others' expense. She moved from Malcolm X's nationalism ('It is impossible for the system . . . to produce freedom for the Black person') to Martin Luther King's challenge to restructure American society, and in that restructuring to find solidarity with other oppressed groups, including women, and thus to bring freedom for all.

Sandra Wilson's address is quoted here at length, for it almost certainly marked the first occasion at which the Church of England was confronted by the challenge of Black Christian theological method.[40]

Rowan Williams, the eminent Oxford theologian, gave a 'White response' to Sandra Wilson. As her lecture had special significance as the first presentation to the Church of England of the dynamic of Black Christianity, so Williams' response, though brief, was an important symbolic act, the first public authoritative White Anglican 'yes' to Black theological reflection.

> The only way in which we can be *concretely* loyal to humanity is by being loyal to particular groups of people who are oppressed. That is how we are loyal to the humanity Christ comes to create.[41]

The Consultation heard two accounts of the current situation, one from Kenneth Leech, the other from Barney Pityana, a refugee from South Africa (where he had been a founder of the South African *Black Consciousness* movement) and vicar of a Birmingham parish. Leech reiterated a profound understanding of racism: its strength was in structures and in the security of acquired power within institutions. He drew attention to the need to keep in touch with the actual experience of Black people in the back streets, and to the need for a serious theological critique of racism.[42]

Pityana similarly called for a prophetic response to injustice and racism. He acknowledged that for Black Anglicans to take an equal place in a plural church they must 'be enabled to build on their cultural faith, commitment and experience to express their true being and identity and seek fulfilment in the church's ministry'. In this he is true to the 'plumblines' of the Black Christian Tradition. However, most of his presentation was concerned with the experience of Black *clergy*, whose relationship with the mass of British Black Anglicans Pityana did not examine.

Pityana was forceful in his plea for a Black theological institute. As we have noted, this is the most promising of the three aims of the A.B.C. noted by James Evans, and has the potential to be a 'bottom-up' enabling institution for the Black Christian community. Again Pityana was most explicit in seeing the potential as a training institution for Black *ordinands*, but he set this in a broader context in two significant ways: firstly, the institute was to be inter-denominational, which had clear advantages in uniting Black Christians on the basis of common experience rather than 'White-led' denominational allegiance; secondly it was to be based on the theological method of the Black Christian community, 'a reflection on the revelation of one universal God through the experiences of Black people'.[43]

The conference is recorded in *Anglicans and Racism*, the 'Balsall Heath' Report. This report concludes with recommendations from workshops; three racially mixed in composition, and one entirely

Black. All three 'mixed' workshop reports made progress in the recognition and empowerment of Black Anglicans. However, the most significant development was the report of the all-Black workshop *Black Theology and Black Anglicans*. Here for the first time in an explicitly Church of England gathering, Black people separated themselves for a while to direct comments not towards the White power structure but towards Black people in the Church and in the nation. Rejecting the academic pursuit of even such promising theological categories as 'Blackness' or 'Liberation', they chose to focus on experience, on the recent experiences of racism suffered by the Black community, and on experience in the Church; on violence, conflict and power in society, and on the experience of *paralysis*, of being a 'dry bone', in the Church of England:

> We experience the Church as a white power structure. We experience it as belonging not to us but to someone else. On the other hand, the Church is the Body of Christ. It doesn't belong to white people. We see this sense of the Body of Christ to be a liberating knowledge.[44]

Out of this process arose questions, and theological reflections on those questions. Here individual Black Anglicans affirmed their history and identity, their own experience of Christ and of the Spirit, and articulated their commitment to develop their own understanding, wider vision and praxis. This was a corporate act of Black theological reflection by Black people within an official Church of England gathering which was then offered to the whole Church through a Church publication. It was the first time this had ever happened.

Finally, we return to the Methodist Church, with which, in considering Milwood's writing, we began this section. Heather Walton's study, *A Tree God Planted*, published in 1985, is a thorough sociological analysis of the distribution of Black Methodists by age, type of church and position in the institution. It gives vivid portrayals of the experience of Black people by presenting case studies of a variety of local churches. Methodism is still the only 'mainstream' Church to have commissioned such a study, and its value as a tool for understanding and for ministry can hardly be overstated. However, it must be noted that the book's historical perspective is limited to recounting memories of the Caribbean; it does not investigate or define the theological tradition which has arisen from the history of Afro-Caribbean people, except in rather phenomenological asides along the way. Thus we learn, for example, that Black people in fellowship groups tend to be quiet in discussion but contribute openly and freely in prayer, but we are offered no historical or theological understanding of this vital observation. Ministers are asked a variety of questions about the role of the Church in issues of race, but none of the questions hint that Black Methodists might constitute a community of faith with traditions and resources of their own and a need for 'free space'. Black Christianity is not named. In 1987 Methodism produced the comprehensive report, *Faithful and Equal*, which includes summaries of 'some initiatives by black Methodists' and 'affirms the right of black Methodists to come together to discuss needs and concerns and to formulate recommendations.' Even this report, however, with its urgent commendation of Black participation in all aspects of Methodist life, not least the ordained ministry, limits its affirmation of the Black inheritance to general and perhaps patronising language about 'the contribution they can offer.'[45]

Renate Wilkinson's Anglican study *A Chance for Change* is much smaller in scope and limited to one diocese. She also uncovers experience by case study as well as presenting statistical analysis. However, through studying the work of Gayraud Wilmore she is able to name the Black Christian Tradition, and thus to suggest in her recommendations that hope for the future lies not only in what 'the Church' does in equal opportunities provision and the like, but in the self-emancipation of Black people:

> (The Church's) primary resource are its own black members, lay and ordained. They embody in themselves the history, the suffering and the spirituality of black people.[46]

In conclusion, it must be noted that the two surveys, *A Tree God Planted* and *A Chance for Change*, were addressed only to ministers, an overwhelmingly White body. To ask White clergy about Black (lay) people in the Church was a necessary task and the only practicable way to uncover certain kinds of information. But it is now necessary for Black Christian experience to be investigated by Black people themselves as a basis for their own theological reflection and strategizing. *A Time to Speak*, a collection of essays by Black British Christians, marks a first step in this task.

I have here examined a number of responses to the 'collision' of Black Christianity with the White Church. They show Black people working to recover their authentic identity and tradition, and a White response which journeys only hesitantly and ambiguously towards repentance and the New Common Life.

It is at the local level where detailed day-to-day building of the Church takes place. I will use the story of the Anglican diocese of Birmingham to illustrate issues which arise generally in the local units of 'mainstream' church life. I have written elsewhere of the response of Birmingham Diocese to the arrival of Anglicans from the Caribbean, including particularly the imaginative ministry of the first 'Chaplain to Overseas People' Rev. Paul Burrough in his mobile caravan (1959–65), and the failure of the Diocese to follow up his work. I described how in the years following Black Anglicans became 'invisible' as successive Community Relations chaplains concentrated their energies on ministries which saw Black people as outside and distanced from the family of the Church of England, as 'people of other faiths', as 'members of Black-led churches', or (particularly at the time of the Church's opposition to the 1981 Nationality Act) as 'victims of social injustice'. These ministries were good and necessary, but sadly were pursued at the expense of responding to those Black Anglicans who, usually in discouraging circumstances, continued to Break Bread at Church of England altars.[47]

The *Race Relations Group* of the Birmingham Diocesan Council for Social Responsibility, was founded in 1980 to promote the CRRU Projects Fund (see p. 145). It was made up largely of White clergy. Following the publication the next year of the 'Leicester Report', the Group concentrated less on wider issues of racial justice, and more on the experience of Black people in the churches of the diocese, and on church structures. Thus the wheel turned full circle in the Diocese; Black Anglicans were becoming 'visible' again in diocesan concerns about race. Between 1983 and 85 the R.R.G. made a deliberate effort to become a less White and clerical group and a more Black and lay group, so that by 1986 the group was much closer to being a Diocesan voice of Black Anglicans.

In June 1983 the R.R.G. sponsored a motion in the Birmingham Diocesan Synod drawing Synod's attention to the report in its entirety. But it subsequently interpreted Synod's resolution requesting it to 'promote discussion' and 'seek implementation of the Report's recommendations where appropriate within the Diocese', almost exclusively in terms of response to the presence of Black Anglicans. This meant concentrating on two sections of the Report, *Racism and Education* and *Church Structures and Policy*, as follows.

Racism and education
Discussion about education, aided by supportive Church school head teachers, concentrated on the expectations of Afro-Caribbean

parents and the experience of their children. Some Black members were acutely aware of the extent to which the education system was failing their children; the Group sought to discover the reasons. Was it because the identity of Black children was insufficiently affirmed in schools? Were expectations of teachers and even some parents not high enough? Why did so few Black children from Church primary and secondary schools appear in Church training colleges? Why did Church schools have so few Black teachers? The Group noted that the Church of England had a 'complete' education system, that is, it was possible to go to Church primary and secondary schools, then to a Church college and back again into a Church school as a teacher.

The R.R.G. had a Synodical mandate to pursue these issues, and therefore sought to enlist the support of the Diocesan Education Council. However, discussion with this body proved difficult; the Group was not able to elicit a positive response to its concern. Meanwhile, the Group had come to the conclusion that nothing less than a complete 'racism audit' of the Church education system was needed, that is, an examination to see whether Black identity and experience was catered for equally with White. This would include examination of curricula, expectations, images, and especially of experience both at primary and secondary levels, as well as monitoring the numbers of Black teachers. Church schools had originally been founded to bring good education to those who had been deprived of it: the Group wanted to pursue a contemporary fulfilment of that purpose in respect of Black people. It was not to be.

Later, the D.E.C. called a day conference in response to *Faith in the City*; an apparently promising forum for taking up the R.R.G.'s concerns. Four R.R.G. delegates attended but came away unconvinced that the Black voice had been heard, still less that the D.E.C. intended to stand alongside the deprived and work out its mission from that priority. Rather, as the R.R.G. delegates' report makes clear, to Black people the atmosphere and agenda of the Conference were decidedly 'colonial':

> We noted that those present were mainly from a professional background, i.e. head teachers, clergy and Church House staff, and few were the ordinary people affected day by day, i.e. parents, parent governors and black teachers. Very little seemed to have been done to ensure a significant black input – particularly from the front. Many of the areas discussed involve high proportions of black people. We quote one of the four other black people who attended: 'I have always felt that the inner-city and U.P.A.'s are

ruled by those living in suburbia. The D.E.C. conference on 4th
October reinforced and confirmed this feeling'.[48]

Church structures and policy
Efforts to secure a response to this section of the *Leicester Report*
met with much greater understanding. The Report had challenged
the institutional racism in the employment and representation of
Black people in church bodies and church government, in the
recruitment and training of Black clergy and in theological education.
With the help of a clear lead and support from the Bishop, Renate
Wilkinson's questionnaire for *A Chance to Change* received an
unusually high 75% response rate, and supplied the R.R.G. with the
information it needed. As we have seen, the study showed that the
proportion of Black 'attenders' was considerable (7% over the
Diocese as a whole, higher in the city itself), that over half the
churches in the Diocese had Black worshippers attending regularly
and that in these the church Electoral Roll numbers were on average
10% Black.

Taking these figures as a base, we should expect to see about 7%
Black participation across the life of the Church. Black people were
indeed reasonably well represented in 'spiritual' and liturgical activities (in Bible study groups, prayer groups, choirs and as altar
servers), but beyond that the patterns of institutional racism became
very clear.[49]

Twelve months later the R.R.G. produced *Building a Black and
White Church*, a statement of recommendations to the Bishop's
Council. It outlines a comprehensive anti-racist strategy for a Church
of England diocese, addressing all significant areas of church life from
employment to liturgy and as such is thought to be unique.[50] The
paper begins by celebrating the Black and White make-up of the
Church as a sign of hope, but goes on to note:

> we have to recognize that black Anglicans were generally badly
> received, that there is still much racism in our church, and that
> positive action is needed if we are to build a hopeful future.

The paper envisages three major diocesan initiatives: (i) a keynote
pastoral letter from the Bishop; (ii) the appointment of a *diocesan
officer* to act as a support and resource to the diocesan staff (i.e.
bishops and archdeacons) and to facilitate and monitor 'positive
action'; and (iii) the adoption by the Diocese of a *statement of
commitment*. The paper then examines: the appointment of clergy
and accredited lay ministers; selection and training for the ministry;

training and educating clergy and laity; the representation of the laity and details of parish life and employment. For each the paper describes the present situation, ascribes responsibility for change to the relevant persons or church council, and lists detailed and specific steps to be taken.

The following three examples indicate its style and scope:

1)   Under 'Selection and Training for Ministry' a number of full-time lay pastoral assistants are envisaged for parishes where there is a large or potential Black presence. Using an existing appointment as a model, this proposal is seen as an expedient short cut to create Black ministry now when it is urgently needed, as a means of developing training which is appropriate to Black ministry, and as a means of challenging and nurturing potential ordinands.

2)   The regular convening of Black Anglicans for worship and mutual support is proposed, as well as an annual Diocesan assembly.

3)   Each mixed-race congregation would be asked to look at its worship to seek the best way of giving expression to elements of the Black Christian tradition, for which a Diocesan resource, for example in music, would be needed.

The response to this paper was a mixture of encouragement and discouragement. The Bishop's Council gave a whole session to examining *Building a Black and White Church*, and to hearing from Black R.R.G. members. The Diocesan Board of Finance adopted an Equal Opportunities Policy,[51] whilst the Diocesan Synod voted almost unanimously to appoint a diocesan officer, the *Bishop's Adviser on Black Ministries*, with his or her own partly elected and partly nominated committee, the *Committee for Black Affairs*. In December 1986 the Diocesan Synod gave overwhelming approval to a resolution which made a statement of commitment, set up a conference 'on the basis of penitence and renewal' for sensitising the Diocese to the situation of Black people in the Church, and asked Bishop's Council to seek to establish a resource centre for Black Anglican development in the Diocese.

Despite all these encouraging developments, however, R.R.G. members sensed that the authorities were losing sight of some of the Group's concerns. The Bishop's Council's response to *Building a Black and White Church* contained a number of reservations which some saw as evasions. For example, the difficult matter of racism in parishes was to be 'included in the Parochial Self-Assessment', the *voluntary* self-assessment proposed in *Faith in the City*, whilst the proposals for action, accountability and monitoring were largely ignored. (Only in 1989 were statistics gathered through the Archdeacon's annual Visitation; it is not clear how the information so gathered will be used.[52]) Above all it became clear that certain decisions, especially concerning the procedure for appointing the Adviser, were being taken without the Group's real participation. This was vital because it raised the key issue of the nature of Black participation in the church: *were Black people still colonial subjects of a White church, or were they equals in a plural church?* Theoretically, the appointment of a Black Adviser was integrated into Diocesan structures, and in the national C.B.A.C. report *Seeds of Hope* was even mentioned as a model of good practice.[53] In practice there was considerable pain and isolation.

The experience of the Birmingham R.R.G. shows that reforming White church structures to allow space for Black Christian presence is a difficult and demanding task. Only when the historic struggle of Black Christians is made the basis for action, and when fellowship and trust develop between Black church members and their White collaborators, is it possible to open up access to resources, to change the 'atmosphere' and the terms of discussion, and to provide a focal point for the anti-racist struggle in the Church. Even then, continual vigilance is essential; the White church structures do not repent of their own accord, and after an apparent step forward can quickly revert to type or fail to see the radical implications of the agreed change.

The appropriate strategy for Black people in a 'mainstream' church is to build up strength from 'below', from the parish base, the local church. Church structures and hierarchy can respond positively to an organized, conscientized body which is already emancipating itself from spiritual colonialism, but church structures and hierarchy will rarely themselves be the means of liberation.

THEOLOGICAL EDUCATION

In 'mainstream' denominations the challenge of the Black Christian Tradition is to the whole continuum of Church life: hierarchy and Sunday School, worship and social witness. In the centre of this continuum, Theological Education for the ordained and accredited ministry is a place where 'above' and 'below', 'centre' and 'periphery' meet.

Concern that Church of England theological education presupposes a middle-class identity and ethos is not new. In so far as the concern is well grounded, 'underside' of the Church suffers a double disadvantage: it is supplied with clergy 'positively unfitted' for such ministry[54] whilst at the same time it sees the ministers it produces lose their roots and identity in training. This is a danger which takes on a new sharpness when the issues of race and culture are added to those of class. Since 1981, however, awareness of three needs has slowly developed: the need to train all students for ministry in a multi-cultural, multi-racial and multi-faith society; the need to prepare White students to minister to Black and multi-racial congregations; and the need to enable Black students to develop their skills, vision and practice of ministry on the basis of a Black identity.

Robinson Milwood's *Let's Journey Together* based its strategy, as we have seen, on the self-affirmation of Black people. His vision for Black ministry, and thus for theological education came from a self-aware Black base in local Methodist churches, circuits and districts. Unfortunately, he did not spell out the implications for theological education, except to say that contact with theological colleges is 'assumed'.[55]

The report, *Blind Leaders for the Blind?*, an enquiry into the way theological students are prepared for ministry in a multi-cultural society, was published in 1981. Though it contained useful findings about awareness among colleges and students and outlined a theology of anti-racism and of ministry in a multi-faith society, it made no mention whatever of Black theology or Black Christians and seems not to have envisaged them as partners in the theological task. The report belongs to the era of Black invisibility.[56]

In 1983, another Methodist document, *Race and Theological Education*, affirmed the multi-racial nature of the Methodist Church, noted the need to tackle 'questions of race and racism' in theological education, and accurately summarized the recent experience of Black Methodists.[57] A brief theological basis for multi-racialism was provided, out of which six guidelines for theological education were given. These involved a shift away from White ethno-centric traditions and values, affirmation of multi-racialism in church and society, and the necessity of experiencing other cultures, including 'experience in churches with a number of black members'. The guiding principle was *permeation* of the course by these insights; the authors were concerned to avoid 'add-on' marginalized courses about race and racism which would leave the main syllabus untouched.

This paper was a marked advance on *Blind Leaders for the Blind?* in that it addressed the inner life and table fellowship of the Church and aimed to avoid marginalisation. However, it had three weaknesses: firstly, it did not list what the 'issues of race and racism' actually are, thus leaving much work to be done on the practical implementation of its principles. Secondly, it failed to recognize that the 'permeation' and the 'add-on' approaches both have advantages as well as disadvantages. An 'add-on' course may be marginal, but by its very focusing and creation of concentrated 'space' it can have

165

power which all but the most thorough permeation would not provide. To be effective, 'permeation' depends on the commitment and awareness of a complete college or course staff, which is simply not a realistic expectation.[58] Thirdly, the faith, culture and resources of Black people were not 'named' or affirmed. The concern to 'fight racism' seems to have obscured a potent weapon for that fight, namely God's revelation of himself to a Black Christian community of faith.

It is only when we come to David Moore's paper, *Pre-Theological College Training*, also written in 1983, that we find a programme of theological education which is both true to the 'plumblines' of Black Christianity and also developed in detail. He advocated a one year full-time pre-college course for Black candidates for ministry. Its educational programme, an integrated pattern of academic study, spiritual life and practical experience, sought to foster in students the development of self-confidence and self-worth on the basis of their own culture and its values. It recognised the importance of Liberation Theology and other contextual theologies for this task and articulated a vision of ministry as 'participation in the struggle of the poor'.

In 1987, Wesley Daniel, a young Black Methodist training for ministry at The Queen's College, Birmingham, wrote *The Question of Race and Theological Education*, a reflection on his time in college. He described how, as a Black student, he had found himself facing two theological agendas, one set by the college and the other arising from his own identity. He was accepted by his colleagues, but only as long as 'thorny issues' of race and racism were not raised. When, in the aftermath of the Brixton and Tottenham disturbances, they *were* raised, he had become isolated as the realisation dawned that his White fellow-students were living in a 'different world'.

He had also come to realise that, although Black Methodists were proud of their Methodist heritage and although the Methodist Church took pride in its Black members, theological students were not being shown the implications of this for ministry. Queen's had only a basic course in Black Theology and ministry; other colleges, it seemed, had nothing at all. His attempts at raising issues of racism had met with resistance both in college and in the wider church; he considered that many White students left college without having resolved even such basic questions as why Black people name themselves as 'Black' or why they need to meet separately (this was often described as 'apartheid in reverse'!). To Daniel, this in effect meant, 'become white, allow us to dictate your course of action', a sentiment reinforced by his experience that theology was taught as substantially a White subject, with Third World or Black Theology a kind of peripheral appendage.

166

The remedy lay in a 'systematic approach to the issue'. Firstly, tutors were needed who are 'able to represent the experience of Black people, their spirituality, tutors with prophetic insight able to put their finger on the nerve of the situation Black people face and interpret it to the church'. Secondly, Black students must study *together*: it was difficult to be the only Black student in college, doubly so when one knew there were other students isolated elsewhere. Whilst numbers remained small, a proper programme should be developed in one place before being duplicated elsewhere. Thirdly, a curriculum should be devised in which the Black Tradition – preaching, pastoral care, music, prayer, socio-economic existence and its relationship to religion – was taught as a unit; the idea that existing courses could be 'permeated' with Black insights was unrealistic. Finally, Daniel was clear that study of the Black tradition was equally important for Black and White students. White students would understand their own identity better, and be better equipped to minister to White and Black. Black students, he concluded 'must be equipped . . . to realise that they can make a significant contribution to the future of church and theology, and that they can provide inspiration to future Black Methodist ministers in this country, through preparation that has taken into account who they are, where they have come from and where they are going.'

Daniel's paper should be recognised as a landmark in the development of theological education. Its starting point was a description of the cost of remaining authentically Black, of remaining true to Black roots, inheritance of faith and upbringing. It developed from that inheritance a liberative praxis, namely a detailed programme by which a neglected 'invisible' community could take its rightful place at the table of theological comprehensiveness. This process would involve pain and cost as White theology was purified and transformed by its encounter with Black theology; but Daniel ended with a universal vision: *both* groups of students would know themselves better, and be better equipped to minister to both communities.

The presentation of this paper to a College staff meeting in July 1987 was perhaps the first occasion in which a specifically Black critique, with demands for action, was made directly to a White theological institution in Britain. The primary challenge was spiritual: could the College 'hear' and 'name' the Black Christian Tradition? Was it willing to acknowledge its own identity in relation to that challenge, take repentant action and so develop a New Common Life? Three developments were agreed: about raising of awareness, about the general curriculum of the college, and about a course specifically for Black students. Firstly, *Racism Awareness Training* was made mandatory in the curriculum; it was later included in staff in-service training.[59] This training has been judged generally successful in its aims, and has had a significant impact on the general consciousness of the College.

Secondly, staff members agreed to a review of courses in the light of the criticism that theology was being taught as a 'White' subject. This was the most sensitive and important area of response since it involved the revision of the syllabuses of individual tutors. Thoroughly pursued, it would involve, for example, acknowledging Black hermeneutic as a distinctive contextual approach to the Bible, or including Black Church History and Black traditions of pastoral care in their respective subject areas. It would involve examining the issue of solidarity with the oppressed, which Black Christianity makes the touchstone of discipleship for White people, in both spirituality and systematic theology classes. Staff agreed to invite Bishop Patrick Kalilombe, the eminent Malawian theologian and Director of the Centre for Black and White Christian Partnership, to assist in the review. Though not all his suggestions have been acted upon, some modifications to the curriculum have taken place.

Thirdly, it was agreed to offer to Black students a *Black Christian Studies Course* with the aims of providing opportunity to study theology and prepare for ministry on the explicit basis of a Black identity, work collaboratively towards a British Black Theology and find mutual support. The course, which commenced in October 1987, explores Black theological method and pursues it in four areas of theology: history, systematics, ministry and mission, and social context. The Course has fulfilled Daniel's criteria by using as far as possible Black and Asian tutors (notably Bishop Patrick Kalilombe), by bringing Black students together, and by devising a Black curriculum undiluted by 'permeation'. It marks distinct progress in that it enables Black students, for the first time in British theological education, to drink unambiguously from their own wells.

Even after these three developments, there were considerable limitations, especially in the teaching programme of the White majority of students. This was acknowledged in the response of the College Principal to a 1988 ACCM enquiry into racism in theological education:

> We would have to acknowledge that some students still go out of College without seriously grappling with the issues or reading the basic literature. Many will have little or no contact with Black Methodist or Anglican congregations or with Black-led Churches. Moreover, our programme . . . is not really a sustained programme,

but is made up of bits and pieces put together over two or three years.[60]

A new curriculum introduced in 1990 sought to address this last issue. In it, the various elements of (i) an experiential Pastoral Studies Course *Christian Ministry in a Multi-cultural Society*, (ii) *Racism Awareness Training* and (iii) the course *Introduction to Black Christianity* are now in a côherent relationship to each other and are part of the core-course taken by all students. Meanwhile, the Black Christian Studies Course has been opened to a small number of White students whilst remaining a Black-majority course. It has attracted Black students from beyond the College and the associated West Midlands Ministerial Training Course and is now open not only to candidates for ministry, but to some Black lay people as well, for example local preachers or others of equivalent theological training.

The crucial task of monitoring the general curriculum remains. Progress is clearer in some subjects than others – evidence of continued dependence on the priorities and consciousness of individual tutors. Most recently the College resolved to act to overcome this problem, and to provide Black leadership for the Black Christian Studies Course, by seeking a full-time Tutor for Black Theology. The appointing in 1992 of Robert Beckford, a young theologian from a Black-led church in Birmingham, as the first such tutor in British theological history, carries the additional promise of building bridges between the 'mainstream' and 'Black-led' communities.

SIMON OF CYRENE THEOLOGICAL INSTITUTE

The opening in September 1989 of the Simon of Cyrene Theological Institute was a significant development not least because of the investment of resources from the 'centre'.[61] We have already noted various steps in the development of this venture, from the original concern of the A.B.C. through David Moore's paper and the 'Young, Gifted and Black' weekends, to Barney Pityana's plea and the proposals of the Balsall Heath Conference.

After the publication of *Anglicans and Racism* (the 'Balsall Heath Report'), ACCM accepted the issue of Black Theological Education as a priority and offered the services of the Secretary of its Committee for Theological Education, to assist in looking for a way forward. A small steering group was formed which in only two years secured ACCM funding, obtained accommodation in Wandsworth in the Diocese of Southwark, turned a purely Anglican committee into an ecumenical body, appointed Sehon Goodridge from Codrington College, Barbados, as the first Principal, and developed a statement of aims and some preliminary course outlines.

The Institute's declared aim is 'research and action towards a just and reconciled society' which it is to promote by developing the articulation of a British Black theology, as well as through 'dialogue' and addressing White church structures. It seeks to train Black lay people and to prepare Black candidates for ministry for training at a theological college or course. It also offers Pastoral Studies Units for students already in training. Although this facility is for 'white and black' students, since the overwhelming majority of students in training are White, the P.S.U.s will in practice be White events. It remains to be seen how this affects the Black identity of the Institute.

The Institute's claim is that it is a facility which is 'devised and developed by black Christians, and one which they can own with the help of the whole Church'.[62] In the lay, ecumenical and social references contained in its statement of aims, as well as in the title of its first P.S.U. 'From the Underside', there is much that is true to the Black Christian Tradition. But the Institute is vulnerable: what if the church structures produce few Black candidates for ministry, or Colleges and Courses give little support so that financial viability is affected? The true 'base' of the Institute is the many thousands of Black Christians still to be found in the 'mainstream' churches. Its success will depend on the extent to which it can inform, conscientize and give hope and direction to them. To be true to its name, it must bear the Cross revealed through Black people and thus become the means of leading a White-led Church, which once accepted slavery and legitimated colonialism, to be transformed into Christ's likeness.

In this chapter we have suggested how the 'plumblines' of Black Christianity may be applied to certain key examples of where Black and White face each other in the Church. The more Black Christian experience is articulated in the Church and the more Black Christians 'name' themselves as a community of faith, especially at the 'base' levels of church life, and the more this is done in response to daily social and political experience; then so much the more can White people be saved from the memory and the present reality of an oppressive identity, and be remade, together with Black people, in the Body of Christ. Only then can Black and White truly be 'one in Christ Jesus' (Gal. 3[28]).

9

Meeting Around the Cross

Not too long ago, I took part in a Saturday evening Festival held in a suburban parish church to celebrate the identities of Black and White Anglicans. First we sang a hymn; then the Vicar, a White man, welcomed us. You are all welcome,' he said, stressing the *all*, 'it doesn't matter whether you are black or white, for we are all one in Christ Jesus.' Instinctively, I winced; it was not a good beginning, for most people present knew that in fact it mattered a great deal. They knew that only Black people could decide if and when a time should come when it mattered no more.

To celebrate our identities in Christ is for Christians a foretaste of salvation, indeed it could be said that the chicken and rice we shared that night was a foretaste of the heavenly banquet. But there is no short cut to that feast; the journey to Resurrection and to a New Common Life in the Spirit procedes through the Cross. The pain of the 'collision' between the two stories takes its meaning from the pain of the Cross; just as the joy of the anticipated feast takes its meaning from the joy of Easter.

VICTIM AND OPPRESSOR MEET

So how do Black and White Christians, and in particular Anglicans, journey together 'through the Cross'? I have argued that the New Testament uses organic imagery ('one flesh' and 'many limbs') to show that the Church is 'one' yet 'many' in its identification with Christ. In Anglican tradition that unity is focused pastorally in the Bishop and liturgically in common prayer, whilst the plurality is expressed in the dialogue between four strands of tradition. However the existing Anglican dialogue is limited theologically by its basis in Western and especially English thought, and pastorally and

171

liturgically by White culture. This is precisely the culture which Black people have experienced as oppressive, for they have been enslaved by Whites, de-cultured by Whites, exploited by Whites and used as instruments to 'make a crop'. Moreover, their position now, which may be described as colonial, is but a modification of the earlier bondage; their concentration at the 'underside' of both society and church shows that, to borrow a lecture title from the German theologian Gerhard Kamphausen, 'the abolition of slavery is an unfinished task'.[1]

From the standpoint of a White national church which has been both the validation and the tool of empire, Black people confront that church as the poor, the outcast and the oppressed. They constitute the people of whom the Bible records, 'they cried to the Lord in their trouble and He delivered them out of all their distress' (Psalm 107[6]). Yet they are far from being the *naked* poor; on the contrary, out of 'no way' God has made a way,[2] and out of the 'things that are not' (1 Cor. 1[28]) Black culture and Black Christian faith have blossomed, thereby shaming the 'wise' and 'strong' and 'bringing to nothing things that are' (1[27]). The 'Living Faith Project' showed how Black Anglicans bring their Black faith and inheritance with them and thereby create cultural pluralism in the Church. But these two stories cannot simply, so to speak, sit alongside the other and make their 'contribution' to the life of the Church, for each bears a sharply dialectical relationship to the other; History forces Black to confront White as *victim to oppressor*.

WHITE IDENTITY: SINGLE, HISTORIC AND CORPORATE

I have defined 'Black' as referring to a historic community of people of African descent who have been subjected to slavery in North America and the Caribbean (p. 4f). 'Black' culture is therefore definable only by reference to Black people's experience of historical encounter with Whites. 'Black' is primarily a term of consciousness; one cannot know oneself as 'Black' except in relation to 'White'. It follows that 'White' also is primarily a term of consciousness grounded in history. One cannot know oneself as 'White' except in relation to Black. This White identity must now be described.

Firstly, it is a *single* identity. White people, including some who would accept my definition of Blackness, frequently object to the use of 'White' in a parallel sense, contending that 'White' refers to a variety of cultures and historical experiences many of which are unconnected with Black people. It is of course true there is cultural pluralism among Whites, not only between nations but also between groups within nations. Poland is not Spain, Cornwall is not Durham. More important, there have been and are serious conflicts between peoples who are White in which it is not difficult to identify oppressor and victim.

Often, however, the story of such conflicts is used by White people to de-historicize the Black experience. 'All have suffered', like 'all have sinned', is a truth which can obscure the sharpness of a particular concrete, historical relationship of oppressor to victim. Peoples who happen to be white-skinned have many experiences, but the term 'White people' is only used because of a history involving 'Black people'. If all people were white-skinned there would be no point in referring to White people. If the relationship between White and Black were as unremarkable and undefined as that between, say, blue-eyed and brown-eyed [white] people then there would be little point in refering to White people. But so long as there is a contemporary form of the historic relationship of oppression between White and Black which has existed now for nearly five hundred years, then the term must be used *to refer to a single identity*. The identity of exploiter, oppressor and colonizer is the corporate identity of the White European response to the 'discovery' of African – and other – Black people. 'White' and 'Black' depend on each other and on history for meaning.

Secondly, White is a *historic* identity. White people, again including some who would accept the validity of speaking of a historic Black identity, often deny the validity of a historic White identity, as for example in the simple statement 'I am not responsible for the sins of my ancestors.' At first sight this is a self-evident moral truth: 'I cannot be guilty of events in which I took no part, and with which I am therefore unconnected'. It is clear that one cannot be guilty of past evil so long as it remains totally in the past (I have never owned a slave), any more than one can take credit for past good so long as it remains totally in the past (I was not part of the campaign for the abolition of slavery).

But the past is connected to the present by the threads of history; threads of cultural tradition and class power. *Cultural tradition* is transmitted from generation to generation in history. White people grow up in a culture where ancient myths about Black people have currency, even if in an altered or modern form. Ancient beliefs about Black physical strength, innate 'rhythm' and inferior intelligence live on in, for example, the (often unconscious) racist assumption in our schools that Black children have a natural aptitude for sport or

173

dancing, but are unlikely to be 'academic'.[3] Sometimes indeed the myth lives in its ancient form; the testimony of a Black mother that when she presented her baby for Baptism in the early 1950's some White people present lifted the child's robe to see whether it had a tail – repulsive and extreme though that is – is far from unique.[4]

In slavery times Black people fulfilled two main roles, domestic service (cooks, cleaners, waiting maids, washer-women, seamstresses and nurses, butlers and coachmen) and labour (the harder toil of the sugar factory and the cane field). Domestic service had higher status and was generally confined to 'brown' or 'coloured' (mixed-race) slaves. It included a high proportion of women, who were not only less threatening to the master than the 'strong' male slave, but were also available for sexual exploitation.[5] Labour and service remain standard White images of Black people in employment today, with service jobs, including those of relatively higher status such as nursing and office work, more accessible to Black women than Black men.[6]

The past is also connected to the present by the threads of *class power* transmitted from generation to generation. The slave trade was an enormously profitable system for the planters whose slaves produced the sugar. It also made the fortunes of the merchant capitalists of Bristol, Liverpool and London who sold them the slaves. A new class of industrial capitalists grew up to supply the manufactured goods with which the slaves were bought (textiles from Lancashire, guns and cutlery from Birmingham, copper rods and bronze rings, as well as silk, felt, sailcloth, beads, spirits, tobacco, beer brewed by Samuel Whitbread and Sir Benjamin Truman).[7] Bankers and commission agents, among them the Quaker Barclay brothers of London, profited from lending money to all of them.[8]

The whole trade became a major source of the accumulation of wealth, a large and at certain points probably decisive contribution to the Industrial Revolution. Fryer shows that funds accumulated from the Triangular Trade helped to finance James Watt's steam engine, the South Wales Iron and Coal industry, the South Yorkshire Iron industry, the North Wales slate industry, the Liverpool and Manchester Railway and the Great Western Railway.[9] Eric Williams, in his historic *Capitalism and Slavery*, published in 1944, observed:

> The commercial capitalism of the eighteenth century developed the wealth of Europe by means of slavery and monopoly. But in so doing it helped create the industrial capitalism of the nineteenth century, which turned round and destroyed the power of commercial capitalism, slavery, and all its works.[10]

174

This view of the foundation of Britain's nineteenth century industrial might in the slave and sugar trade of the preceding century, as well as the shift in economic power which underlay Abolition, is as Basil Davidson puts it, 'a view that has not been overturned'.[11]

The fruit of slavery then was the industrial might of nineteenth century Britain, and its attendant colonialism.[12] From these spring the modern wealth and economic power of Britain and the consequent affluence enjoyed by much of the British population. Britain is perhaps no longer the outstanding example of European wealth but shares nevertheless with the countries of North America and Western Europe the fruits of ongoing exploitation of Third World resources for their own benefit, and in particular for the benefit of a powerful rich minority within those nations.[13] This relationship, termed 'neo-colonialism' since direct political colonialism has ended, underlies both famine in Africa[14] and modern struggles in South Africa. It is the economic basis for on-going racism and continued antagonism between Black and White. Helmut Gollwitzer writes of 'the common burden of colonial guilt, from which all of us* have drawn gigantic profits.'[15]

Some past struggles between oppressor and victim are now 'dead' history; they have no appreciable living connection to the present. But the cultural tradition of White racism and the slave/colonial/neo-colonial class and power structures on which it is based are 'live' history; they are alive both within Britain and in the relationship of Europe and North America to the Third World. 'White' is therefore a term which denotes a *historic reality*, involving White people of the past and present together. I am responsible for my response in the present to a situation in which the past lives.

Thirdly, White is a *corporate* identity. Some Whites object to the validity of a 'White-oppressor' identity by arguing that moral responsibility is a matter of individual responsibility. In its moderate form this objection allows the force of the argument that 'White' is a single and historic identity defined by its relationship with 'Black', but seeks to exempt individuals or groups by virtue of their moral outlook or political praxis in history. 'Not all White people are bad', the argument runs, 'what about Wilberforce, John Brown, Lancashire Cotton workers in the 1860's, Mother Theresa . . . ?'[16]

In its more radical form the validity of *any* corporate identity is denied: 'The individual alone is responsible for his or her actions'. 'Only individuals can believe, repent, grow in holiness . . .' It is

---

* i.e. White Europeans. Gollwitzer, writing in Germany in 1970, assumes an entirely White European readership.

indeed individuals who act, individuals who believe, and it is in the individual that the movement of repentance must take place.[17] But this sovereignty of the individual must be qualified in two ways. Firstly, the identity of an individual is an interpretation of personal history shaped by the memory within the 'interpretative horizon' of a tradition or traditions. These form the structures within which decisions are made, our beliefs are formed and our repentance takes place. The identity deriving from, for example, my birth into a particular family or nationality is indestructible, even if formally renounced. Secondly, what may be understood as the 'free' decisions of an individual may be shown in sociological investigation to be part of a general social trend or movement of which at the time he or she was unaware.

The Bible and the Liturgy abound with evidence that the Judaeo-Christian tradition regards the corporate as fundamental to the understanding of identity. Eichrodt in his *Theology of the Old Testament* writes of a 'living individuality' in Israel existing in fruitful tension with the 'striking fundamental characteristic of Israel, namely the strength of their sense of solidarity'. This 'affects the individual and motivates his conduct'.[18] Thus Israel is a people with whom God makes a covenant; they can be described as a son (Hosea 11[1]), or as a vineyard ripe for destruction (Isaiah 5[7]). Repeatedly, the whole people of Israel is addressed as one morally responsible entity, as in Isaiah 48 where the 'house of Jacob' is severely rebuked. The nation is so obstinate that its neck is an 'iron sinew' and its forehead 'brass' (verse 4), whilst its disobedience has consequences that will be felt by its descendants (verses 18–19).

A commentator observes:

> The essential principle to grasp is that the Israel of the past and the present is one Israel. This is the conception which has aptly been called that of 'corporate personality' (Wheeler Robinson) – and 'such a physical whole has an extension in time as well as space, so that the mystic bond which unites society may be conceived retrospectively as regards its ancestors and prospectively with regard to future generations' (A.R. Johnson). There is therefore no contradiction in addressing Israel at one moment as a rebel, at another chastened, at another the Lord's righteous servant. By this principle the prophet is able to address the Israel he knows, about to return to Jerusalem forgiven, and yet to describe her as a rebel from birth, and to speak of her sin as that which merited the judgement of exile.[19]

New Testament imagery for the solidarity of the Church and its union with Christ have already been described (see pp. 88ff.). The Liturgy, whilst affirming individuality in the distribution of the elements one by one to each believer who receives, sets this act in a context of solid corporate identity in confession of sin, absolution, affirmation of faith, and celebration of a common peace:

We have sinned against you . . .
We believe in one God . . .
We are the body of Christ. In one Spirit
     we were all baptized into one body . . .
Though we are many, we are one body,
     because we all share in one bread.

The particularity of an individual's life and faith is not denied by these affirmations. He or she lives that life and holds that faith within a historic continuity of corporate identity.

As with the identity of Israel and the Church in the Old and New Covenants, so with the identity of 'Black' and 'White' in relation to each other. The individual is free, and indeed required, to make moral decisions, but within the variety of corporate identities which form his or her person. To inherit the 'White' identity in Britain is to inherit a living tradition of the oppression and exploitation of Black people. To fail to recognize oneself as inevitably part of that tradition is to fail to know oneself. Keith Sinclair, an Anglican priest in Birmingham, tells of his own discovery of corporate 'White' identity. He was already a converted evangelical Christian when he began to worship regularly with a Black-led Pentecostal congregation:

Bit by bit with the welcome, the worship, the joy of new friendships and experiences, the reality of something else was dawning upon me. It wasn't expected and it came from no observable source, but it dawned nonetheless, and as it dawned, it sickened me and I felt ashamed. This thing I call racism – the discovery that I was poisoned. I found thoughts and assumptions coming to my mind quite often, they were all to do with a sense of being superior because I was white and everyone else was black . . . In the middle of a conversation, a sermon, a song, a prayer, it came. And I made a discovery. I saw something with devastating clarity. I called myself a Christian, born again and so on. But I had not realised how much of the way I thought, behaved, responded, had to do not with the new birth but the old one. I realised how much I actually operated as someone who was white, English, middle class. That these things were actually first, that being a child of God was not. And as I realised this in myself, I couldn't see anything else the same way again.

It was one of the most devastating experiences of my life; and it came because I was welcomed and accepted as a brother by those who daily had been humiliated and degraded by the very things that I found rising up in me. And what rose up in me had shaped our country and society, and has been shaping it for a long time. I tell you I went up to that altar rail often for prayer. And that which was most devastating became the way through to liberation; I was able to recognise it, even eventually to talk with my friends about it and see them react as if they knew all about it and had just been waiting for me to realise – oh, the grace of God! Racism is pervasive in white culture and society; it is in the air we breathe. You can read about it in books, study it in statistics, even watch it on the TV screen, but it is nearer than that; it is in our very being as white people. The long history before and since the generations of slavery and colonisation mean that truly the sin of the father has been visited on the children . . .

A whole part of my education, even my evangelical education, just fell apart – English history was so basically good, wasn't it? Weren't we really so kind? Didn't we achieve so much in the end? How could I have focused so much on the Abolition movement and not asked what was happening in the 200 years from the Reformation to its beginning? . . . 10 million slaves from Africa to the American and Caribbean colonies, the basis of the whole British economic, political and cultural 'greatness' of the nineteenth century![20]

This kind of testimony is often dismissed as a destructive and paralysing 'wallowing in guilt'. It would be better regarded, however, as a 'confession of guilt', by which is meant the articulating, corporately or individually, of awareness of sin in the light of God's goodness. Confession is a necessary part of Christian prayer, a common and basic liturgical activity, without which very little Christian worship proceeds to the praise of God or to intercession. Confession is not destructive and paralysing, – for two reasons. Firstly, to admit to the identity of 'White oppressor' is not an acknowledgement of total depravity. Personhood is formed by a variety of identities, many of which may be positive and creative. God does not desire the death of sinners; no person coming into the world is devoid of His light. Secondly, admitting to the identity of

'White oppressor' is, like all other confession, the beginning of a process which lies at the heart of Christian experience: repentance, forgiveness and restoration. This process of dying and rising is certainly painful, but the promise is of a new life that exceeds Eden, is better than innocence.[21] It is an experience of God's 'amazing grace':

> Amazing grace! How sweet the sound
> That saved a wretch like me!
> I once was lost but now am found,
> Was blind, but now I see.[22]

IDENTITIES AND THE CROSS

Paul's first letter to the Corinthians was addressed to a congregation divided over the gift of tongues, sexual immorality and abuse of the Lord's Supper, and split into partisan factions, each claiming the name of one of the missionaries to Corinth, or even of Christ Himself. Modern scholarship has brought socio-historical tools to the understanding of these divisions, and insists that they are not simply individual 'personality clashes' on the one hand, nor controversies of 'pure' theology on the other, but that they reflect different social and cultural strata in the congregation.[23]

Paul brings to these conflicts his spiritual authority as an apostle; he has no personal episcopal or imperial sanctions he can use against them, they are as independent of him as he, a 'tent-maker', is of them. His appeal to them begins as an apparent moral exhortation; he appeals 'that all of you agree and that there be no dissensions among you' (1 Cor. 1^{10}). It is soon clear however that the integration of this community depends not on submission to a 'law' of unity backed by Paul's authority, nor on debate with each other to find an agreeable compromise. Instead he directs the community to be reconciled by looking towards the source of grace, towards the *Cross*, towards 'Christ crucified . . . the power of God and the wisdom of God' (1 Cor. 1^{24}). The imperfections of the community are placed in the context of God's redemptive eschatological purpose. Within this purpose the different sections of the community discover that they do not all stand in the same relationship to God. Some are, so to speak, closer to the Cross than others. The formation of the Body of Christ depends not only upon each person (or group) recognising the Cross, but also upon each recognizing where the other stands in relation to the Cross. It is a dialectical interaction between these plural identities which transforms them into one Body. In that process there has to be both a painful negation of oppressive identities and a determined preservation of liberating resources.

It is the 'not wise', the 'not powerful', the 'not of noble birth', the foolish, weak, low and despised, 'even the things that are not' (1 Cor. 1^{26-28}), that most partake of the wise foolishness of God in the Cross. Dialectical interaction with those who are powerful in the world extends the redemptive power of the cross in history:

> God chose what is foolish in the world to *shame* the wise, God chose what is weak in the world to *shame* the strong, God chose what is low and despised in the world, even the things that are not, to *bring to nothing* [negate] the things that are. (1 Cor. 1^{27-28})

Gerd Theissen comments:

> From the preaching of the Cross, Paul derives a revaluation of all norms of social rank. It is precisely the nobodies, those who are weak and have no standing, whom God has chosen.[24]

As we have seen, White people holding the power of this world to oppress, have made Black people to be 'foolish', 'low' and 'despised' relative to the norms of the powerful. The denial of Black humanity in slavery times, and the 'psychological genocide' that denied baptism and gave no identity but that of 'replaceable tool', have turned human beings into 'things that are not'.

Baptism and the Lord's Supper are mentioned in Paul's writing in a similar way; they are the means and the expression of turning away from worldly status to the reordering which is brought about by the 'foolishness' of the Cross. The *priority of the poor* is affirmed in respect of both sacraments. In the case of Baptism, Paul first writes that 'Jews or Greeks, male or female, slave or free' (Gal. 3^{27-28}) were all baptised into Christ, i.e. into His death, to be transformed into the body of Christ. But the image of the 'body of Christ' being made up of various categories of humanity depends, elsewhere, on a comparison with the human body being made up of various kinds of organs, some of which are more 'honourable' than others. In the human anatomy, 'God has so adjusted the body, giving the greatest honour to the inferior part' (1 Cor. 12^{24}). Similarly, in the body of Christ, as C.K. Barrett says commenting on this verse, 'weaker and humbler members of the church should not be despised but treated with special honour.'[25]

In respect of the Lord's Supper, when Paul hears that the

Corinthian church is failing to share properly the common meal which precedes the Supper, he denounces them for 'despising the *ecclesia* of God' and 'humiliating those who have nothing' (1 Cor. 11^{22}). It is this failure which constitutes 'unworthy' eating and drinking in the Lord's Supper (11^{27}). The community should rather wait, and then share (11^{33}), so that the poor are not humiliated. In the Lord's Supper, Paul reminds them, the Body of Christ is being repeatedly formed as they 'proclaim the Lord's death until He comes' (1 Cor. $11^{33,26}$).

In Paul's great hymn of love (1 Cor. 13) this divine preference for the poor is not explicitly stated. Elsewhere, however, (e.g. Rom. 5^8) the love of Christ is defined in terms of the Cross, and this love 'controls us' and redirects our lives away from worldly status:

> For the love of Christ controls us, because we are convinced that one has died for all, therefore all have died. And he died for all, that those who live might live no longer for themselves but for Him who for their sakes died and was raised. (2 Cor. $5^{14,15}$)

'All' affirms various cultural and theological groups within the Church, those (social activists?) who give their body to be burned, those (intellectuals?) who understand all mysteries and all knowledge, and those (Charismatics?) who speak in tongues (1 Cor. 13^{1-3}). It is the love of Christ in the death of Christ, entered into at Baptism and proclaimed repeatedly in the Lord's Supper, that withers these imperfections till 'the perfect comes' (1.Cor. 13^{10}), and Christ's people are made one with Him. That process is not an undialectical, universal, human response to love, however; *it is the grace of God using the 'things that are not' to bring to nothing the things that are.*

THE PERFECT VICTIM

The first preaching of the Gospel, as Luke presents it to us in the familiar narratives of Acts 2^4, proclaimed Jesus as Lord, and urged those who heard it to repent and believe. Often overlooked, however, is the attribution of guilt which precedes it: guilt not of 'sins', still less of 'sin', but of *one historical, specific and concrete offence.* Those who hear the message are the ones who judged, condemned and crucified Jesus (Acts 3^{13-14}).

Guilt is attributed particularly to the rulers and leaders, but also to the 'men of Judea' and all who dwell in Jerusalem, to Gentiles present, and to Pilate representing 'the kings of the earth gathered together against the Lord and against his anointed' as in Psalm 2 (Acts 4[26]). This is not, of course, a theory of generic Jewish guilt, but it spells out a defined audience of the guilty, focused on the imperial power and its local puppet-monarch, whilst suggesting that they represent the whole of humanity in accordance with God's purpose. Precisely to these presumptuous judges Jesus comes in the preaching as a judge, but his judgement is a saving, rescuing and forgiving one. Christ rescues and vindicates his own oppressors, who in accepting that judgement are accepted and set free to live:

> Repent and be baptised every one of you, in the name of Jesus Christ for the forgiveness of your sins, and you shall receive the Holy Spirit (Acts 2[38]).

The preaching of the Resurrection message is, in Rowan Williams' phrase, to *'recognise one's victim as one's hope.'*[26] Historic guilt far from being bypassed in the salvation process, 'builds on and from it'.[27]

God has identified Himself with the suffering victim, and as Williams points out not *the* victim in the abstract, but *our* (or my) victim, the one *we* have oppressed. The Resurrection is the archetype (the 'significant pattern' to use Rowan Williams' phrase[28]), because Jesus is, in New Testament teaching, *pure* victim; he alone is only victim, a man perfectly obedient to the Father, consistently refusing the role of oppressor. Jesus is totally and unambiguously described as 'pure Victim', a designation which is not modified or qualified by some other identity in a different set of relationships.[29]

In ordinary human relationships the boundary between oppressor and victim is never so clear. Certainly it is possible to be both oppressor and victim even within one relationship. Nevertheless, if the Resurrection message is to be effective in history rather than on some ideal or spiritual plane, then oppression as a historical category must be defined. Rowan Williams' definition is simple, but very radical:

> What is at issue is simply the transaction that leads to exclusion, to the severance of any reciprocity.[30]

This is true even if the oppressor's *cause* is right, and even if the victim's cause is *wrong*. Williams quotes a Rumanian novelist's verdict on the suicide in his prison cell of a young Moluccan terrorist: 'Anyone hanged in his cell is Jesus Christ on his cross'. This is offensive to all human sense of justice, but Williams continues:

Our necessary justice does not repair the breach in the world created by a terrorist's massacre, it creates a fresh breach . . . But if God is the enemy of all human diminution, he is there too . . . guaranteeing that we shall not forget even the most despised and loathed of victims. He judges our justice: not condemning it or inverting it, but transcending. It is the secret Paul learned of a divine justice, righteousness, which acts only to restore . . . the justice which will not act against us, that is incapable of aggression or condemnation: the righteousness that makes righteous.[31]

The same point is compellingly made in an anonymous poem which was left in a Toronto church by a woman who as a child had been sexually abused. It was written in response to a figure hung beneath a cross, the figure of a woman with arms outstretched as if crucified. The figure helps the victim of assault to move from shame to realisation that God was with her 'as the violated girl caught in helpless suffering.' She continues:

The chains of shame and fear
no longer bind my heart and body,
A slow fire of compassion and forgiveness is kindled.
My tears fall now
for man as well as woman.

You, God,
can make our violated bodies
vessels of love and comfort
to such a desperate man.
I am honoured to carry this womanly power
with my body and soul.

You were not ashamed of your wounds.
You showed them to Thomas
as marks of your ordeal and death.
I will no longer hide these wounds of mine.
I will bear them gracefully.
They tell a resurrection story.[32]

Our examination of the history suggests that the victim-oppressor relationship of Black to White is relatively unambiguous: Black as victim and White as oppressor needs little qualification. However, we must affirm that this and other great wrongs of history, however morally clear, do retain a degree of ambiguity. The suffering of the victim is never totally identified with suffering of the 'pure Victim'.

The Cross can never be a total divine moral approval of the oppressed's position; it is never a weapon of justification which the victim can use to return violence on the oppressor and so continue the cycle of oppression, what Rowan Williams calls a 'magnifying mirror for his condition.[33] We cannot suffer in order to be innocent.

But the Cross is the presence of God with the oppressed in their suffering, making sense of it, and giving significance to it. The presence of the crucified Christ, taking the suffering upon himself, is vital to the victim's endurance and survival, especially where the oppression is so severe that all human hope fails and there is only 'hope against hope'.

> If the Lord had not been on our side, now may Israel say; if the Lord had not been on our side when men rose up against us, then they would have swallowed us up alive . . . Blessed be the Lord who has not given us as prey to their teeth . . . (Psalm 124[1-3,6])

Precisely in this manner the Black Christian Tradition looks to the Cross. James Cone asks the question 'Who is Jesus Christ for us today?' and explains why the answer for Black Christians must always begin with the affirmation 'Jesus is Who He was', with the historical Jesus. Cone protests against the separation of the Christ of Faith from the Jesus of history, whether among the Early Fathers or in Kierkegaard, Bultmann and much of Barth.[34] Jesus' ministry was with and to the poor, one of total identification ('he had to be made like his brethren in every respect' Hebrews 2[17]). Cone writes:

> Black folks . . . were impressed by the Passion because they too had been rejected, beaten and shot without a chance to say a word in defence of their humanity. In Jesus' death black slaves saw themselves, and they unleashed their imagination, describing what they felt and saw.

He illustrates from the spirituals:

> Oh dey whupped him up de hill, an 'he never said a mumbalin' word,
> He jes' hung down his head an' he cried.
>
> Oh see my Jesus hangin' high!
>
> Were you there when they crucified my Lord?

Cone continues:

Through the experience of being slaves, they encountered the theological significance of Jesus' death: through the crucifixion Jesus makes an unqualified identification with the poor and the helpless and takes their pain upon himself. If Jesus was not alone in his suffering, they were not alone in their slavery. Jesus was with them! He was God's Black Slave who had come to put an end to human bondage. Herein lies the meaning of the resurrection . . . Through Jesus' death, God has conquered death's power over his people.[35]

CONVERSION — ENCOUNTER WITH THE VICTIM'S CRY

How does the grace of God use the people who 'are not' to bring to nothing the things that are? The process begins when a cry of the oppressed is heard, when, in our case, the White church encounters and hears the cry of 'God's Black Slave' from the Cross. This cry is the cry of the murdered victim Abel for vindication, which God hears (Genesis 4^{10}). It is the cry of the Israelites in Egypt for relief and liberation (Exodus 3^{23-25}). It is the cry for justice of any poor person, widow, orphan or the stranger outside Israel, outside the community of faith (Ex. 23^{23-24}) and it is the cry of the righteous poor against oppression within the community of faith (Psalm $34^{15,17}$). It is the agonized cry for justice long waited for, the cry of the oppressed who, whilst not doubting God's sovereignty, ask for understanding of His ways in history (Habakkuk 1^{2-4}). It is the silent cry of God's suffering servant in Isaiah 53 and it is Jesus' radical cry of desertion:

My God, my God, why hast thou forsaken me?
(Matthew 27^{46}).

This Biblical cry is echoed in Black songs and writings. The spirituals abound with cries to God for help and anguished statements of suffering, though usually intertwined with confidence and joy:

Oh my Good Lord! Keep me from sinking down.

Nobody knows the trouble I've seen, Glory, Hallelujah!

I must walk my lonesome valley, I got to walk it for myself . . .
Jesus walked His lonesome valley, He had to walk it for Himself.[36]

Nineteenth century Black writers and preachers made clear their difficulties in reconciling the justice of God with human slavery.

Bishop Daniel Payne of the African Methodist Episcopal Church (elected 1852) asked:

> Is he a just God? Is He a holy Being? If so, why does he permit a handful of dying men thus to oppress us?[37]

To this cry from within the community of faith must be added the cry of the Black unbeliever. Payne wrote:

> They hear their masters professing Christianity . . . and they know that oppression and slavery are inconsistent with the Christian religion; therefore they scoff at religion itself – mock their masters and distrust both the goodness and justice of God. Yes I have known them even to question His existence.[38]

The 'seculars', the Black musical tradition known as the *blues*, contains evidence of open rebellion against God. Blacks, James Cone tells us, changed 'Live a humble to the Lord' to 'live a humbug', and sang:

> Our father, who is in heaven
> White man owe me eleven and pay me seven
> They kingdom come, they will be done,
> And if I hadn't took that, I wouldn't had none.[39]

as well as more reflectively:

> They say we are the Lawd's children, I don't say that ain't true
> They say we are the Lawd's children, I don't say that ain't true
> But if we are the same like each other
> Oooh, well, well, why do they treat me like they do?[40]

Cone describes how the lack of a satisfactory Christian answer to that question led to direct rebuking of God, for example for W.E.B. DuBois in 1906.

> We raise our shackled hands and charge Thee, God by the bones of our stolen fathers, by the tears of our dead mothers, by the blood of thy crucified Christ: *What meaneth this?*[41]

Whilst some Black people found a new religious home in various forms of Islam, Black intellectuals became secular humanists:

I know full well now
Jesus could not die for me –
That only my own hands
Dark as the earth
Can make my earth-dark body free
(Langston Hughes).[42]

All these are to the White church the cries of the Black oppressed. Because Jesus is with and in the suffering, they constitute the appeal of Jesus crucified to White Christians.

The cry has two aspects. Firstly, it is the cry of *judgement*; it is the cry which accuses the crucifiers and makes plain to them what they have done. It locates God *with* Black people as far as their relationship with Whites is concerned, and it declares that He is *for* Black people (even as some of them reject Him). It places God *apart from* White people as far as their relationship with Blacks is concerned, and declares that He is *against* them (even as they honour Him with their lips). As Karl Barth writes:

> The human righteousness required by God and established in obedience . . . has necessarily the character of a vindication of right in favour of the threatened innocent, the oppressed poor, widows, orphans and aliens. God always takes his stand unconditionally and passionately on this side and on this side alone: against the lofty and on behalf of the lowly; against those who already enjoy right and privilege and on behalf of those who are denied and deprived of it.[43]

It must again be emphasised that Black people are the location of God's presence relative to Whites, only because God loves those whose cry for deliverance He hears, not because Black people (or any other oppressed group) have intrinsic or earned moral merit with which to please Him. God did not set His love on Israel because they had any strength or virtues with which to impress Him, for they were 'the fewest of all peoples' (Deuteronomy 7[7]). God's love for Black people is derived solely from His sovereign righteousness and His consequent promise to save the oppressed ('the oath which he swore to your fathers' (Deuteronomy 7[8]). Therefore He redeems 'from the house of bondage'.

This has important consequences for the White response to the 'cry' of judgement against them. The response to judgement is penitence, yet this penitence must avoid the oft-felt need to see penitence towards the victim as an admission that the victim is morally superior. This, as Rowan Williams points out, 'reduces my violence to a kind of mistake: had I but recognised the virtue of my victim, I should have seen that I had no 'right' to act as I did'.[44] Black people are not 'better' than Whites, neither physically, culturally nor spiritually. Any such claim sentimentalizes them, and removes them from real history by ignoring the plurality of identities which make up the personhood of all individuals, Black or White. People who are Black may, in other dimensions of their being, be oppressors; for example, as rulers, husbands, landlords or capitalists.

It is a mistake, therefore, for White people as an expression of their penitence to attribute cultural superiority to Africans, or to claim that Black people are intrinsically 'more spiritual'.[45] It is often claimed that racism is *only* a White problem, and that there is no such thing as Black racism. On our understanding that 'White' and 'Black' have meaning only in relationship to each other as 'oppressor' and oppressed', it is certainly the case that racism can only be attributed to Whiteness. But this should not be understood as a claim that people with black skins never exercise oppressive power over others of a different racial group. (However, it must be acknowledged that many of these oppressive relationships have been historically conditioned by White oppression, for example when the main or only role model experienced is that of the White oppressor, or where violence is – or is believed to be – necessary for survival, or where anger felt against White oppression is internalised by Black individuals or communities and then projected onto others).

Hearing and accepting the judgement that they are guilty does not in itself absolve White people. That would indeed be to 'wallow in guilt'. It would be to say 'I am feeling guilty; this proves that I am wicked and my victim is therefore, my moral superior'. It would hand to Black people the oppressive whip which was formerly used against them. It would not transcend oppression, only reverse it. The White offence is that they have oppressed *other human beings*, not that they have oppressed good ones.

The second aspect of the cry is that it makes an *appeal for repentance* to White people and especially to White Christians. It declares that Whites not only should repent but may and can repent. They too belong to God, they too may obtain His mercies, they too are human; it is not beyond them to make the 'quantum leap' in imagination to grasp what their victims have suffered and to be moved from within. The familiar Old Testament text can be placed on the lips of the Black Jesus:

Is it nothing to you, all you that pass by? Behold and see if there is any sorrow like my sorrow (Lamentations 1[12]).

Hearing the cry is indeed the moment of judgement ('Now is the judgement of this world' John 12[31]), when the White church either repents or does not repent. As at the first preaching of the Gospel, and through the ages, some will find the Cross foolishness and a stumbling block (1 Cor. 1[23]). Others will begin the spiritual journey of repentance that leads to new life. I am reminded of an evening spent showing the British Council of Churches' film strip *The Enemy Within* – a vivid portrayal of the Black experience in Britain – to a group of White Christians. Some responded defensively, even angrily, others were silent and thoughtful. One priest, however, remains in my memory as having been much moved: 'To think', he said, 'that this is what we have done to them.' This repentance is the gateway to new life.

We are here describing the experience of *conversion*. White people who repent turn to their victim and find there, through and within the suffering of the victim, a true and pure Victim once crucified who does not return oppression and violence. This promises to transform, and not merely continue or invert, the previous relationship.[46]

White people come to the point (or process) of conversion in different ways. It may be a sudden encounter with Black suffering, of the kind described above. Many begin at an earlier stage: they encounter Black people as an extra, even exotic, dimension of their existing spiritual lives, one which adds excitement and variety, but leaves their existing spiritual 'base' intact and unthreatened. At this stage the humanity of Black people has not really been encountered; they remain in a sense objects, cultural phenomena, (including *Christian* cultural phenomena!) to be experienced and enjoyed. Then, at best, the spiritual lives of White and Black run parallel to each other, with perhaps occasional 'bridging' exercises for those whose lives otherwise never meet. At this stage we visit each other, taste each other's food, have enjoyable days out, and from time to time have a joint Eucharist. All these events are good, but this kind of connection does not change the fact that the roads are only parallel. To describe such events as instant 'Christian fellowship' is to make fellowship a shallow experience, where whole dimensions of human interaction and dialectic are precluded.

At worst, this stage gives White people, because their superior wealth and power remains intact, the chance to dominate, patronize, and 'take up the Black cause'. The response of Black people to this kind of White liberalism has often been described. For James Cone it is wanting to 'change the heart of the racist without ceasing to be his friend', wanting 'progress without conflict', 'enjoying all the privileges of being White and yet being loved by blacks'.[47] Whatever form this first stage takes, and however embarrassing or painful for Black people, it is a stage that few White people avoid, and, perhaps, few totally leave. But those who admit the charge of the just judge, ('to think, this is what we have done to them') have already begun to realise that the Christ they affirm in Church is the Christ they have encountered in Black suffering. Gustavo Gutierrez, writing of the parallel relationship between Latin American Christians (here meaning clergy, religious and laypeople of a secure middle class or wealthy background) and their own poor says:

> For many Latin American Christians at the present time the possibility of following Jesus depends on their ability to make their own the spiritual experience of the poor. This requires a deepgoing conversion: they are being asked to make their own the spiritual experience of the poor.[48]

This is indeed to see God through receiving a vision of the suffering Christ. This alone can convert, as Martin Luther wrote:

> It is not good enough for anybody, nor does it help him that he recognises God in His glory and majesty, unless he recognised Him in the abasement and ignominy of the cross (Heidelberg Disputations)

This first stage of White conversion, described now at length, may be summarized as *an encounter with the suffering of Christ in the suffering which they themselves cause by virtue of their identity as oppressors, to the people they oppress.*

This is precisely the first stage of a New Testament paradigm of conversion: Paul at Damascus. Like Whites, Saul the Pharisee is dominating his victims and denying their identity. Thus 'breathing out threats and murder', he encounters Christ who reveals that Paul's persecution of the Christians is a continued persecution of Christ Himself, 'I am Jesus whom you are persecuting'. (Acts 9[1–5]).

CONVERSION – THE CRISIS EXPERIENCE

The encounter with Jesus in one's own victim is of course a disturbing and traumatic experience. One's existing spiritual foundations are revealed as the base on which oppression was built. Old securities, therefore, collapse, and fixed reference points crumble away; the spiritual base is no longer intact. Familiar paths lead nowhere, whilst the life of the White church, continuing as if it had no dialectical relationship with Black people (and often no relationship at all!), comes to seem meaningless and arid. The old theology no longer speaks, definitions of key-words (salvation, sanctification, fellowship) believed and lived over many years, wither. The time is painful for it entails a sense of loss:

> As I pour out my soul I recall other times:
> How I entered the sanctuary and prostrated myself towards the altar,
> Amid songs of joy and thanksgiving
> Amid the bustle of the feast.
> (Psalm 42[5])[49]

The old wineskins burst, and wine is spilt. The time is, as Gutierrez says, one of 'passing through a desert'.[50] The old prayer no longer speaks, there is grief for the lost unity of life. There is also separation from previous fellowship; friends notice that something has happened but cannot 'see what it is'. It is necessary to go on alone, at the mercy of events as they happen, submitting oneself to them. Submitting to 'events' means submitting to the community of one's victims; they lead and show the former oppressors where they are to go. And in submitting to them they submit to Christ. At this stage particularly, there is very little idea what His will is, but they are never left without some sense of His presence, some assurance that the way will become clearer. If they can pray at this time, it is simply to pray to trust, to trust Him to lead them. As Gutierrez says, the desert may be a foreign land, but it is not one from which God is absent. In it 'the seeds of a new spirituality can germinate'.[51]

This second stage of conversion may be summarized as *a time of crisis, loss, and separation from one's roots, a time of submission to one's victims, and in them to God's leading*. Again we note the clear parallels with Paul's conversion: his crisis and loss ('when his eyes were opened he could see nothing . . . for three days he was without sight, and neither ate nor drank'); separation from his roots: ('The men who were travelling with him stood speechless, hearing the voice but seeing nothing'); submission to his victims ('they led him by the hand') and assurance that God will lead ('rise, enter the city, and you will be told what you are to do') (Acts 9[7-9]).

CONVERSION – REDEMPTION OF MEMORY AND THE NEW FUTURE

White ministers of a Black congregation soon learn how badly its members were, in general, received in 'mainstream' churches on arrival in England. Although this rejection took place in the context of rejection in the wider society of the 'Mother Country', it is the one which hurt the most for the faithful Christian. As one woman revealed to the author, 'I learned to cope with racism everywhere else, but I was shocked to find it in the church'. Clergy will doubtless decide that their first task is to reverse this situation by a ministry of welcome to Black people, and by encouraging other White people to do the same. Since such a change in the life of a parish has invariably elicited a positive response from previously lapsed or disillusioned Anglicans of the first generation, clergy may easily conclude that once the change has taken root, all will be well.

The power of this change must not be overlooked. Many Black Anglicans have testified how good pastoral ministry in time of crisis 'brought us back to the Church'. For Black and White such a change has allowed the 'milk of human kindness' to flow again. For Black people it has restored familiar marks of ecclesial identity from the past, albeit a colonial past; it has become an oasis in the otherwise 'endless pressure' of contact with Whites. For the White church it is the first vital step to conversion and thus to reconciliation. Without it, the Black presence in the Church of England would be insignificant.

For clergy, this may be the stage at which they are fascinated by the discovery of a 'new' Christian tradition within their own flock: it is the stage of the 'extra, even exotic, dimension' to their existing spiritual life). But, as they experience Black social life and the Black Christian Tradition powerfully communicated through family celebrations, funeral services and in the singing of certain hymns, they will begin to ask, 'where is this coming from?' At that moment, though yet unrecognised, their meeting with the Black Christ has begun. In meeting the Black Christ in the history, culture and identity of Black people they are also compelled to begin a new encounter with their history, culture and identity, with the memory of their own people and their own church.

If they were to reject this encounter with the Black Christ in favour of a superficial friendliness where, as it is put, 'colour is irrelevant', they would be making the serious error of trying to create a new community in the Church without regard to history. They would be attempting an exercise of the *will* without regard to the history which formed it, an act of 'pure reason' devoid of memory. For although Christ daily offers a new beginning, this can be received only by dying daily and rising with Him, by bearing the verdict of the Cross on their historic identity. A church that forgets history as it tries to create a new presence of welcome and acceptance for Black people will inevitably find that power remains in White hands, and thus that

White identity, culture and liturgy continue to dominate. The environment may now be kindly where once it was oppressive, but the message underlying it will be (as a Black priest has remarked) 'Forget your own culture, forget who you are, feel like us'.[52] Blacks may now be recognised as human beings and as fellow *Christians*, but the question of *identity*, for which memory is crucial, will be avoided. This will be precisely the *colonial* church which Noel Erskine describes (p. 70). As the Black community develops and forms its various responses to life in Britain, it is clear that colonial consciousness is dying very fast, and with it will go the Black presence in any White-led church which seeks to keep its Black members in 'colonial' dependence.

The experience of the White Christians who do allow themselves to look at their own history and identity through the 'cry' of the oppressed is certainly a sharp one. For me it included tales of rejection in churches and of the difficult early days of immigration, as well as many stories of the day to day struggle which were then as startling to me as they were commonplace and obvious to those who told me. It was for instance a new experience to hear a group of women describe how each guarded her dignity in such workaday situations as making sure the White person sitting on the same bus seat and waiting to get past would acknowledge her politely ('If he don't say, 'Excuse me', me just look in mi handbag'!) It was startling to hear the grown-up son of an eminently respectable family respond to a mention of the police by saying, 'Mind you, my mother hates the police for what they have done to us'.

Reflection on the 'cry' even within 'ordinary' pastoral ministry, recovers for the White priest, and thus for the White church, *the suppressed memory of the oppressive past*. Thus the Black singing of hymns recalls the origin of Black Christian music in the spirituals of slavery times. An old slave said:

> My master call me up and order me a short peck of corn and a hundred lash. My friends see it and is sorry for me. When dey come to de praise meetin' dat night dey sing about it.[53]

The funerals recall the 'sweet chariot', welcome because it comes 'for to carry me home' – yet it leaves a 'motherless child' behind. The family events recall the solidarity of a community formed in oppression. Baptisms celebrated today recall baptisms refused or discounted in previous centuries; today's marriages recall the informal and precarious arrangements under slavery, and pressures on Black family life ever since.

How can White people face this suppressed memory? How can they face the recall of a past of wrong and hurt? It is a frightening counsel, promising apparently only terror and further despair, a fruitless, paralysing encounter with guilt. To be confronted with the judgement of God is painful; how can we stand before Him? The answer is to be found in the context in which the memory of the past is recalled, namely the Resurrection and, therefore, in the Eucharist in which the Resurrection is celebrated. Rowan Williams shows that in St. John's Gospel the disciples' recognition of Jesus is much more than the slow recognition of a familiar figure, it is also the slow return of their buried past of desertion and failure, Simon recognizing himself as betrayer, part of the past that makes him who he is.[54] And when God's judgement is 'revealed and embodied and 'specified' in Jesus, the victim who will not condemn, we can receive it'. For Jesus, even as he returns our memory, waits on our love ('Simon, son of John, do you love me?') and he sits and eats with us ('Come and have breakfast'). This meal clearly recapitulates not only earlier table-fellowship but also the memory of betrayal on the night of the Last Supper. Yet it is the meal of welcome and forgiveness; it is the meal where a new call, a new vocation is given ('feed my sheep' . . . 'another will gird you and carry you where you do not wish to go'.) (John 21[12–19])[55]

These elements are built into every Eucharist: we who sit at table with Christ are still his betrayers and, by extension, judges and crucifiers. Rowan Williams again:

> The Eucharist is never a simple fellowship meal, not even a simple fellowship meal with Jesus. Its imagery always and necessarily operates between the two poles of Maundy Thursday and Easter Sunday . . . All meals with Jesus after Calvary speak of the *restoration* of a fellowship broken by human infidelity.[56]

As we learn how tragic the past has been, at that very moment a new hope and a new vocation is revealed to us.

If the relationship of White to Black is one of oppressor to victim, then the presence of Black Anglicans at Anglican Eucharists is likewise an encounter with the presence of the risen Christ. White Anglicans see Black Anglicans staying with them, and recognise that as *miracle* – a triumph over death (destruction of humanity, destruction of identity), and therefore a sign of resurrection. It indeed recovers the painful memory of White betrayal (those who said, 'Why don't you go to "your" church down the road?' must face what they have done when Black people nevertheless persist in presenting

194

themselves at the Lord's Table), but it does so *in the presence of Jesus*. This is signified by the ready participation in key liturgical acts. To 'the Lord be with you' Black Christians respond, 'And also with you'; they confess their sins together with White people, they exchange a hand of peace, eat from the same plate and drink from the same cup, – Sunday by Sunday, year after year, in buildings which embody their past and present oppression. For White people who recognise what is happening and who face the story of their own past, this is nothing less than *the restoration of fellowship broken by their own infidelity*. It is one of the most powerful signs of hope within the Christian churches; though fragile it remains a telling witness to the love of Christ.

This should not be understood as a White insistence that Black Christians, let alone Black people, have a 'duty' to 'forgive' their oppressors. Only in a context of deep repentance can a White Christian even begin to talk of being forgiven. It must also be noted that many Black Christians remain unable to continue in the denomination of their upbringing, and cannot but remain deeply hurt by the experiences that caused their exodus. (In spite of this, Black-led denominations invariably give a warm and vivid welcome and affirmation to visiting White Christians). Others have ceased active membership of any church, and on occasions express their hurt, as I once discovered at a party when conversing amicably with a woman who had come to England twenty years earlier. On learning that I was an Anglican priest her attitude changed immediately and she snapped angrily at me: 'I will *never* come to your church'. On attempting to renew her Anglican Church membership on arrival in England she had been rudely asked to leave.

To say that the continuing presence of Black Anglicans at Anglican Eucharists is an encounter with the risen Christ must be understood carefully. It must be reiterated that 'Black' and 'White' take their meaning only from their relationship with each other. Black people are Christ for Whites only because they have been oppressed by Whites. In other dimensions of their lives they are as much under judgement and in need of forgiveness as Whites. But when Black Christians greet Whites at the Eucharist, then the oppressed one is greeting the oppressor with a judgement that is forgiveness in the resurrection feast.

This third stage of conversion may be summarized as *an encounter with the memory of one's identity as oppressor in the miraculous Resurrection context of forgiveness and acceptance*. Again, this stage is present in Paul's conversion in the visit of Ananias:

The Lord Jesus who appeared to me on the road by which you came, has sent me that you may regain your sight and be filled with the Holy Spirit (Acts 9[17]).

Ananias is, for White Christians, the type of the Black Christian who comes representing Jesus, and who tells them 'what (they) are to do' (9[6]). So the Lord who has vindicated the oppressed comes through them, as Rowan Williams puts it, 'in their words and hands to save their oppressors who are his as well'.[57]

CONVERSION — THE NEW LIFE, AN EXCHANGE OF GIFTS

So the White oppressive past is returned to White people 'in the presence of Jesus' through the judgement, acceptance and forgiveness given by the persistent presence of Black Christians at the altar. This 'Easter' has only been possible because of a 'Good Friday' experience. Now we move on to the New Life of the two communities together, to life in the Spirit.

I am sometimes asked, 'What is it like in a congregation where Black and White get on well together?' For our purposes I take 'get on well' to mean a situation where the historic identities have been faced, where the mutual recognition of victim and oppressor has happened and where some measure of White repentance and Black forgiveness has been articulated at the Lord's Table. Does one identity predominate? Is something entirely new fashioned? It must be conceded that this situation is much harder to write about from practical experience than all that has gone before. What is written so far has in some measure been lived here and there in the Church; even in these places, however, we stand only at the first frontier of 'what God has prepared for those who love Him'.

Three marks of the new life in Christ can, however, be tentatively described. Firstly, the new life involves *continuity of identity* for both Black and White, and therefore continued encounter with each other, but now in Christ. Neither White nor Black should desire – or fear – the annihilation of their identity. To be in the Body of Christ is always to be present with our humanity – our cultural, social, sexual and racial identities. So our identity as Black or White lives on, but now in Christ. The shame and the suffering is still there, but in Him, ('Lord, when did we see you hungry . . . or thirsty . . . or a stranger . . . ?').

Rowan Williams points out that there is a common element to

all the Resurrection narratives, namely the otherness, the unrecognizability, the *strangeness* of Jesus. As we continue to live in Him and find ourselves identified with Him, we also find Him *strange to* us. Our identity is definite and assured, we stand on firm ground in Christ, yet we are not 'completed'. Christ calls us – and this is our new vocation – to new encounters, to new interactions, so long as we remain in an imperfect world:

> Jesus grants us a solid identity, yet refuses us the power to 'seal' or finalize it, and obliges us to realize that this identity only exists in endless responsiveness to new encounters with him, in a world of unredeemed relationships: to absolutize it, imagining that we have finished the making of ourselves, that we have done with desire and restlessness, is to slip back into that un-redeemed world; to turn from the void of the tomb to the drama of a cheapened Calvary for the frustrated ego.[58]

The Church is sometimes spoken of as the 'extension of the incarnation', a kind of continuation of Jesus. The image of the Body of Christ is particularly susceptible to this kind of interpretation. Yet it is important to experience the Church as the place of *continued* encounter with Jesus the stranger. It is not an 'undialectical' extension of Christ; as Rowan Williams puts it:

> the Church is not the assembly of the disciples as a 'continuation' of Jesus, but the continuing group of those engaged in dialogue with Jesus, those compelled to renew again and again their confrontation with a person who judges and calls and recreates.[59]

Far from being annihilated, the two identities continue to react to and with each other, an interaction now of promise and creativity, not of threat of diminution.

Secondly, this interaction consists in the *exchange of gifts*. This does not mean that the gifts of each tradition are thrown into some kind of spiritual melting pot where they are made bland by a process of dehistoricizing (Black choirs singing in White cathedrals and no questions asked!). Rather each tradition itself is a gift, a gift made up of stories in history, (a good Black preacher is one who can 'tell the story'; Black Theology, says James Cone, is 'an investigation into the raw materials for our pilgrimage, telling the story of 'how we got over'.) In the New Life of the Body of Christ the Spirit gives the gift of speech so that each group can tell its story and offer it, not to be submerged or 'melted down' but *exchanged* in the community.

My particular past is there, in the Church, as a resource for my relations with my brothers and sisters – not to be poured out repeatedly and promiscuously, but as a hinterland of vision and truth and acceptance out of which I can begin to love in honesty.

My gift . . . is my*self*, my story given back, to give me a place in the net of exchange, the web of gifts, which is Christ's Church.[60]

Fundamental to selfhood is to have a name, and fundamental to selfhood in the Church is to be named by Christ in the Body. In the New Life we can openly 'name White as White and Black as Black', for we can tell our story having the full courage to 'own' our identity, forgiven slavemasters-colonizers-oppressors and delivered slaves-colonized-victims, both delivered from the destructive consequences of sin, but from different 'sides'. Our identity is now grounded in recognition by the perfect Victim, and this generates trust and openness between those formerly estranged, as we struggle in the Spirit to enable each other, and not to dominate.

Thirdly, for both identities, the interaction involves a process of *purification* ('for he is like a refiner's fire' Mal. 3^2). White Christian tradition is purified in all its details from its oppressive and imperialistic stance. This involves both the explicitly Christian tradition of the Church of England, and the traditions and values of the nation with which the Church is historically identified. So we will find White Christians struggling to deliver their undoubted cultural achievements, moral values and social institutions – including their churches – from bondage to an exploitative economic system with its accompanying racism. For example, part of the British story is to cherish the value of freedom, equality under the law, toleration and democracy. Can these values be purified of imperialism and racial superiority? Again, part of the Church of England's story is to cherish the fruits of scholarship, liturgy, music and architecture, missionary commitment, zeal for social reform, and (especially in modern times) critical commentary on unjust legislation. Can these fruits be purified of racism, and of an easy and uncritical acceptance of oppressive social structures? Purification will involve a host of detailed and practical reforms. For instance, a cherished and compellingly beautiful part of the Anglican spiritual inheritance is the musical tradition of its cathedral worship. Yet this tradition is substantially dependent on the private school system. This disturbing alliance of 'things spiritual' with unjust social structures can hardly survive a genuinely repentant turning to the oppressed Christ.

It is beyond the scope of this book to develop a detailed programme of struggle, though some examples of anti-racist activity in the

Church were described in Chapter Eight. I am not aware of much writing on the purification of White tradition, but the following quotation from Archbishop Runcie's 1982 address to the Birmingham Community Relations Council should be noted:

> I both cherish our national story, shorn of its imperial pretensions, and believe that this story, now illuminated by the vision of the brotherhood of all races rooted in the universal fatherhood of God has a power to move men and women to acts of friendship and self-sacrifice.[61]

This would be a radical shearing! Nonetheless, forgiven and restored into communion with their Black brothers and sisters, White Anglicans would continue to be recognizably themselves with their culture, heritage and identity. 'Naming Black as Black' involves a kind of *purification in reverse*. Because the Black identity is one of victim, its 'impurities' are the result of the internalization of the White values. Black identity is in this purification *restored*; to be Black is no longer inferior, weak, ugly, unintelligent, incompetent or even simply unconfident. We rejoice unequivocally to hear that to be Black is to be 'proud', 'beautiful' or 'strong' whereas, although we ultimately desire that White people affirm the same of themselves, it will be some time before they can use such words easily and unoppressively (compare for example the utterly different overtones of 'I'm proud to be Black' and 'I'm proud to be White').

CONVERSION – THE VOCATION OF THE NEW LIFE

Because we have begun to be truthful to each other – but truthful *in Christ*, 'in the presence of Jesus' – we have hope, hope for ourselves and for the wider human community. That is to say, because our past and present have been restored, we can have a creative future in *mission* to the world. This is our vocation from God, to extend out into the world the new life which we begin to experience and celebrate in the Church; so we bring the resources of our hope to other entrenched victim-oppressor relationships. We do this not as a 'duty' taken up by a deliberate act of will, (although there will have to be a conscious choice of particular liberation projects), but as an inevitable consequence of the Spirit's activity in enabling the New Common Life.

Conversion of the oppressor to the victim leads us beyond

reformation of the Church to mission to the world. This is so for at least three reasons. Firstly, the Church of England has been bound up so closely with the historic oppressive White identity that it would be impossible, even if it were desirable, to separate Church from society as the area in which the purifying Spirit of God is at work. Secondly, as we have seen, the very words 'Black' and 'White' take their meaning from a history that was enacted on a world and not just a church stage, so the hope cannot be confined to the Church. Thirdly, the victim-oppressor relationship of Black and White is intimately bound up with other oppressions. Thus we find, for example, that Black women who become 'conscious' of White oppression, are also led to examine its relationship with the oppression of women by men, and of Black women by Black men.[62] Black people who become conscious of White oppression are led to examine the relationship of their experience with that of the White working class. This is not because of a moral comparison ('there are other oppressions which it is our duty also to look at'), but because the various oppressions are intimately intertwined in history. There is no White racism which does not also have a sexist and classist dimension. This takes us inevitably into these areas in hope – provided that we do not make the mistake of thinking that racist oppression is comprehensible entirely under the categories of gender or class struggle.

In its mission to the world the Church points men and women to Christ, to Jesus Christ made victim of our sins, and therefore to be discovered in and through all victims of oppression. It is through the victim that forgiveness is mediated, enabling the New Common Life to emerge, which is not a reversal of the old oppression but rather a new creation. By pointing to this Christ and testifying to the joy of our experience of Him, we transmit our hope to the world. We become the leaven, the salt and the light; we have a Gospel, and by living out our hope we proclaim it.

ABBREVIATIONS

A.B.C.	Association of Black Clergy.
ACCM	Advisory Council for the Church's Ministry.
A.C.S.	American Colonization Society.
AFFOR	All Faiths For One Race.
A.M.E.	African Methodist Episcopal Church.
A.M.E.Z.	African Methodist Episcopal (Zion) Church.
ACUPA	Archbishop's Commission on Urban Priority Areas.
B.C.C.	British Council of Churches.
B.S.R.	Board of Social Responsibility of the Church of England.
CADEC	Christian Action for Development in the Caribbean.
CARAF	Christians against Racism and Fascism.
CARJ	Catholic Association for Racial Justice.
C.B.A.C.	Committee for Black Anglican Concerns.
C.C.C.	Caribbean Conference of Churches.
C.I.I.R.	Catholic Institute for International Relations.
C.I.O.	Church Information Office.
CRRU	Community and Race Relations Unit of the British Council of Churches.
C.T.I.	Claiming The Inheritance.
D.E.C.	Diocesan Education Council.
D.S.R.	Division of Social Responsibility of the Methodist Church.
D.C.S.R.	Diocesan Council for Social Responsibility.
J.C.W.I.	Joint Council for the Welfare of Immigrants.
L.N.S.M.	Local Non-Stipendiary Ministry.
M.S.C.	Manpower Services Commission.
P.S.U.	Pastoral Studies Unit.
R.R.G.	Race Relations Group.
S.o.C.T.I.	Simon of Cyrene Theological Institute.

SCM   Student Christian Movement (Press).
S.P.G.   Society for the Propagation of the Gospel in Foreign
            Parts.
U.T.C.W.I. United Theological College of the West Indies.
V.S.O.   Voluntary Service Overseas.
W.C.C.   World Council of Churches.

NOTES

PREFACE

1. ROSWITH GERLOFF, *A Plea for British Black Theologies: The Black Church Movement in Britain in its transatlantic Cultural and theological interaction with special reference to the pentecostal Oneness (Apostolic) and Sabbatarian Movements*, (Studies in the Intercultural History of Christianity no. 77, 2 vols), Verlag Peter Lang, 1992.

   Bongani Mazibuko, *Education in Mission – Mission in Education: a Critical Comparative Study of Selected Approaches*, (same publisher as Gerloff, vol. 47) 1987.

   Iain MacRobert, *The Black Roots and White Racism of Early Pentecostalism in the USA*, Macmillan, 1988; and MacRobert, *Black Pentecostalism in Britain*, St Andrew Press, 1992.

   Walter J. Hollenweger, 'Interaction Between Black and White in Theological Education', *Theology* 90/737, Sept. 1987, pp. 341–50.

2. 'The supplying our Plantations with Negroes is of that extraordinary advantage to us, that the planting of Sugar and Tobacco and carrying on Trade there could not be supported without them, which Plantations . . . are the great Cause of the Increase of the Riches of the Kingdom' (Joshua Gee, *The Trade and Navigation of Great Britain Considered*, 1729; quoted in this work on p. 19).

CHAPTER 1: A NEW PEOPLE IS BORN (pages 1–6)

1. See Albert J. Raboteau, *Slave Religion: the 'Invisible Institution' in the Antebellum South*, Oxford University Press, 1978, p. 96.
2. See Peter Fryer, *Staying Power: the History of Black People in Britain*, Pluto Press, 1984, p. 372ff.
3. See, however, James H. Evans, 'The Struggle for Identity: Black People in the Church of England', in J. Wilkinson, R. Wilkinson and James H. Evans, *Inheritors Together*, B.S.R. of the Church of England, 1985; and

Louis-Charles Harvey, 'From Immigration to Integration' and 'From Rejection to Liberation' in 'Claiming the Inheritance', *Racial Justice* No. 6, Evangelical Christians for Racial Justice, (12 Bell Barn Shopping Centre, Cregoe Street, Birmingham B15 2DZ), 1987.

4. See Walter J. Hollenweger, 'Towards an Intercultural History of Christianity', *International Review of Mission*, Vol. CXXVI, No. 304, October 1987, p. 526.

5. See Myrna Lubin, *My Life as a Black Catholic*, in Patrick Kalilombe et al., *Black Catholics Speak*, CARJ, 1991.

6. The progress of 'theology from the underside' into western consciousness is interesting to observe. As recently as 1963 John Macquarrie published *Twentieth Century Religious Thought* (SCM, 1963), in which no reference is made to theology outside Europe and North America. A more recent survey by David Ford (*The Modern Theologians, an Introduction to Christian Theology in the Twentieth Century*, Blackwell, 1989) includes accounts of Latin American, Black, Asian, Feminist and other 'underside' theologies. These are all in a second volume, however; European theology has a volume to itself in which fourteen celebrated names are given a chapter each. For a European attempt to map out a new ecumenical 'paradigm' for theology in the light of twentieth century developments, see Hans Küng, *Theology for the Third Millennium: an Ecumenical View*, Doubleday, 1988.

7. For statements of the quarrel of Third World and other 'underside' theology with Western theology, see Kwesi A. Dickson, *Theology in Africa*, Darton, Longman & Todd and Orbis, 1984, pp. 1–10; Jon Sobrino, *The True Church and the Poor*, SCM, 1985; Choan-Seng Song, *Theology from the Womb of Asia*, Orbis, 1988, p. xiii; James Cone, *God of the Oppressed*, Seabury, 1975, pp. 45ff.

8. See Theo Witvliet, *A Place in the Sun: an Introduction to Liberation Theology in the Third World*, SCM, 1985, p. 1.

9. See David R. Hughes, 'The Biology of Race' in Clifford S. Hill and David Matthews, *Race, a Christian Symposium*, Victor Gollanz, 1968, and Charles Husband '"Race": The Continuity of a Concept' in C. Husband (ed.) *'Race' in Britain: Continuity and Change*, Hutchinson 1982, pp. 11–27.

10. See Gayraud S. Wilmore, *Black and Presbyterian: The Heritage and the Hope*, Geneva Press, Philadelphia, 1983, pp. 37ff.

11 Wilmore, *Black and Presbyterian*, p. 52.

12. Black Theology in South Africa is a related development. The social and political thrust of the term distinguishes it from 'African theology' further north where the reference is primarily to the relationship of Christianity and African culture. See *A Place in the Sun*, chapters 3 and 4, and Adrian Hastings, 'On African Theology', *Scottish Journal of Theology*, Vol. 37, No. 3, pp. 359ff.

In the United States, 'Afro-American' and more recently 'African-American' have become widely used as a more culturally positive way of denoting the Black American community.

13. The tension between the two uses of the word 'Black' in Britain is not yet resolved. On the one hand it is used to include all 'non-whites'. This use, depending as it does on a common experience of racism, refers to political identity and struggle. On the other hand, terms such as 'Black and Asian', arise out of the linguistic and religious complexity of the various communities and refer primarily to cultural identity. See 'Faithful and Equal', Report of the Division of Social Responsiblility, *Agenda of the 1987 Methodist Conference*, 2.5, Methodist Church 1987, p. 159. Recently the political use of 'Black' has been challenged as a means by which white political activists suppress the true cultural and religious identity of Asian people. See Tariq Modood, 'Alabama Britain', *The Guardian*, May 22nd, 1989.

CHAPTER 2: DISCOVERING BLACK CHRISTIANITY (pages 7–17)

1. See my *Black Anglicans in Birmingham*, 1984, pp. 30–39, unpublished paper for St. George's House, Windsor.
2. Ibid, pp. 22–29.
3. Unfortunately these lectures were not published.
4. John V. Taylor, *The Primal Vision*, SCM, 1963; see also Geoffrey Parrinder, *West African Religion* (2nd edition), Epworth, 1961; John Mbiti, *African Religions and Philosophy*, Heinemann, 1969
5. Christianity came very early to North Africa and to Ethiopia, but most of the rest of the continent had no contact with Christianity until the European expansion of the sixteenth century and later.
6. See Josiah U. Young, *Black and African Theologies: Siblings or Distant Cousins?*, Orbis Books, 1986, pp. 62–69; and Iain MacRobert, *The Black Roots and White Racism of Early Pentecostalism in the USA*, Macmillan, 1988, pp. 11–15.
7. See James H. Cone, *The Spirituals and the Blues*, Harper and Row, 1972, p. 17.
8. For a collection of the best known spirituals, see *Songs of Zion*, Abingdon Press, Nashville, 1981, nos. 74–171. The spiritual quoted here is No. 170.
9. Quoted in Cone, op. cit., p. 36.
10. Cone, *God of the Oppressed*, p. 121.
11. For a Latin American expression of this key characteristic of a liberation theology, see Jon Sobrino, *The Spirituality of Liberation*, Orbis, 1988, p. 26.
12. Martin Luther King, 'Loving your Enemies' in *Strength to Love*, Harper and Row, 1963, p. 46.
13. Maya Angelou, *I Know Why the Caged Bird Sings*, Virago Press, 1984, p. 123.
14. Cone, *The Spirituals and the Blues*, p. 97.
15. Cone, *God of the Oppressed*, p. 242.

16. The Black Christian Studies Course began at Queen's College, Birmingham in October 1987. (See chapter 9, p. 168.) The Simon of Cyrene Centre, an ecumenical venture, opened in September, 1989 under its principal, Dr. Sehon Goodridge, a former Principal of Codrington College, Barbados.

17. *C.M.S. Newsletter*, October 1985.

CHAPTER 3: ENGLISH CHRISTIANITY AND BLACK PEOPLE (pages 18–35)

1. Peter Fryer, *Staying Power: The History of Black People in Britain*, Pluto Press, 1984, p. 135.

2. Joseph Jones, 'The "Distressed" Negro in English Magazine Verse', *Studies in English* No. 17, University of Texas Bulletin No. 376, 8 July 1937, p. 103, quoted in Fryer, *Staying Power*, p. 145.

3. See John H. Griffin, *Black Like Me*, Signet Books, 1960.

4. Fryer, op. cit., p. 16.

5. Joshua Gee, *The Trade and Navigation of Great Britain Considered*, 1729, quoted in Fryer, op. cit., p. 17.

6. The word 'racism' is often popularly misused to mean discrimination or simply prejudice against Black people. Its earliest meaning, traced back to only 1942, is the same as Fryer's, namely the doctrine or theory of racial superiority. Kenneth Leech notes a shift in emphasis more recently to political and social structures, which the older meaning need not necessarily include. This is made clear by the term 'institutional racism', which, strictly speaking is a tautology. Leech points out the vital importance of the W.C.C. Consultation on Racism at Notting Hill in 1969 for the development of this understanding, and quotes Elizabeth Adler: 'It was deemed imperative that they no longer concentrate on improving race relations at an individual level but on striving for racial justice and a new balance of power at the level of institutions'; Adler, *A Small Beginning*, Geneva, 1974, p. 12, quoted in Leech, '"Diverse Reports" and the meaning of "Racism",' *Race and Class*, Vol. 28, No. 2, Autumn 1986, pp. 82–88. In references to contemporary racism, for example in the Church, I use the word in its full structural sense.

7. Morgan Godwyn, *The Negro's and Indians Advocate*, 1680, quoted in Fryer, op. cit., p. 146. See also A.C. Dayfoot, *The Shaping of the West Indian Church*, unpublished D.Th.thesis, Toronto School of Theology, 1982, p. 275ff.

8. Fryer, ibid, p. 149.

9. Ibid, pp. 151f.

10. George Metcalf, Introduction to E. Long, *History of Jamaica*, Cass Library of West Indian Studies No. 12, Frank Cass, 1970, p. xi, quoted in Fryer op. cit., p. 160.

11. Carl Linnaeus, *The Animal Kingdom or zoological system of the*

celebrated Sir Charles Linnæus, trans. Robert Kerr (J. Murry and R. Faulder, 1792), p. 45, quoted in Fryer, ibid, p. 166.

12. Ibid, p. 169.

13. Ibid, pp. 170–190.

14. For a Black examination of this theory see Cain H. Felder, *Troubling Biblical Waters*, Orbis, 1989, pp. 38–41. For a Black survey of the history of its interpretation, see Charles B. Copher, 'Three Thousand Years of Biblical Interpretation with Reference to Black Peoples', in Gayraud S. Wilmore (ed.), *African American Religious Studies: an Interdisciplinary Anthology*, Duke UP, 1989, pp. 105ff.

15. Robert Knox, *The Races of Men: a philosophical enquiry into the influence of Race over the Destinies of Nations*, second edition, (Henry Renshaw, 1852), p. 246, quoted in Fryer, op. cit., p. 175.

16. Fryer, ibid, p. 185.

17. Quoted in Fryer, ibid, p. 187.

18. Ibid, p. 190.

19. Fryer, ibid, p. 46. Alexander and David Barclay were among the number.

20. Stanley Elkins, *Slavery*, University of Chicago Press, 1968, p. 76.

21. Ibid, p. 77.

22. R. Greenwood and S. Hamber, *Emancipation to Emigration*, Macmillan Caribbean, 1980, p. 33.

23. Gayraud Wilmore, 'Identity Crisis: Blacks in Predominantly White Denominations' in William Howard, (ed.), *Colloquium on Black Religion*, Reformed Church in America, New York, 1976, p. 5.

24. Quoted in Albert J. Raboteau, *Slave Religion: The 'Invisible Institution' in the Antebellum South*, New York: OUP 1978. See also A.C. Dayfoot, op. cit., pp. 303ff.

25. David Jenkins, *Black Zion: The Return of Afro-Americans and West Indians to Africa*, Wildwood House, 1975, p. 129.

26. See Alex Haley, *Roots*, Hutchinson, 1977. A historical basis for the scene depicted in the film is found in the life of John Newton; see John Pollock, *Amazing Grace*, Hodder and Stoughton, 1981, pp. 94–97.

27. Quoted in Fryer, op. cit., p. 146.

28. Leslie, *History of Jamaica*, 1740, quoted in Augier and Gordon, *Sources of West Indian History*, Longmans, 1962, p. 142.

29. Augier, Gordon, Hall and Reckord, *The Making of the West Indies*, Longmans, 1960, p. 136. On the Church of England in the Caribbean in this period see A.C. Dayfoot, op. cit., pp. 288–333.

30. For the origins of the S.P.G. and its work in the American colonies, see H.P. Thompson, *Into All Lands: the History of the Society for the Propagation of the Gospel in Foreign Parts, 1701–1950*, S.P.C.K., 1951, pp. 3–91.

31. Circular letter of D. Humphreys, S.P.G. Secretary, 1725, MSS A.XIX. 113, S.P.G. archives, quoted in Thompson, ibid., p. 45.

32. Quoted in Raboteau, *Slave Religion*, p. 104.

33. Frank J. Klingberg, *Anglican Humanitarianism*, pp. 122–123, quoted in Raboteau ibid, p. 128.

34. F.A. Hoyos, *Barbados, A History from the Amerindians to Independence*, Macmillan Caribbean, 1978, p. 86. See also Frank J. Klingberg (ed.), *Codrington Chronicle: An Experiment in Anglican Altruism in a Barbados Plantation* (University of California Publications in History, Vol. 37), University of California Press, 1949; and Dayfoot, op. cit., pp. 333ff.
35. Noel L. Erskine, *Decolonizing Theology: A Caribbean Perspective*, Orbis, 1981, p. 31.
36. See Sehon S. Goodridge, *Facing the Challenge of Emancipation: a Study of the Ministry of William Hart Coleridge*, Cedar Press, 1981; and Dayfoot, op. cit., pp. 486ff.
37. See John Gilmore, *Toiler of the Sees: A Life of John Mitchinson, Bishop of Barbados*, Barbados National Trust, 1987.
38. Francis J. Osborne and Geoffrey Johnston, *Coastlands and Islands; First Thoughts on Caribbean Church History*, United Theological College of the West Indies, 1972, pp. 200ff.
39. Erskine, op. cit., p. 71.
40. Ibid, p. 72.
41. Cited by David Divine addressing *Claiming the Inheritance*, July, 1987. See *Celebrating the Black Family*, Claiming the Inheritance, 1988, p. 20.
42. From Bob Marley and the Wailers, 'Redemption Song', *Uprising*, (gramophone record ILPS 9596), Island Records Inc., 1980.
43. Frantz Fanon, *Black Skin, White Masks*, Grove Press, 1967. The quotation (from p. 7) is fron Aimé Césaire, *Discours sur le Colonialisme*.
44. Kortright Davis, *Emancipation Still Comin': Explorations in Caribbean Emancipatory Theology*, Orbis Books, 1990, p. 35.
45. Ashley Smith, *Educational Priorities: a Caribbean Perspective* (unpublished), 1987.
46. Fryer went as reporter and is the author of the well-known article entitled, 'Five Hundred Pairs of Willing Hands'; see Fryer, op. cit., p. 373.
47. See Fryer, op. cit., p. 373. Particularly notable among the invitations was the appeal for nurses from the Minister of Health, Enoch Powell.
48. John Rex and Robert Moore, *Race, Community and Conflict*, O.U.P., 1967, p. 157.
49. Accordng to a survey in the late 1960's, three-fifths of White British people saw themselves as superior to Africans and Asians. Nicholas Deakin, *Colour, Citizenship and British Society*, Panther, 1970, p. 325, cited in Kenneth Leech, *Struggle in Babylon*, Sheldon, 1988.
50. For general delineation of the extent of racial disadvantage and discrimination, see Colin Brown, *Black and White Britain, the Third P.S.I Survey*, Gower, 1984. For an earlier account, see David J. Smith, *Racial Disadvantage in Britain: the P.E.P. Report*, Penguin, 1977. On education, see the classic, Bernard Coard, *How the West Indian Child is made Educationally Sub-Normal in the British School System*, New Beacon Books, 1981; also, *West Indian Children in our Schools: interim report*, (the 'Rampton' Report), Cmnd. 8273 HMSO, 1981; *Education for All: The Report of the Committee into the Education of Children from Ethnic*

Minority Groups, the 'Swann' Report, (Cmnd. 9452) HMSO, 1985; and *Talking Chalk: Black Pupils, Parents and Teachers Speak about Education*, AFFOR, Birmingham, 1981. On policing, see, *Police against Black People*, Institute of Race Relations, 1979; and S. Hall et al., *Policing the Crisis: Mugging, the State and Law and Order*, Macmillan, 1978. For a general Black account, based on life in Bristol, see Ken Pryce, *Endless Pressure*, Penguin, 1979.

51. See Ann Dummett, *A Portrait of English Racism*, Penguin Books, 1973, pp. 157ff.

52. On the fallacy of the 'numbers game', see Leech, op. cit., p. 175.

53. At the independence of the larger Caribbean territories, settlers in Britain lost British citizenship and were given citizenship of their newly independent country of origin. By the time most became aware of the change, registration as a British citizen was costing £60 per person. As chairman of our church Advice Centre in Aston I regularly witnessed the anger and dismay of those who were thus compelled to undergo this costly process, a powerful symbol of rejection. It is interesting that, at the independence of St. Kitt's-Nevis, not long after the Nationality Act came into force in 1983, the Government was persuaded to grant automatic citizenship to all Kittitians and Nevitians who had 'right of abode' in Britain.

    Prominent among current manifestations of racism in government practice is the difficulties faced by visiting relatives from the Caribbean.

54. J.H. Oldham, *Christianity and the Race Problem*, SCM, 1924. See R. Elliott Kendall, *Christianity and Race*, B.C.C., 1983, and James H. Evans Jr. 'The Struggle for Identity: Black People in the Church of England' in J.L. & R. Wilkinson and James Evans, *Inheritors Together*.

55. C.S. Hill and D. Matthews (ed.), *Race, a Christian Symposium*, Victor Gollancz, 1968.

56. Testimony of a former resident of Handsworth to the author.

57. *The New Black Presence in Britain: a Christian Scrutiny*, B.C.C., 1976, p. 28.

58. R. Wilkinson, *A Chance to Change*, full version (unpublished), p. 37, abbreviated in J.L. & R. Wilkinson, op. cit.

59. The figures given here relate only to the 75% of parishes which responded to the questionnaire. The true absolute number of members and regular attenders in the diocese (though probably not the percentage) will therefore be higher. For a fuller account of the findings of *A Chance to Change* see ch. 8, p. 270, 275.

60. Heather Walton, *A Tree God Planted: Black People in British Methodism*, Ethnic Minorities in Methodism Working Group, D.S.R., 1985.

61. Ibid, p. 1.

CHAPTER 4: BLACK CHRISTIANITY BEFORE EMANCIPATION (pages 36–52)

1. James H. Cone, *Black Theology and Black Power*, Seabury, 1969; 20th Anniversary edition with new preface, Harper and Row, 1989.
2. Cone, *God of the Oppressed*, p. 5.
3. W.E.B. Dubois, *The Negro Church*, Atlanta University Press 1903; and *The Souls of Black Folk*, A.C. McClurg, 1929. Melville Herskovits, *The Myth of the Negro Past*, Beacon, 1958.
4. Gayraud Wilmore, *Black Religion and Black Radicalism*, Orbis, 2nd Edition, 1983, p. 26.
5. Ibid, p. 15; see John V. Taylor, *The Primal Vision*, SCM, 1963; Geoffrey Parrinder, *West African Religion* (2nd edition), Epworth, 1961; John Mbiti, *African Religions and Philosophy*, Heinemann, 1969.
6. Albert J. Raboteau, *Slave Religion, The Invisible Institution in the Antebellum South*, OUP, 1978, p. 8.
7. Wilmore, op. cit., p. 18.
8. Wilmore, (ibid, p. 22) notes that anti-social magic and 'witchcraft' was the particular form available to slaves of a universal human need to find outlets for fears, jealousies and hatred.
9. Mayal = 'to grasp the evil', i.e. to grasp and destroy the evil produced by obeah. Pukkumina is customarily spelt 'Pocomania' (the Spanish for 'a little madness', a wrong derivation which almost certainly stems from antipathy to the cult). See Ivor Morrish, *Obeah Christ and Rastaman*, James Clark, 1982, pp. 40–67; Leonard E. Barrett, *The Rastafarians*, Sangsters Book Stores and Heinemann, 1977, pp. 16–28; and Edward Seaga, 'Revival Cults in Jamaica: Notes towards a Sociology of Religion', *Jamaica Journal* Vol. 3, No. 2, June 1969, reprinted by Institute of Jamaica Publications, 1982.
10. Wilmore, op. cit., p. 26. See Raboteau, *Slave Religion*, pp. 59–75 for discussion of the African roots of shouting, dancing, singing and motor-behaviour. Of the spirituals Raboteau writes, 'Despite the African style of singing, the spirituals . . . were performed in praise of the Christian God. The names and words of the African gods were replaced by Biblical figures and Christian imagery. African style and European hymnody met and became in the spiritual, a new, Afro-American song to express the joys and sorrows of the religion which the slaves had made their own' (p. 74).
11. Raboteau, ibid, p. 127.
12. See Raboteau, ibid, p. 127, cf. Wilmore op. cit., p. 8.
13. Le Jau to the Secretary of the Society for the Propagation of the Gospel, 1710, quoted in Raboteau, ibid, p. 103; cf. the Bishop of London in 1727: 'Christianity . . . lays them under stronger Obligations to perform those duties with the greatest Diligence and Fidelity; not only from the Fear of man, but from a sense of Duty to God, and the Belief and Expectation of a future account'; quoted in Raboteau, ibid, p. 103.

14. Cf. C. Eric Lincoln, *The Black Church Since Frazier*, Schocken Books, 1974, p. 174.
15. See A.C. Dayfoot, *The Shaping of the West Indian Church*, pp. 367ff.
16. Ibid, pp. 379–381 and 394ff.
17. See Raboteau, ibid, pp. 128ff.; Kamphausen, 'The Rise of Black Christianity', *Cadbury Lectures* (unpublished), University of Birmingham, 1982; and Nathan O. Hatch, *The Democratization of American Christianity* Yale UP, 1989.
18. Raboteau, *Slave Religion*, p. 131. Methodists recorded 12,215 Black members in 1797, almost a quarter of the total. Baptist membership was estimated at 18,000 in 1793.
19. Greenwood and Hamber, *Emancipation to Emigration*, p. 70; and Dayfoot, op. cit., pp. 367ff.
20. Ibid, pp. 379–381 and 395ff.
21. Raboteau, *Slave Religion*, p. 141; Erskine, *Decolonizing Theology*, pp. 41–45; Dayfoot, op. cit., pp. 389ff., and Clement Gayle, *George Liele: Pioneer Missionary to Jamaica*, Jamaica Baptist Union, 1982.
22. Quoted in Raboteau, ibid, p. 66.
23. Ibid, p. 67.
24. Ibid, p. 68.
25. On the historian's dependence on White sources, see Wilmore, op. cit., pp. 29ff., and Michael Craton, *Testing the Chains: Resistance to Slavery in the British West Indies*, Cornell University Press, 1982, pp. 15 and 24ff.
26. Craton, ibid, p. 35.
27. Ibid, p. 25.
28. Ibid, p. 33.
29. See W.N. Katz, *Black Indians: a Hidden Heritage*, Atheneum, 1986, pp. 49ff.
30. The Black Caribs developed on the windward side of St. Vincent where shipwrecked Africans from slaveships, supplemented by a steady stream of runaways from Barbados, had mixed with the native Caribs. Although they lived more as small farmers than Carib warrior fishermen, and although African physical characteristics soon predominated, the Black Caribs remained culturally substantially Carib in language, religion and social customs. They became formidable adversaries for the new British colonizers after the cession of St. Vincent in 1763 and adeptly formed alliances with the rival French. Finally defeated in 1796, they were deported to Rattan, off the coast of Honduras, whence they have settled on the Honduras mainland, in Guatemala and in Belize. I myself had several Black Caribs ('Garifuna') among my pupils in Dangriga, Belize in 1965–67, and found the Garifuna language and cassava-based culture very much alive, with traditional religious practices continuing beneath a Catholic exterior. The survival and present strength of the Garifuna is a remarkable story.
31. See Craton, op. cit., pp. 67ff. and 211ff.
32. Craton, ibid, p. 66.
33. Edward Long, *History of Jamaica*, London, 1774, vol. II, pp. 447–448, cited in Craton, op. cit., p. 127. The recently published journal of

plantation overseer Thomas Thistlewood gives a vivid account of the 'dreadful apprehension' of a White man caught in the midst of the fighting, but also of the 'loyalty' of the Maroon and non-Coromantee slaves; see Douglas Hall (ed.), *In Miserable Slavery: Thomas Thistlewood in Jamaica*, Macmillan, 1990, pp. 92ff.

34. When the Hanover Plot of 1776 was uncovered in Jamaica, Whites were shocked by the participation of this group in planning rebellion. The French revolutionary period saw a large-scale rebellion in Grenada (1795–97) which was led by a Catholic and French-speaking coloured planter Julien Fédon, who like others of his class was aggrieved at the White British Protestant new order. Fédon captured the Governor and by 1796 had to all intents and purposes established in Craton's phrase, 'a black republic under arms' (op. cit, p. 241). The second Carib War meanwhile developed in St. Vincent, and both islands were only finally subdued in late 1797. This is also the period of the Final Maroon War in Jamaica. See Craton, op. cit., pp. 161ff.

35. Craton, ibid, pp. 261ff.

36. See Craton, ibid, pp. 277ff; and Cecil Northcott, *Slavery's Martyr*, Epworth, 1976.

37. See Craton, ibid, pp. 296ff; and C.S. Reid, *Samuel Sharpe: From Slave to Jamaican Hero*, Bustamante Institute, 1988.

   It was left to the Methodist missionary Henry Blaby to give the martyr's accolade to Sharpe, to whom it belonged: 'I was amazed at the power and freedom with which he spoke, and the effect which was produced upon his auditory . . . He thought, and he learned from his Bible, that the whites had no more right to hold black people in slavery than black people had to make the white people slaves.' Blaby noted Sharpe's disappointment that the revolt had gone out of control, and recorded his final words: 'I would rather die upon yonder gallows than live in slavery.' (Henry Blaby, *The Death Struggles of Slavery*, London 1853, pp. 115f., cited in Craton, p. 321).

38. Ibid, p. 242.

39. Ibid, p. 28.

40. On Quakers and slaveholding see Raboteau, ibid, pp. 109–110; on Quakers and the origins of the Abolition movement, see Wilmore, op. cit., pp. 78–83.

41. Raboteau, *Slave Religion*, pp. 143–145.

42. Wilmore, op. cit., p. 25.

43. See Carol V.R. George, *Segregated Sabbaths: Richard Allen and the Rise of Independent Churches*, O.U.P., 1973.

44. Wilmore, op. cit., p. 48.

45. Ibid, pp. 53–74.

CHAPTER 5: THE BLACK CHRISTIAN TRADITION — A TRIPLE INHERITANCE (pages 53–86)

1. Raboteau, *Slave Religion*, p. 141.

2. See Carol V.R. George, *Segregated Sabbaths: Richard Allen and the Rise of Independent Churches*, O.U.P., 1973.

3. Wilmore, *Black Religion and Black Radicalism*, p. 90.
4. Ibid, p. 93.
5. Elder Hawkins, 'Whence Have We Come?' in *Black Presbyterians United, Report to the Session*, Black Presbyterians United, Office of Black Mission Development, United Presbyterian Church, 475 Riverside Drive, New York, N.Y. 10115. See *Periscope*, 'Black Presbyterianism Yesterday, Today and Tomorrow, 175 Years of Ministry 1807–1982', Office of Black Mission Development, 1982, for a historical survey of Black Presbyterianism; and Gayraud Wilmore, *Black and Presbyterian, the Heritage and the Hope*, Geneva Press, Philadelphia, 1983.
6. See J. Carleton Hayden, 'Alexander Crummell: Afro-Anglican Pioneer in the United States, England and Liberia, 1819–1898' in *Linkage*, No. 5, Dec. 85/Jan. 86, Office of Black Ministries, Episcopal Church Center, 815 Second Avenue, New York, N.Y. 10017.

   Other publications available from the same address include *Black Clergy in the Episcopal Church: Recruitment, Training and Deployment*, 1981, and *The Recruitment of Black Clergy for the Episcopal Church. Some Biblical, Theological and Practical Considerations*, 1982.
7. *Lift Every Voice and Sing*, Church Hymnal Corporation, 800 Second Avenue, New York, N.Y. 10017, 1981. For the United Methodist Church's *Songs of Zion*, see bibliography.
8. The first Reformed Church Colloquium was held in 1975. Lectures include: William Bentley, 'Black Christianity: A Historical Overview'; Noel Erskine, 'The Fundamentals of Black Theology' (1975); Gayraud Wilmore, 'Identity Crisis: Blacks in Predominantly White Denominations' (1976); James Cone, 'The Social Context of Black Theology', and 'A Black Perspective on America: A Theological Interpretation' (1977); Howard Dodson, 'Strategies for Liberation (1978); Lawrence Jones, 'The Turning of the Wheel: An Historical Overview of Black White Relations in the Churches of America', and 'An Agenda for a Black Congregation in a Majority White Denomination' (1980); Lawrence Carter, 'The Dancers of Single Issue No-fault Morality'; McKinley Young 'Preaching in the 80's: The View of a local Pastor' (1981); Cornel West, 'The Sixties and Afro-America' (1983); Black Council of the Reformed Church in America, 1823 Interchurch Center, 475 Riverside Drive, New York, N.Y. 10115. For Black Catholic thought see *Ministry Among Black Americans*, St. Meinrad School of Theology, St. Meinrad, Indiana 47577; Clarence J. Rivers, *Soulfull Worship*, National Office for Black Catholics, 1234 Massachusetts Avenue NW., Washington D.C. 20005.
9. 'The New Black-led Pentecostal Churches in Britain' in Paul Bradham (ed.), *Religion State and Society in Modern Britain*, Edwin Mellen Press, 1989. See Wilmore, *Black Religion and Black Radicalism*, pp. 152–157.
10. Wilmore, op. cit., p. 232. See Walter Hollenweger, *Pentecost between Black and White*, Christian Journals, 1974, pp. 13ff. For reflection on the relationship of Black Pentecostalism to Black Power in the U.S.A., and the work of the Pentecostal pastor Arthur Brazier and the Woodlawn

Association in Chicago, see Rose Jackson, *The Nature and Role of Black Gospel Music in the Black Pentecostal Worship Service*, D. Min. dissertation (unpublished) for University of Chicago, 1986; and 'The Role of the Black Church' in *Celebrating the Black Family*, Claiming the Inheritance, Birmingham, 1988. Jackson was formerly Minister of Music at the Apostolic Church of God, Woodlawn, Chicago, where Brazier is Minister. When I visited this church on study leave in 1990, I was able to worship with its congregation of over 2000 members, to listen to critically aware interpretation of the Bible which was acutely relevant to the 'ghetto', and to study its social outreach ministry.

11. Louis-Charles Harvey, 'From Rejection to Liberation: The Development of the Black Church in Great Britain and the United States' in 'Claiming the Inheritance', *Racial Justice* No. 6, Evangelical Christians for Racial Justice, p. 19.
12. See Wilmore, op. cit., p. 36.
13. Ibid, pp. 38ff.
14. Ibid, p. 121.
15. James W. Hood, *One Hundred Years of the African Methodist Episcopal Zion Church*, A.M.E.Z. Book Concern, 1895, quoted in Wilmore, op. cit., p. 121.
16. Daniel Coker to Jeremiah Watts, April 3rd 1820, from 'Journal of Daniel Coker', quoted in Wilmore, op. cit., p. 105.
17. See Wilmore, pp. 109ff.
18. See ibid, pp. 113ff.
19. Ibid, p. 122ff.
20. Ibid, p. 134.
21. See Booker T. Washington, *Up from Slavery*, Carol, 1989 (reprint); and Robert M. Franklin, *Liberating Visions: Human Fulfilment and Social Justice in African-American Thought*, Fortress, 1990, pp. 11ff.
22. See ibid, pp. 145ff.; Barrett, The Rastafarians pp. 64–67, 76–81; Rupert Lewis, *Marcus Garvey: Anti-colonial Champion*, Karia Press, 1987; Tony Martin, *Marcus Garvey, Hero: a First Biography*, Majority Press, 1983; and Amy Jaques-Garvey (ed.), *The Philosophy and Opinions of Marcus Garvey*, Arno Press, 1969.
23. St. Clari Drake and Horace Clayton, *Black Metropolis*, Harcourt, Brace, 1945, p. 381, quoted in Wilmore, op. cit., p. 162.
24. Wilmore, ibid, p. 172.
25. See Wilmore, ibid, pp. 174ff.; Theo Witvliet, *The Way of the Black Messiah*, SCM, 1987, pp. 117ff.; John J. Ansbro, *Martin Luther King Jr.: the Making of a Mind*, Orbis, 1982; and James Cone, *Martin, Malcolm and America: a Dream or a Nightmare?*, Orbis, 1991.
26. See James H. Cone, *Martin, Malcolm and America: a Dream or a Nightmare?*, Orbis, 1991, pp. 213ff.
27. James Baldwin, *The Fire Next Time*, Penguin, 1964, p. 81.
28. See Wilmore, op. cit., pp. 183ff.; Witvliet, op. cit., pp. 137ff.; and Cone, op. cit., pp. 38ff.
29. This analysis of the role of the Black Church is relevant also to Britain,

where it finds echoes among secular Black radicals, and, from a different standpoint, among Rastafarians: see Ernest Cashmore, *Rastaman*, George Allen and Unwin, 1979, p. 73.

30. Harvey, 'From Immigration to Integration: The Exodus Experience of Black People in the United States and Great Britain', *Racial Justice*, No. 6, p. 8.

31. Wilmore, op. cit., p. 188.

32. See ibid, pp. 192ff., and Gayraud Wilmore and James Cone (eds.), *Black Theology, A Documentary History, 1966–1975*, Orbis, 1979. On the consequences in theological education, see Gayraud S. Wilmore, *The Historical Mandate for African American Theological Education*, unpublished mss., 1989; and Charles Shelby Rooks, *Revolution in Zion: Reshaping African-American Ministry, 1960–1974*, Pilgrim, 1990.

33. See Wilmore and Cone, op. cit., pp. 80–89.

34. James H. Cone, *Black Theology and Black Power*, Seabury, 1969; 20th anniversary edition with new preface, Harper and Row, 1989.

35. Ibid, pp. 39f.

36. Jon Sobrino, 'Theological Understanding in European and Latin American Theology', in *The True Church and the Poor*, SCM, 1985, p. 16.

37. James Cone, *A Black Theology of Liberation*, 2nd Edition, Orbis, 1986.

38. James Cone.

39. See Helmut Gollwitzer, 'Why Black Theology?' in Wilmore and Cone, *Black Theology*, pp. 152–173. Gollwitzer acknowledges white guilt and the necessity for practical repentance, but makes the criticism that the significance of the Cross is God's judgement on all people, black and white, though different in concrete form.

40. Paul Lehmann, in 'Black Theology and Christian Theology' in Wilmore and Cone, op. cit., pp. 144–151, asks whether Cone has neglected the mutual need of oppressed and oppressor for forgiveness.

41. Ibid, p. 101f.

42. Ibid, p. 181.

43. Wilmore, *Black Religion and Black Radicalism*, p. 215.

44. Witvliet, *The Way of the Black Messiah*, p. 176.

45. Wilmore, op. cit., pp. 218–219.

46. Ibid, pp. 223–224.

47. See Cone, Introduction to the Second Edition of *A Black Theology of Liberation*, pp. xvii–xx; *For My People, Black Theology and the Black Church*, Orbis, 1984, chapters 6, 7 and 8; Witvliet op. cit., pp. 239–242; and Wilmore and Cone, *Black Theology* Part V. See Jaquelyn Grant, *White Women's Christ and Black Women's Jesus: Feminist Christology and Womanist Response*, Scholars Press, 1989; Renita Weems, 'Reading Her Way through the Struggle: African American Women and the Bible', in Cain H. Felder, *Stony the Road We Trod: African American Biblical Interpretation*, Fortress Press, 1991; and writings of Kelly Brown, Clarice Martin, Cheryl Sanders, Delores Williams.

48. See Cone, *For My People*, pp. 175–188.

49. Cornel West, in Sergio Torres and John Eagleson (eds.), *Theology in*

the Americas, Orbis, 1976; quoted in Witvliet, *The Way of the Black Messiah*, p. 238.

50. Cone, *For My People*, pp. 186–187.
51. Witvliet, *The Way of the Black Messiah*, p. 239.
52. Part of the task of 'decolonizing' Caribbean theology is to replace the colonial consciousness of the 'West Indies' with consciousness of the 'Caribbean Basin', with its varied and separated territories and four principal languages of French, Dutch, Spanish and English, as well as related *patios*; see Ashley Smith, "Christ the Hope of the Caribbean" in *Real Roots and Potted Plants*, Mandeville Publishers, Jamaica, 1984, pp. 9–16. See bibliography for developments in Caribbean theology and Theo Witvliet, *A Place in the Sun*, SCM, 1985, pp. 104–117, for an overview.
53. Erskine, *Decolonizing Theology*, p. 75.
54. Ibid, p. 71.
55. Ibid, p. 70; see also Philip D. Curtin, *Two Jamaicas: The Role of Ideas in a Tropical Colony 1830–1865*, Harvard UP, 1955, (reprinted New York: Atheneum, 1970).
56. C.E. Lincoln, *The Black Experience in Religion*, Doubleday, 1974, p. 336, quoted by Louis-Charles Harvey in *Black Religion in USA and Great Britain* (unpublished manuscript), ch. 2, p. 34; see Leonard Barrett, *The Sun and The Drum*, Sangsters Book Stores/Heinemann, 1976, pp. 17–24.
57. Ivor Morrish, *Obeah, Christ and Rastaman*, James Clarke, 1982, p. 42; see Leonard Barrett, *Soul-Force: African Heritage in Afro-American Religion*, Doubleday, 1974, p. 319; and Barrett, *The Sun and The Drum*, pp. 24–27.
58. Walter Hark, *Breaking of the Dawn*, 1754–1904, Jamaica Moravian Church, 1904, p. 88, quoted in Erskine, *Decolonizing Theology*, p. 79.
59. Erskine, *Decolonizing Theology*, p. 77.
60. Morrish, *Obeah, Christ and Rastaman*, p. 92.
61. See Barrett, *The Rastafarians*, pp. 51ff.
62. Ibid, pp. 22ff.; Morrish, op. cit., pp. 40–67.
63. Iain MacRobert, "The New Black-led Pentecostal Churches in Britain" in Paul Badham, *Religion State and Society in Modern Britain*, Edwin Mellen Press, 1989, pp. 121ff.
64. *Statistic Yearbook of Jamaica*, Department of Statistics, Kingston, 1974, quoted in MacRobert, ibid.
65. MacRobert, ibid, p. 126.
66. On Rastafarians in Jamaica, see Barrett, *The Rastafarians*; Cashmore, *Rastaman*, pp. 13–37, Ivor Morrish, *Obeah, Christ and Rastaman*, James Clark, 1982; and Joseph Owens, *Dread: the Rastafarians of Jamaica*, Sangster, 1976.
67. On Rastafarians and the Ethiopian Orthodox Church in Jamaica, see Barrett, op. cit., pp. 201–209; in England, see Cashmore, op. cit., pp. 52–69.
68. Morrish, op. cit., p. 85.

69. See Barrett, *The Rastafarians*, pp. 193ff.; Cashmore, *Rastaman*, pp. 98ff.
70. Cashmore, *Rastaman*, pp. 52–53.
71. For other such testimonies see John Wilkinson, Renate Wilkinson and James Evans: *Inheritors Together*, Board of Social Responsibility of the Church of England, 1985, pp. 13 and 29–36. Also, Sylvia Estridge, "I Came to England" in *Celebrating the Black Family*, Claiming the Inheritance, Birmingham, 1988.
72. Ira Brooks, *Where do we go from here?*, New Testament Church of God, 1983, p. 13.
73. See Iain MacRobert, *Black Pentecostalism in Britain*, St Andrew Press, 1992.
74. Paul Burrough, *West Indians in Britain*, newspaper article in Birmingham Diocesan archive.
75. See S.E. Arnold, *From Scepticism to Hope*, Grove Books, 1992.
76. Roswith Gerloff, *The Development of Black Churches in Britain Since 1952*, paper presented to History Workshop on Religion and Society, 1983, pp. 14ff. See also Gerloff, *A Plea for British Black Theologies*, Verlag Peter Lang, 1992.
77. Harvey, *Black Religion in USA and Great Britain* (unpublished ms.), ch. 3, p. 26.
78. Gerloff, op. cit., pp. 10ff.
79. Ira Brooks, *Another Gentleman to the Ministry*, 1985.
80. Heather Walton, *A Tree God Planted*, p. 48 (ministers), pp. 40–41 (other leaders). For the most recent Methodist reflection on this situation, see "Faithful and Equal", Report of the Methodist D.S.R., *Agenda of the 1987 Methodist Conference*, Methodist Church, 1987, pp. 156–193.
81. Renate Wilkinson, "A Chance to Change", M.Sc. thesis for the University of Aston (1984), abbreviated in *Inheritors Together*, B.S.R. of the Church of England, 1985. The Diocese of Southwark has produced *Black Anglicans in the Southwark Diocese*, Southwark Diocesan Race Relations Commission, 48 Union Street, London SE1 1TD. On only a 50% return, this survey shows: 15% of Anglicans in Southwark are Black, 3.6% of people in positions of responsibility, 4.1% of Deanery Synod members, 3.4% of Diocesan Synod members, 2 out of 15 General Synod members (13%), and 1.7% of clergy (8 out of 461).
82. Cashmore, *Rastaman*, p. 149.
83. Ibid, p. 73.
84. Harvey, *Black Religion in USA and Great Britain*, ch. 3, p. 29.

CHAPTER 6: COMPREHENSIVENESS AND BLACK CHRISTIANITY (pages 87–100)

1. David Moore, *Invisible People*, 1984, unpublished paper for Race, Pluralism and Community Group, Church of England.
2. The classic Anglican statement on the Authority of Scripture is the sixth of the Thirty-Nine Articles, "Holy Scripture containeth all things necessary to salvation . . ." (1571, from the Forty-two Articles of 1553). The

article reflects the wider movement of both the Lutheran and the Swiss Reformations. It is the basis of the second question asked of clergy at ordinations, and similar to the second sentence of the Declaration of Assent ("The Church of England . . . professes the faith uniquely revealed in the Holy Scriptures . . ."), which is also required of clergy.

In modern times the Church of England has shared the wider debate within theology in response to the rise of critical scholarship, notably the Biblical Theology school. Many students have been particularly influenced by the Congrgationalist theologian C.H. Dodd (see his *The Authority of the Bible*, Nisbet, 1928) and by Barth's distinction between The Word of God and Scripture as the witness to God's activity in history (Karl Barth, *Church Dogmatics*, T. & T. Clarke, 1936–1969, I/1: p. 126. For an influential article by a noted Anglican, see A.M. Ramsay, "The Authority of the Bible", in *Peake's Commentary on the Bible*, Nelson, 1962. See also, L. Hodgson *et al.*, *On the Authority of the Bible*, S.P.C.K., 1960, and J. Muddiman, *The Bible, Fountain and Well of Truth*, Blackwell, 1983.

3. Alan Richardson, *An Introduction to the Theology of the New Testament*, SCM, 1958.
4. *Oxford Book of Carols*, O.U.P., 1928.
5. Richardson, *Theology of the New Testament*, pp. 284f.; see also Walter J. Hollenweger, *Conflict in Corinth*, Paulist Press, 1982, p. 5.
6. Richardson, ibid, pp. 268–7.
7. Ibid, p. 266.
8. Ibid, p. 258ff.
9. Ibid, p. 257.
10. Ibid, pp. 254ff.
11. Ibid, p. 288.
12. Ibid, p. 289.
13. Rudolph Bultmann, *Theology of the New Testament*, Vol. 1, SCM, 1952, p. 93.
14. ibid, p. 100.
15. Ibid, p. 101.
16. Stephen Neil, *Anglicanism*, Penguin, 1958, pp. 417–434; W. Wolf (ed.) *The Spirit of Anglicanism*, T. and T. Clark, 1982.
17. A.M. Ramsay, *The Gospel and the Catholic Church*, Longmans, 1936, p. 220.
18. John Whale, *The Future of Anglicanism*, Mowbrays, 1988, p. 90.
19. Wolf (ed.) *The Spirit of Anglicanism*, p. 165.
20. Ibid, p. 153.
21. Charles Gore, *Roman Catholic Claims*, Murray, 1892, p. xii, cited in Wolf, ibid, p. 155.
22. See the *Thirty-Nine Articles* in the Book of Common Prayer. They reached their present form in 1571, but are substantially the work of Cranmer. They owe much to the Lutheran Augsburg Confession of 1530, and define clearly, but not unduly narrowly, the Anglican position against medieval Catholic corruption, as well as against the more

extreme Calvinism and Anabaptist teachings. See especially articles *v* (Scripture), *viii* (Creeds), *xxiv* (Language), *xi* (Grace), and *xxxi* (Christ's One Oblation).

23. Richard Hooker, *The Laws of Ecclesiastical Polity* II & VII.5. For an extended consideration of Hooker, see Wolf (ed.). *The Spirit of Anglicanism*, chapter 1.

24. Quoted in Wolf, ibid, p. 144.

25. For a summary of Wesley's spiritual struggle leading to his conversion, the influence of the Moravians, see Maldwyn Edwards, "John Wesley" in R.E. Davies and E.G. Rupp, *A History of the Methodist Church in Great Britain*, Vol. I, pp. 46–50. Wesley's own description of his conversion is: "About a quarter before nine, while he was describing the change which God works in the heart through faith in Christ, I felt my heart strangely warmed. I felt I did trust in Christ alone for my salvation, and an assurance was given me that he had taken away my sins, even *mine* and saved me from the law of sin and death."

26. The first English Prayer Book was issued in 1549; the subsequent 1552 book was a revision in much more Protestant direction. The ecclesiastical settlement of 1662 failed in its attempt to include the Puritan clergy of the Commonwealth Church, thus making the publication of the 1662 Book as much an occasion of exclusion as of comprehension. Nonconformists became a deprived "nation within a nation", see Neil, *Anglicanism*, pp. 164–166.

27. John S. Habgood, "On Being a Liturgical Reviser", *Theology*, March 1979, p. 97.

28. Ibid, p. 98.

29. John S. Pobee, "Newer Dioceses of the Anglican Communion – Movement and Prospect", in *The Study of Anglicanism*, ed. Stephen Sykes and John Booty, S.P.C.K., 1988, p. 397.

30. Ibid, p. 402.

31. Cornel West, "Black Theology and Marxist Thought" in Gayraud S. Wilmore and James H. Cone, *Black Theology: A Documentary History 1966–1979*, Orbis, 1979, p. 554.

32. See Klaus Wengst, *Pax Romana and the Peace of Jesus Christ*, SCM, 1987.

33. See Tissa Balasuriya, *The Eucharist and Human Liberation*, SCM, 1977, especially pp. 36–41, and pp. 79ff.

34. See G. Cope "Vestments" in J.G. Davies (ed.) *A New Dictonary of Liturgy and Worship*, SCM, 1985. The Christian use of the stole derives from a scarf worn by Roman officials as a badge of rank; the chasuble and cope both derive from the outer garment generally worn in the Graeco-Roman world. The alb is directly derived from the 'tunica alba' of classical times.

35. See W.H.C. Frend, *The Donatist Church*, O.U.P., 1952, especially pp. 333ff.

36. See J.N.D. Kelly, *Early Christian Doctrines*, A. and C. Black, 1958, pp. 338–343; and Maurice Wiles, *The Christian Fathers*. Hodder and Stoughton, 1966, p. 80, for passing reference to political factors.

37. Interestingly, a stream of modern Black Pentecostals reject orthodox Trinitarian doctrine. Roswith Gerloff in a recent examination of the Oneness (Apostolic) tradition suggests that it is a response of the dispossessed and poor to confusion over a dogma which has lost its meaning and suggestive power to the masses, and continues, "the re-examination of Trinitarian dogma is part and parcel of the conscious and unconscious struggle of Black people against white impositions" (Roswith Gerloff, "Blackness and Oneness (Apostolic) Theology", paper presented to the Annual Conference of the Society for Caribbean Studies, 1985). Of course neither Black Anglicans nor most Black Pentecostals hold to the 'Oneness' doctrine. But the example shows how close to the 'core' the Black challenge may ultimately be. See also "Towards a Common Expression of Faith: A Black North American Perspective" from the Richmond (Virginia) Consultation, 1984, reviewed in *Christian Century*, June 1985. The statement contrasts the Black traditions of Unity, Holiness, Catholicity and Apostolicity with white Euro-centric tradition: "We deplore the fact that the profession of universality has actually meant that the norms of what is considered acceptable to the Church had to originate in the West. For years anything that white Christians . . . did not interpret as catholic lay outside the realm of true faith and proper order. Such assumptions . . . permitted the gospel to be used to divide people rather than free them to express the fullness of the faith in their own cultural styles and traditions."

38. See two hymnals from majority white "mainstream" churches in the United States: *Lift Every Voice and Sing* (Church Hymnal Corporation, New York, 1981), a U.S. Episcopalian collection of hymns, songs and spirituals from the Black tradition – *Songs of Zion* (Abingdon Press, Nashville, 1981), a "songbook from the Black religious tradition" from the United Methodist Church. This extensive collection has three main sections, hymns, spirituals and Black gospel, together with songs for special occasions and service music. J. Jefferson Cleveland's introduction to the section describes how white evangelical hymns from Watts and Wesley down to the Sankey era were "made over", converted and adapted into Black hymns. "Amazing Grace", "Jesus, Lover of my Soul" and "Leaning on the Everlasting arms" are three famous examples from a long list. See also Viv Broughton, *Black Gospel: an Illustrated History of the Gospel Sound*, Blandford Press, 1985, pp. 11–27; and Rose C. Jackson, *The Nature and Role of Black Gospel Music in the Black Pentecostal Worship Service*, dissertation submitted to the University of Chicago Divinity School for D. Min. degree, 1986 (unpublished), chapter 1.

39. See James H. Cone, *God of the Oppressed*, Seabury 1975, pp. 30ff.

40. cf. Cone, ibid, p. 128: "I am baffled that many American white theologians still continue to do theology independently of the oppressed of the land."

41. On the Black Interpretation of the Bible see also Felder, *Troubling*

Biblical Waters; Felder (ed.), *Stony the Road We Trod*; and, Itumeleng J. Mosala, *Biblical Hermeneutics and Black Theology in South Africa*, Grand Rapids: Eerdmans, 1989.

42. Lesslie Newbigin, *The Other Side of 1984*, W.C.C., Geneva, 1984, p. 48.
43. Cone, *God of the Oppressed*, pp. 19–20.
44. Preface to the *Book of Common Prayer*, 1662.
45. See for example, from North America, Norman K. Gottwald, *The Tribes of Yahweh*, Orbis 1979, pp. 9f.; and, from Latin America, Jon Sobrino, *The True Church and the Poor*, SCM 1985, pp. 7–38.
46. Cone, *God of the Oppressed*, p. 46.
47. Ibid, p. 49.
48. Ibid, p. 55.
49. Barney Pityana, "A Black Anglican Perspective", in *Anglicans and Racism*, Board of Social Responsibility, Church of England, 1986.

CHAPTER 7: NAMING BLACK AS BLACK
(pages 101–132)

1. Graham Leonard, Bishop of London, letter to James Evans, 1983, quoted in James Evans, 'The Struggle for Identity: Black People in the Church of England', in J. Wilkinson, R. Wilkinson, J. Evans, *Inheritors Together*, p. 61.
2. Ibid, p. 61.
3. The crowd in Acts 2 name the apostles as Galileans, whilst the crowd itself is named as Parthian, Mede, Elamite and so on. Those who had crucified Jesus were a conspiracy of similarly international identities ('Herod and Pontius Pilate conspired with the Gentiles and the peoples of Israel,' Acts 4:27).
4. Undertaken in 1985.
5. But see chapter 9 for recent developments, and for details of the Centre for Black and White Christian Partnership.
6. A remark made in conversation with the author.
7. This paragraph summarizes my own experience as a parish priest, and includes details not specfically mentioned in the Project group.
8. See chapter 2, p. 8.
9. See Balasuriya, *The Eucharist and Human Liberation*, pp. 74ff. for the inadequacy of reform of the externals of worship as a response to the experience of young people in Sri Lanka.
10. This does not quite mean that present distresses are actually the final battle of God against the forces of evil as seen in the vision of St. John the Divine, but that we are experiencing a time which indicates that the end will come soon. The little Apocalypse in the Synoptic Gospels is most often quoted in this connection: 'you will hear of wars and rumours of wars: see that you are not alarmed; for this must take place but the end is not yet. For nation will rise against nation, and kingdom against kingdom, and there will be famines and earthquakes in various places: all this is but the beginning of the sufferings. Then . . . you will be hated

by all nations for my name's sake . . . many will fall away . . . most men's love will grow cold. But he who endures to the end will be saved. And this gospel will be preached throughout the whole world . . . and then the end will come' (Matthew 24[6–14]).

CHAPTER 8: PLUMBLINES AND NEW BUILDING
(pages 133–170)

1. Cf. the title of the Birmingham Anglican diocese's R.R.G. paper, *Building a Black and White Church, Recommendations to the Bishop's Council of the Diocese of Birmingham*, 1985.
2. Cornel West, 'Black Theology and Marxist Thought' in Wilmore and Cone, *Black Theology*, p. 554.
3. But see Paul Grant and Raj Patel, *A Time to Speak: Perspectives of Black Christians in Britain*, Racial Justice (E.C.R.J.)/ Black Theology Working Group, 1990; and *A Time to Act*, Racial Justice (E.C.R.J.)/ Black and Third World Theology Working Group, 1992.
4. Louis-Charles Harvey, 'From Rejection to Liberation: the Development of the Black Church in Great Britain and the United States,' in 'Claiming the Inheritance', *Racial Justice* No. 6, Spring 1987, E.C.R.J., p. 23.
5. The term 'Black Church' is American; the preference in Britain is for 'Black-led'. Harvey writes, 'The feeling presented to me (by Black church leaders) was that Black signifies separation and not together-ness . . . this problem of nomenclature is reflective of [the] problem the black church in Britain is wrestling with, that is the problem of relating belief to active and substantial protest against their economic exploita-tion and racial suffering.' Harvey, *Black Religion in the U.S.A. and Great Britain* (unpublished mss.), ch. 3, p. 9).
6. C.T.I. arose partly out of the *Living Faith Project* and partly out of a response of the Community Relations Committee of the Methodist Church in Birmingham to the needs of its younger Black members.
7. See Roderick Hewitt, *Reflections on the Handsworth Riot*, unpublished mss., 1985.
8. see Fryer, *Staying Power*, pp. 98–112.
9. On Wilberforce, see John Pollock, *Wilberforce*, Lion, 1977. On the relative importance of economic and humanitarian factors in the abolition of slavery, see Fryer, *Staying Power*, pp. 207ff. and Eric Williams, *Capitalism and Slavery*, University of North Carolina Press, 1944. Sharp's work brought about the famous Mansfield judgement (1772) on the case of James Somerset, that no slave could be returned to the West Indies from Britain against his or her will; see Fryer, op. cit., pp. 115–126.
10. Louis-Charles Harvey, 'From Rejection to Liberation: The Develop-ment of the Black Church in Great Britain and the United States'; and 'From Immigration to Integration: The Exodus Experience of Black People in the United States and Great Britain'; in 'Claiming the Inheritance'.

11. Sybil Phoenix, 'The Black British Family in the Church', in *Celebrating the Black Family*, Claiming the Inheritance, 1988.

12. David Divine, 'The Black British Family in Society', in *Celebrating the Black Family*.

13. Rose Jackson, 'The Role of the Black Church' in *Celebrating the Black Family*.

14. See Kenneth Leech, *Struggle in Babylon*, Sheldon Press, 1988, pp. 64ff.; Peter Fryer, *Staying Power: The History of Black People in Britain*, Pluto Press, 1984, pp. 376ff., and Paul Rich, 'The Politics of Race Relations,' in (ed.) Peter Jackson, *Race and Racism: Essays in Social Geography*, Allen and Unwin, 1987.

    At Smethwick Peter Griffiths stood for the Conservatives on an openly racist platform with the notorious slogan, 'If you want a nigger neighbour, vote Labour'. The sociologist Stuart Hall describes this as 'the first moment when racism is appropriated into the official policy and programme of a major political party and legitimated as the basis of an electoral appeal' ('Racism and Reaction' in *Five Views of Multi-Racial Britain*, 1978, p. 29 cited in Fryer, op. cit., p. 382).

15. See Sheila Patterson, *Immigration and Race Relations in Britain 1960–67*, Institute of Race Relations and Oxford University Press, 1969; John Rex and Sally Thompson, *Colonial Immigrants in a British City, a Class Analysis*, Routledge and Kegan Paul, 1979, and Fryer, op. cit., pp. 381ff.

16. Roswith Gerloff, *A Plea for British Black Theologies*, (Studies in the Intercultural History of Christianity no. 77, 2 vols), Verlag Peter Lang, 1992.

17. Roswith Gerloff, in 'Dialogue between Revd. Roswith Gerloff and Revd. Bongani Mazibuko,' *10 Years of Spiritual Challenge*, Centre for Black and White Christian Partnership, Birmingham, 1988.

18. For examples of Black criticism of society see Gus John: *Because They're Black*, Penguin, 1971; and *Race in the Inner City*, Runnymede Trust, 1972. An early work in the field of education, one which gave rise to considerable public debate, was: Bernard Coard, *How the West Indian Child is made ESN in the British School System*, New Beacon Books, 1972.

19. *The New Black Presence in Britain: a Christian Scrutiny*, B.C.C., 1976, pp. 17ff.

20. *The New Black Presence*, p. 23.

21. See David Sheppard, *Bias to the Poor*, Hodder and Stoughton, pp. 65–66, and 103. A history of the work of CRRU in the 21 years of its life, which is being prepared by its former Executive Secretary, David Haslam, should be available in 1993.

22. Ian Martin, 'The Racism of Present Immigration Policy,' in *Vigil: What about Immigration?*, Christian Action, Winter 1981.

23. See *Report of Proceedings* Vol. 8, No. 2, July 1977, CIO, pp. 513ff.

24. *Report of Proceedings* Vol. 9, No. 3, November 1978, CIO, pp. 1144ff.

25. 'Immigration and Racial Justice: a Christian Statement', *Vigil*, p. 17.

26. The Archbishop of Canterbury attacked the Bill as 'seriously defective', criticizing it as a source of anxiety and fear to minority communities which was, moreover, difficult to understand, would create a need to

register where none had existed before, and raised the spectre of Black people being challenged to prove their citizenship in the course of ordinary life. He made the important point that reactions to the Bill must be understood 'in the context of experiences the ethnic minorities have been through'. They needed security, whereas the Bill contained not even a preamble affirming the multi-racial nature of the national identity. *Parliamentary Debates (Hansard), House of Lords*, Vol. 421 (8 June–26 June 1981), pp. 875f.

27. Robinson Milwood, *Let's Journey Together*, Methodist D.S.R., 1980, p. 15.
28. See *Report of Proceedings*, Vol. 8 No. 2 (1977), pp. 513–564.
29. Ibid, p. 16.
30. David Moore, *Invisible People: Black People in the Church of England*, (unpublished) 1984, pp. 16–18.
31. *Inheritors Together*, p. 31.
32. Ibid, p. 68.
33. Ibid, p. 67.
34. Kenneth Leech lists several important weaknesses of the report: the 'tendency to raise problems and run away from them'; circumlocutory terminology at sensitive points; a weak understanding of racism and class; and an ignoring of the Church of England's class and cultural role in the nation. Perhaps the most serious indictment is of its theology, or rather lack of it: 'beyond brief allusions . . . there is no gospel in the report. We are told nothing of incarnation, redemption, transformation or sanctification. There is no Kingdom theology beyond the two brief references . . . ACUPA begs the question of whether the role of the Church is to witness to a different set of values and therefore to a different ordering of society which will embody those values more adequately.' *Struggle in Babylon*, pp. 140–150.
35. *Faith in the City*, p. 42, pp. 96–100.
36. Ibid, pp. 107, 120, 135.
37. See *Report of Proceedings*, Vol.17, No.1, February 1986, CIO. The rejection (by a very small majority) of the proposal for a Standing Commission caused great hurt among Black Anglicans. The Standing Committee of General Synod was given the task of formulating alternative proposals which were adopted at the July Synod of 1986 (*Report of Proceedings* Vol. 17, No. 2); see also *Faith in the City: Minority Ethnic Groups, Report by the Standing Committee*, (GS 753). Feelings there were clearly running high; Canon Ivor Smith-Cameron, one of Synod's very few Black clergy, said that the earlier recommendation of the Standing Committee, an all-White body, to support all 61 recommendations of *Faith in the City* except the one for a Black Commission (see *Faith in the City: the General Synod's Response, Report by the Standing Committee*, GS 715) had sent 'a wave of bewilderment, distress, frustration and horror through the black constituencies both in the Church and in society outside the Church.'
38. On a straight vote there was a majority of Synod in favour of the measure

(200–161). It was defeated by a procedural measure: Penny Grainger of the Diocese of Ely called for a division by houses and the Measure went down to an adverse vote in the House of Laity (80–96), [cf. Clergy 103–62 and Bishops 17–3.] Anger among Black members was exacerbated by the means used, and because White Synod members who had helped prepare the legislation were among those who voted against it. *Church Times*, 10 February 1989.

39. James H. Cone, *Black Theology and Black Power*, Seabury Press, 1969, p. 66; quoted in *Anglicans and Racism* (the 'Balsall Heath Report'), p. 7.
40. *Anglicans and Racism*, pp. 5–15.
41. Ibid, pp. 16f.
42. Ibid, pp. 18–22.
43. Ibid, pp. 23–32.
44. Ibid, p. 40.
45. Heather Walton. *A Tree God Planted*, Methodist Church DSR, 1985; *Faithful and Equal* (a report adopted at the Portsmouth Methodist Conference, 1987), Methodist Church DSR, 1987. See also: Ethnic Minorities in Methodism Working Party, 'Race, Racism and the Life of the Church,' *Epworth Review* Vol. 11, No. 2, May 1984, which supplies a Biblical understanding of 'race' and the need to build a racially just society and church, and acknowledges that the church is culturally plural, but is not explicit about the Black Christian Tradition or its dialectically critical role in relation to a 'mainstream' White church.
46. Renate Wilkinson, 'A Chance to Change,' in Wilkinson, Wilkinson and Evans, *Inheritors Together*, p. 41.
47. *Black Anglicans in Birmingham*, pp. 22–29 and 40–44.
48. *D.E.C. ACUPA Day Conference, Response by Diocesan Race Relations Group*, (report of R.R.G. delegates to the R.R.G.), 1986, (unpublished).
49. Black attenders were less likely than White attenders to be on the Electoral Roll (the list of registered members) – the ratio of attenders to members was: Whites 10:13.7, Blacks 10:5).

Black Sunday School children were the same proportion of all Sunday School children as Black adult members were of total membership (9%), but Black teachers were under-represented (7% taking mixed congregations only).

Black people were under-represented on Parochial Church Councils; over half the churches with mixed congregations had no Black P.C.C. members).

Black people were under-represented among church officers (7% of church-wardens, 1.5% of treasurers, no P.C.C. secretaries), 14 out of 276 paid employees – 8 of whom were cleaners), in synods (2 out of 135 Diocesan Synod lay representatives), and in the stipendiary ministry (1 only).

– statistics from 'A Chance to Change' (abbreviated version), in J.L. & R. Wilkinson and James Evans, *Inheritors Together*, Church of England B.S.R., 1985, pp. 22–28.

New statistics were collected in 1989 through the Archdeacons' annual

Visitation. Unfortunately the questions asked were not linked to those of *A Chance to Change* and direct comparisons are in most cases not possible. Some improvement was evident: 2 of the 6 General Synod representatives were Black; 3 of the Bishop's Council – good in absolute terms; 5 stipendiary clergy and 5 Diocesan Synod members – better than 1983, but far from 7%; Black membership of P.C.C.s was in some deaneries encouragingly near that of Black membership of the Electoral Roll, and in two cases actually higher. Black people constitute 5.4% of all the Diocese's Electoral Rolls (cf. *A Chance to Change*'s 10% of mixed congregations only). The Archdeacons did not enquire about attendance, so no comparison with the 7% figure is possible. It should be born in mind, however, that Black people are much more likely to be regular attenders but not formally members than White people.

– statistics from *Black People's Participation in the Anglican Diocese of Birmingham*, Diocesan C.B.A., 1989.

The numbers do not suggest a significant erosion of Black Anglican numbers as a proportion of White, but neither do they show significant progress in eliminating institutional racism.

50. *Building a Black and White Church, Recommendations to the Bishop's Council of the Diocese of Birmingham*, 1985. For resources available from other dioceses see: *Seeds of Hope: Report of a Survey on Combatting Racism in the Dioceses of the Church of England* (GS 977), General Synod of the Church of England, 1991, pp. 29ff.

51. *Equal Opportunity Policy for the Birmingham Diocesan Board of Finance*, Birmingham D.B.F., 1986.

52. see above, note 49.

53. *Seeds of Hope*, p. 10.

54. *Faith in the City*, pp. 119f.

55. Milwood, *Let's Journey Together*, p. 26.

56. Kenneth Cracknell, David Jennings and Christine Trethowan, *Blind Leaders for the Blind? Theological Education in Today's Plural Society*, AFFOR, 1981.

57. Peter Russell, George Mulrain, Maurice Hobbs, and Heather Walton, *Race and Theological Education, a Discussion Paper*, Methodist Church D.S.R., 1983. At that time Peter Russell was Principal of Kingsmead College (Methodist Overseas Division), Maurice Hobbs was Chair of the Evangelical Race Relations Group (now E.C.R.J.), and Heather Walton was Research Officer for the Working Party on Ethnic Minorities in Methodism.

58. See for example, *Partners in Practice*, A Discussion Document produced by the B.C.C., arising from the visit of Overseas Theological Educators during 1987, B.C.C. 1989, passim.

59. The 1987 Methodist Conference, in approving the D.S.R.'s report *Faithful and Equal*, 'urged' racism awareness training for all ordinands and for ministers who are to become Circuit Superintendent or Chairman of District; Methodist Conference Agenda, 1987, p. 188.

60. James Walker, in a letter to Brian Russell, Secretary to the ACCM Committee for Theological Education, 11 November, 1988.

61. Simon of Cyrene, the African who was 'compelled' to bear the cross (Mt. 27[32]), is here seen as the representative figure of the Black Church; cf. Rose Jackson, 'The role of the Black Church', in *Celebrating the Black Family*, pp. 24–26.
62. *Simon of Cyrene Theological Institute*, introductory leaflet, S.o.C.T.I., p. 6.

CHAPTER 9: MEETING AROUND THE CROSS
(pages 171–200)

1. Gerhard Kamphausen, 'Cadbury Lectures', University of Birmingham, 1982 (unpublished).
2. See Cone, *The Spirituals and the Blues*, p. 36.
3. See *West Indian Children in our Schools: interim report of the committee of enquiry into the education of children from ethnic minority groups* (the 'Rampton' Report), Cmnd. 8273, HMSO, (1981), pp. 13,55; *Education for All: The Report of the Committee into the Education of Children from Ethnic Minority Groups* (the 'Swann' Report), Cmnd. 9452, HMSO, 1985, p. 15; and *Talking Chalk: Black Pupils, Parents and Teachers Speak about Education*, AFFOR, Birmingham, 1982, p. 39.
4. Testimony of a church member in Edgbaston, Birmingham, to the author.
5. See Orlando Patterson, *The Sociology of Slavery*, McGibbons Kee, 1967, pp. 56–65. Patterson describes a three-fold hierarchy of domestics, skilled workers and field slaves. The skilled workers included boilermen, smiths, carpenters, coopers, doctors and nurses. There was a general correlation of status and colour, with deference paid to lighter shades and to slaves who worked in proximity to Whites.

   This colour gradation was of great psychological importance to the 'coloured' slaves, whose whole identity depended on it. As the black slaves taunted then, 'you brown man hab no country . . . only de neger and buckra (White man) got country.' Blacks themselves did not internalize these colour ideals, nor did they necessarily regard the higher status jobs as desirable. Some such as nurse were much coveted because of its 'emoluments,' but most domestic jobs made a slave vulnerable to the constant and capricious demands of the master or – even worse – his wife. A field slave had a relatively secure routine including leisure hours.
6. See Hazel V. Carby, 'Black Feminism and the Boundaries of Sisterhood', in Centre for Contemporary Cultural Studies, *The Empire Strikes Back*, Hutchinson, 1982, pp. 215, 219. A distinctly larger percentage of Afro-Caribbean women have 'higher' qualifications than do men (18% in the 25–44 age range, as against 11% for men in Spring 1985; see *Employment Gazette*, Vol. 95, No. 1, Department of Employment, Jan. 1987, pp. 165ff.). However, the importance of nursing as a source of employment for Black women is shown by the fact that ⅖ of higher qualifications obtained by West Indian women are in nursing (ibid.). On the exploitation of Black women in the Health Service despite the status

of nursing as a profession, see Ron Ramdin, *The Making of the Black Working Class in Britain*, Wildwood House, 1987, pp. 309ff. Nevertheless, 'qualified West Indian women' are the only category of Black people in employment who have a higher overall job level than their White equivalents (1984, see Colin Brown, *Black and White Britain: the third PSI survey*, Gower, 1985, p. 158.

7. Fryer, *Staying Power*, pp. 14–15.
8. Ibid, p. 46.
9. Ibid, p. 17.
10. Eric Williams, *Capitalism and Slavery*, Chapel Hill, University of North Carolina Press, 1944.
11. Basil Davidson, *Black Mother: Africa and the Atlantic Slave Trade*, Penguin, 1980, p. 83. Davidson is responding to the controversy Williams' thesis aroused.
12. For discussion of the theoretical understanding of European domination of the Third World, see R. Owen and B. Sutcliffe (eds) *Studies in the Theory of Imperialism*, Longmans; 1972, especially case studies in part 3.
13. For the economic relationship between North America and Western Europe and the Third World, and the ultimate threat posed to both groups of nations, see Brandt Commission *North South: A Programme for Survival*, 1979, and *Common Crisis North-South: Co-operation for World Recovery*, Pan Books, 1983.
14. *Common Crisis* pp. 121f.
15. Helmut Gollwitzer, *The Rich Christians and Poor Lazarus*, Saint Andrew Press, 1970, p. 9.
16. See John Pollock, *Wilberforce*, Lion, 1977; and W.E.B. DuBois, *John Brown*, New York: International, 1972.
17. Gollwitzer, op. cit., p. 10.
18. Walter Eichrodt, *Theology of the Old Testament* Vol. 2, SCM, 1962, p. 232.
19. D.R. Jones, 'Commentary on Isaiah II and III', in *Peake's Commentary on the Bible*, Nelson, 1962, pp. 523–4.
20. Keith Sinclair, *Theological Reflections on Racism*, unpublished paper delivered at Queen's College, Birmingham, June 1986.
21. See p. 88 above.
22. The author of the popular hymn, *Amazing Grace*, is John Newton, see ch. 3 note 26.
23. See Gerd Theissen, *The Social Setting of Pauline Christianity*, T. and T. Clark, 1982, pp. 69–137; and Hollenweger, *Conflict in Corinth*.
24. Theissen, op. cit., p. 56.
25. C.K. Barrett, *A Commentary on the First Epistle to the Corinthians*, A. & C. Black, 1968, p. 291.
26. Rowan Williams, *Resurrection*, Darton, Longman and Todd, 1982 p. 11.
27. Ibid, p. 12.
28. Ibid, pp. 13–16.
29. Ibid, pp. 13–16.
30. Ibid, p. 16.

31. Ibid., p. 19.
32. A.K. Hammar and A. Käppeli (eds), *Women in a Changing World* No. 25, W.C.C., 1988, quoted in Bridget Woollard, 'Mary had a Boy Child,' *Anvil* Vol. 5, No. 3, 1988.
33. Ibid, p. 79.
34. Cone, *God of the Oppressed* pp. 115ff.
35. James H. Cone, *The Spirituals and the Blues*, Harper and Row, 1972, pp. 52–54.
36. Ibid, pp. 63ff.
37. Ibid, p. 70.
38. Ibid, p. 69.
39. Ibid, p. 69.
40. Ibid, p. 136.
41. Cone, *God of the Oppressed*, p. 185.
42. Ibid, p. 186.
43. Karl Barth, *Church Dogmatics III*, T & T Clark, 1957, p.386, quoted in Allan Boesak, *Black and Reformed*, Orbis, 1984, p. 91.
44. Williams, op. cit., p. 16.
45. On this point see Maya Angelou, *The Heart of A Woman*, Virago, 1986, pp. 172ff.
46. In speaking of not returning violence I am not presuming to instruct Black people, or any other oppressed group, that they are obliged to forgo violence in their just cause. It is not for White people as oppressors to presume to determine what means are moral in the struggle against themselves! The real and terrible moral responsibilities involved here belong to the oppressed.
47. James H. Cone, *Black Theology and Black Power*, Seabury, 1968, pp. 26–28.
48. Gustavo Gutierrez: *We Drink From Our Own Wells*, SCM, 1984, p. 30.
49. Ibid, p. 18.
50. Ibid, p. 19.
51. Ibid, p. 19.
52. Quoted in Renate Wilkinson, 'A Chance to Change', in *Inheritors Together*, p. 34.
53. Cone, *The Spirituals and the Blues*, p. 42.
54. Williams, *Resurrection*, p. 34.
55. Ibid, pp. 34–42.
56. Ibid, p. 40.
57. Ibid, p. 10.
58. Ibid, p. 84.
59. Ibid, p. 84.
60. Williams, op. cit., p. 43.
61. Robert Runcie (Archbishop of Canterbury) *Address to the Birmingham Community Relations Council*, C.I.O., 1982.
62. See James Cone, *For My People: Black Theology and the Black Church*, Orbis, 1984, pp. 122–139.

Bibliography

A. CARIBBEAN

i) History, general

ALLEYNE, Mervyn, *Roots of Jamaican Culture*, London: Pluto, 1988.

AUGIER, F.R., GORDON, S.C., HALL, D.G. and RECKORD, M., *The Making of the West Indies*, Longman Caribbean, 1960.

AUGIER, F.R., GORDON, S.C., *Sources of West Indian History*, London: Longmans, 1962.

BECKLES, Hilary, *Black Rebellion in Barbados: the Struggle Against Slavery, 1627–1838*, Bridgetown: Carib Research and Publications, 1987.

BLACK, Clinton V., *History of Jamaica*,Kingston: Longman Jamaica, 1990.

BUSH, Barbara, *Slave Women in Caribbean Society 1650–1838*, Kingston, Jamaica: Heinemann, 1990.

CRATON Michael, *Testing the Chains: Resistance to Slavery in the British West Indies*, Ithaca: Cornell University Press, 1982.

CURTIN, Philip D., *Two Jamaicas: The Role of Ideas in a Tropical Colony 1830–1865*, Cambridge, Mass: Harvard UP, 1955, (reprinted New York: Atheneum, 1970).

FANON, Frantz *Black Skin, White Masks*, New York: Grove Press, 1967.

GREENWOOD, R. and HAMBER, S., *Emancipation to Emigration*, Macmillan Caribbean, 1980.

HART, Richard, *Black Jamaicans' Struggle Against Slavery*, Institute of Jamaica, 1977.

HOYOS, F.A., *Barbados, A History from the Amerindians to Independence*, Macmillan Caribbean, 1978.

PATTERSON, Orlando, *The Sociology of Slavery*, London: MacGibbon & Kee, 1967.

REID, C.S., *Samuel Sharpe: from Slave to National Hero*, Kingston, Jamaica: Bustamante Institute, 1988.

SMITH, Keithlyn B. and SMITH, Fernando C., *To Shoot Hard Labour: the*

Life and Times of Samuel Smith, an Antiguan Workingman, 1877–1982, Scarborough, Ontario: Edan's Publishers, 1986.

WATSON, Karl, *The Civilised Island Barbados: a Social History, 1750–1816*, Barbados, 1979.

ii) Religion, general

BARRETT, Leonard E, *The Sun and the Drum*, Kingston, Jamaica: Sangster's Book Stores and Heinemann, 1976.
  The Rastafarians, Kingston, Jamaica: Sangsters Book Stores and Heinemann, 1977.

FOSTER, Byron, *Spirit Possession in the Garifuna Communities of Belize*, Benque Viejo del Carmen, Belize: Cubola Productions, 1986.

MORRISH, Ivor, *Obeah, Christ and Rastaman*, Cambridge: James Clark, 1982.

OWENS, Joseph, *Dread: the Rastafarians of Jamaica*, Kingston, Jamaica: Sangster, 1976.

SEAGA, Edward, 'Revival Cults in Jamaica: Notes towards a Sociology of Religion', *Jamaica Journal* Vol.3 No.2, June 1969, reprinted by Institute of Jamaica Publications, 1982.

iii) Theology and Church History

BISNAUTH, Dale, *History of Religions in the Caribbean*, Kingston, Jamaica: Kingston Publishers, 1989.

> *Called to Be*, Bridgetown, Barbados: CADEC, 1973.

> *Consultation for Ministry in a New Decade, 17–21 November, 1984*, Bridgetown, Barbados: C.C.C., 1985.

CUTHBERT, Robert W.M., *Ecumenism and Development*, Bridgetown, Barbados: C.C.C., 1986.

DAVIS, Kortright, *Moving into Freedom*, Barbados: Cedar Press, 1977.
  Mission for Caribbean Change, (Studies in the Intercultural History of Christianity, No.28), Frankfurt: Verlag Peter Lang, 1982.
  Cross and Crown in Barbados, Studies in the Intercultural History of Christianity, No.20), Frankfurt: Verlag Peter Lang, 1983.
  Emancipation Still Comin': Explorations in Caribbean Emancipatory Theology, Maryknoll: Orbis Books, 1990.

DAYFOOT, A.C., *The Shaping of the West Indian Church: Historical Factors in the Formation of the Pattern of Church Life in the English-speaking Caribbean 1492–1870*. D.Th. thesis for Toronto School of Theology, unpublished, 1982.[1]

ELLIS, J.B., *The Diocese of Jamaica*, London: S.P.C.K., 1913.

ERSKINE, Noel L., *Decolonizing Theology: A Caribbean Perspective*, Maryknoll: Orbis Books, 1981.

EVANS, E.L., *A History of the Diocese of Jamaica*, Jamaica, 1977.

GAYLE, Clement, *George Liele: Pioneer Missionary to Jamaica*, Kingston: Jamaica Baptist Union, 1982.

GILMORE, John, *The Toiler of the Seas: a Life of John Mitchinson, Bishop of Barbados*, Bridgetown, Barbados: Barbados National Trust, 1987.

GOODRIDGE, Sehon S., *Facing the Challenge of Emancipation*, Bridgetown, Barbados: Cedar Press, 1981.

GUMBS, Wycherley, *Methodism: its Root and Fruit*, 1986.

HAMID, Idris (ed.), *Troubling of the Water*, Trinidad: San Fernando Press, 1973. *Out of the Depths*, Trinidad: San Fernando Press, 1977.

HENDERSON, George E., *Goodness and Mercy: a Tale of a Hundred Years*, printed in Kingston, Jamaica, 1967.

KLINGBERG Frank J. (ed.), *Codrington Chronicle: An Experiment in Anglican Altruism in a Barbados Plantation* (University of California Publications in History, Vol. 37), University of California Press, 1949.

LEWIS, A. Kingsley, *The Moravian Mission in Barbados, 1816–1866: A Study of the Historical Context and Theological Significance of a Minority Church among an Oppressed People* (Studies in the Intercultural History of Christianity, No.37), Frankfurt: Verlag Peter Lang, 1985.

MULRAIN, George, *Theology in Folk Culture: A Study of the Theological Significance of Haitian Folk Religion*, (Studies in the Intercultural History of Christianity, No.33) Frankfurt: Verlag Peter Lang, 1984.

NORTHCOTT, Cecil, *Slavery's Martyr, John Smith of Demerara and the Emancipation Movement 1917–24*, London: Epworth Press, 1976.

OSBORNE, Francis J. and JOHNSTON, Geoffrey, *Coastlands and Islands: First Thoughts on Caribbean Church History*, Kingston, Jamaica: U.T.C.W.I. 1972,

SMITH, Ashley, *Real Roots and Potted Plants*, Williamsville, Jamaica: Mandeville Publishers, 1984.
Educational Priorities: a Caribbean Perspective, 1987.

WATTY, William, *From Shore to Shore: Soundings in Caribbean Theology*, Kingston, Jamaica, 1981.

B. SOUTH AFRICA

BOESAK, Allan, *Black Theology, Black Power*, London: Mowbrays, 1978.
Farewell to Innocence, Maryknoll: Orbis Books, 1983.
Black and Reformed, Maryknoll: Orbis Books, 1984.

> *Challenge to the Church: A Theological Comment on the Political Crisis in South Africa* (The Kairos Document), Braamfontein: The Kairos Theologians, and London: C.I.I.R. and B.C.C., 1985.

MAZIBUKO, Bongani, *Education in Mission – Mission in Education*: a Critical Comparative Study of Selected Approaches (Studies in the Intercultural History of Christianity no. 47), Frankfurt: Verlag Peter Lang, 1987.

MOORE, Basil (ed.), *Black Theology, the South African Voice*, London: C. Hurst & Co., 1973.

MOSALA, Itumeleng J., *Biblical Hermeneutics and Black Theology in South Africa*, Grand Rapids: Eerdmans, 1989.

C. OTHER THIRD WORLD THEOLOGY

i) General

HOLLENWEGER, Walter J., 'Intercultural Theology', *Theological Renewal*, October, 1978.
'Towards an Intercultural History of Christianity', *International Review of Mission*, Vol.LXXVI, No. 304, Oct.1987, pp.526ff.
WITVLIET, Theo, *A Place in The Sun: an Introduction to Liberation Theology in the Third World*, London: SCM Press, 1985.

ii) Asia

BALASURIYA, Tissa, *The Eucharist and Human Liberation*, London: SCM Press, 1979.
SONG, Choan-Sen, *Theology from the Womb of Asia*, London: SCM Press. 1988.

iii) Latin America

CARDENAL, Ernesto, *Love in Practice, The Gospel in Solentiname*, London: Search Press, 1977.
GUTIERREZ, Gustavo, *We Drink from Our Own Wells*, London: SCM Press, 1984.
SOBRINO, Jon, *The True Church and the Poor*, London: SCM Press, 1985.
TORRES Sergio and EAGLESON John (eds.), *Theology in the Americas*, Orbis, 1976.

iv) Africa

DICKSON, Kwesi, *Theology in Africa*, London: Darton, Longman and Todd, 1984.
HASTINGS, Adrian, 'On African Theology', *Scottish Journal of Theology*, Vol.37, No.3.
MBITI, John S., *African Religions and Philosophy*, London: Heinemann, 1969.
PARRINDER, Geoffrey, *West African Religion* (2nd edition), London: Epworth, 1961.
TAYLOR, John V., *The Primal Vision*, London: SCM, 1963.

E. UNITED STATES

i) History, general

BREITMAN, G. (ed.), *Malcolm X Speaks: selected speeches and statements*, New York: Grove Press, 1965.
The Last Year of Malcolm X, New York: Pathfinder, 1967.

DAVIDSON, Basil, *Black Mother: Africa and the Atlantic Slave Trade*, London: Victor Gollancz, 1961.

DOUGLASS, Frederick. *Life and Times of Frederick Douglass, (revised edition of 1892)*, New York: Collier Macmillan, 1962.

DUBOIS, W.E.B. *John Brown*, New York: International, 1972.

ELKINS, Stanley M., *Slavery*, University of Chicago Press, 1968.

GRIFFIN, John H., *Black Like Me*, New York: Signet Books, 1960.

HATCH, Nathan O., *The Democratization of American Christianity*, Newhaven: Yale UP, 1989.

KAMPHAUSEN, Gerhard, Cadbury Lectures for the University of Birmingham, 1982 (unpublished).

KATZ, William Loren, *Black Indians, a Hidden Heritage*, New York: Atheneum Macmillan, 1986.

WASHINGTON, Booker T. *Up from Slavery*, New York: Carol, 1989 (reprint).

X, Malcolm, *The Autobiography of Malcolm X*, New York: Grove Press, 1965.
By Any Means Necessary, New York: Pathfinder, 1970.

ii) African Heritage

BARRETT, Leonard E, *Soul-Force: African Heritage in Afro-American Religion*, Garden City, New York: Anchor Press/Doubleday, 1974.

DUBOIS, W.E.B., *The Negro Church*, Atlanta University Press, 1903.
The Souls of Black Folk, Chicago: A.C. McClurg & Co., 1929.

GENOVESE, Eugene D., *Roll, Jordan, Roll*, New York: Pantheon Books, 1974.

HALEY, Alex, *Roots*, London: Hutchinson, 1977.

HERSKOVITS, Melville, *The Myth of the Negro Past*, Boston: Beacon, 1958.

JENKINS, David, *Black Zion: The Return of Afro-Americans and West Indians to Africa*, London: Wildwood House, 1975.

MacROBERT, Iain, *The Black Roots and White Racism of Early Pentecostalism in the USA*, London: Macmillan, 1988.

RABOTEAU, Albert J., *Slave Religion: The 'Invisible Institution' in the Antebellum South*, New York: Oxford University Press, 1978.

iii) Black Literature

ANGELOU, Maya, *I Know Why the Caged Bird Sings*, 1984,
Gather Together in My Name, 1985,

Singin' and Swingin' and Gettin' Merry like Christmas, 1985,
The Heart of a Woman, 1986,
All God's Children Need Travelling Shoes, 1987.
London: Virago Press.

BALDWIN, James, *The Fire Next Time*, London: Penguin, 1964.

JAQUES-GARVEY Amy (ed.), *The Philosophy and Opinions of Marcus Garvey*, New York: Arno Press, 1969.

LEWIS, Rupert, *Marcus Garvey: Anti-colonial Champion*, London: Karia Press, 1987.

MARTIN, Tony, *Marcus Garvey, Hero: a First Biography*, Dover, Mass: Majority Press, 1983.

iv) Black Theology and Church History

ANSBRO, John J., *Martin Luther King, Jr.: the Making of a Mind*, Maryknoll: Orbis, 1982.

CONE, James H., *Black Theology and Black Power*, Minneapolis: Seabury Press, 1969; 20th anniversary edition with new preface, Harper and Row, 1989.
A Black Theology of Liberation, (originally published 1970) 2nd Edition Maryknoll: Orbis Books, 1986.
The Spirituals and the Blues, San Francisco: Harper and Row, 1972.
God of the Oppressed, Minneapolis: Seabury Press, 1975.
For My People: Black Theology and the Black Church, Maryknoll: Orbis Books, 1984.
My Soul Looks Back, Maryknoll: Orbis Books, 1985.
Speaking the Truth, Grand Rapids, Mich: Eerdmans, 1987.
Martin, Malcolm and America: a Dream or a Nightmare?, Maryknoll: Orbis, 1991.

FELDER, Cain Hope, *Troubling Biblical Waters*, Maryknoll N.Y.: Orbis, 1989.

FELDER, Cain Hope (ed.), *Stony the Road We Trod: African American Biblical Interpretation*, Minneapolis: Fortress Press, 1991.

FRANKLIN, Robert Michael, *Liberating Visions: Human Fulfilment and Social Justice in African-American Thought*, Minneapolis: Fortress, 1990.

GEORGE, Carol V.R., *Segregated Sabbaths: Richard Allen and the Rise of Independent Churches*, New York, O.U.P., 1973.

GRANT, Jaquelyn, *White Women's Christ and Black Women's Jesus: Feminist Christology and Womanist Response*, Atlanta: Scholars Press, 1989.

HARDING, Vincent, *Hope and History: Why We Must Share the Story of the Movement*, Maryknoll N.Y.: Orbis, 1990.

JACKSON, Rose C., 'The Role of the Black Church' in *Celebrating the Black Family*, Birmingham: Claiming the Inheritance, 1988.

KING, Martin L. Jr., *Why We Can't Wait*, New York: Signet Books, 1964.
The Trumpet of Conscience, London: Hodder and Stoughton, 1967.
Where Do We Go from Here: Chaos or Community? New York: Harper and Row, 1967.

Strength to Love, San Fransisco: Harper and Row, 1963.

A Testament of Hope: the Essential Writings of Martin Luther King, Jr., ed. James Washington, San Francisco: Harper and Row, 1986.

LINCOLN, C. Eric, *The Black Experience in Religion*, Garden City N.Y.: Anchor Press/Doubleday, 1974.

The Black Church Since Frazier, New York: Schocken Books, 1974.

LINCOLN, C. Eric & LAWRENCE, H.M., *The Black Church and the African-American Experience*, Durham NC: Duke UP, 1990.

ROOKS, Charles Shelby, *Revolution in Zion: Reshaping African-American Ministry, 1960–1974*, New York: Pilgrim, 1990.

STOKES, Olivia Pearl, 'Black Theology: A Challenge to Religious Education' in Thompson, Norma H, *Religious Education and Theology*, Birmingham, Alabama: Religious Education Press, 1982.

> *Towards a Common Expression of Faith: A Black North-American Perspective*, report on the Consultation at Virginia Union University, Richmond, Va., 1984.

WEEMS, Renita, 'Reading **Her Way** through the Struggle: African American Women and the Bible', in Cain H. Felder, *Stony the Road We Trod: African American Biblical Interpretation*, Minneapolis: Fortress Press, 1991.

WEST, Cornel, *Prophesy Deliverance!, An Afro-American Revolutionary Christianity*, Philadelphia: Westminster Press, 1982.

WILMORE, Gayraud S., *Black and Presbyterian, The Heritage and the Hope*, Philadelphia: Geneva Press, 1983.

Last Things First, Philadelphia: Westminster Press, 1982.

Black Religion and Black Radicalism, An interpretation of the religious history of Afro-American People, (originally published 1973), second edition, Maryknoll: Orbis Books, 1983.

WILMORE, Gayraud S. (ed.), *African American Religious Studies*, Durham NC: Duke University Press, 1989.

WILMORE, Gayraud S. and CONE, James H., *Black Theology, a Documentary History, 1966–1979*, Maryknoll: Orbis, 1979.

WITVLIET, Theo, *The Way of the Black Messiah*, London: SCM Press, 1987.

v) Episcopal Church

Episcopal Church publications, (Episcopal Commission for Black Ministries, Episcopal Church Center, 815 Second Avenue, New York, N.Y.10017):

Linkage, (journal of Office of Black Ministries).

Black Clergy in the Episcopal Church: Recruitment, Training and Deployment, 1981.

The Recruitment of Black Clergy for the Episcopal Church, Some Biblical, Theological and Practical Considerations, 1982.

But We See Jesus: a Pastoral Letter from the Black Episcopal Bishops to Black Clergy and Laity in the Episcopal Church, 1990.

> *Institutional Racism Audit*, General Theological Seminary, New York, 1983.

vi) Roman Catholic

> *Ministry Among Black Americans*, St. Meinrad School of Theology, St. Meinrad, Indiana 47577.
RIVERS, Clarence J., *Soulfull Worship*, National Office for Black Catholics, 1234 Massachusetts Avenue NW., Washington D.C. 20005.
> 'What we have Seen and Heard', (Pastoral letter of Black Catholic Bishops of U.S.), *Origins*, October, 1987.

vii) Presbyterian

Presbyterian Church of U.S.A. publications, (475 Riverside Drive, New York, N.Y.10115):
'Whence Have We Come', *Report to Session*, Black Presbyterians United, 1977.
Black Presbyterianism Yesterday, Today and Tomorrow, 175 Years of Ministry 1807–1982, Office of Black Mission Development, 1982.

viii) Reformed Church

Reformed Church in America publications, (Black Council of the Reformed Church in America, 1823 Interchurch Center, 475 Riverside Drive, New York, N.Y.10115):
Bentley, Williams, 'Black Christianity: A Historical Overview';
Erskine, Noel, 'The Fundamentals of Black Theology', 1975.
Wilmore, Gayraud, 'Identity Crisis: Blacks in Predominantly White Denominations', 1976.
Cone, James, 'The Social Context of Black Theology', and 'A Black Perspective on America: A Theological Interpretation', 1977.
Dodson, Howard, 'Strategies for Liberation', 1978.
Jones, Lawrence, 'The Turning of the Wheel: An Historical Overview of Black White Relations in the Churches of America', and 'An Agenda for a Black-Congregation in a Majority-White Denomination', 1980.
Carter, Lawrence, 'The Dangers of Single Issue No-fault Morality', and Young, McKinley, 'Preaching in the 80's: The View of a local Pastor', 1981.
West, Cornel, 'The Sixties and Afro-America', 1983.

E. BRITAIN
i) History, General

FILE, Nigel and POWER, Chris, *Black Settlers in Britain 1555–1958*, London: Heinemann Educational Books, 1981.

FRYER, Peter, *Staying Power: The History of Black People in Britain*, London: Pluto Press, 1984.

POLLOCK, John, *Amazing Grace*, London: Hodder and Stoughton, 1981. *Wilberforce*, London: Lion, 1977.

ii) Society, General

BROWN, Colin, *Black and White Britain, the Third P.S.I. Survey*, Aldershot, Hants: Gower, 1984.

BRYAN, Beverley, DADZIE, Stella, and SCARFE, Suzanne, *The Heart of the Race: Black Women's Lives in Britain*, London: Virago, 1985.

CLARKE, Peter B., *Black Paradise; the Rastafarian Movement*, Wellingborough: the Aquarian Press, 1986.

COARD, Bernard, *How the West Indian Child is made Educationally Sub-Normal in the British School System*, London: New Beacon Books, 1981.

DIVINE, David, 'The Black British Family in Society', in *Celebrating the Black Family*, Birmingham: Claiming the Inheritance, 1988.

DUMMETT, Ann, *A Portrait of English Racism*, London: CARAF Publications, 1984.

Europe and 1992: Focus on Racial Issues, London: CARJ, 1990.

HUSBAND, Charles (ed.), *'Race' in Britain: Continuity and Change*, London: Hutchinson, 1982.

JOHN, Augustine, *Because They're Black*, London: Penguin, 1971.

Race in the Inner City, London Runnymede Trust, 1972.

LEECH, Kenneth, 'Diverse Reports' and the Meaning of 'Racism', in *Race and Class*, Vol. 28, No. 2, Autumn, 1986.

Struggle in Babylon, London: Sheldon, 1988.

MARTIN Ian, 'The Racism of Present Immigration Policy', in *Vigil*, Christian Action, 1981.

PANTI-AMOA Leonie, 'The Educational Needs of Black Women in Britain', in 'Claiming the Inheritance' *Racial Justice*, No. 6, Spring 1987, Evangelical Christians for Racial Justice.

PATTERSON, Sheila, *Immigration and Race Relations in Britain 1960–67*, London: Institute of Race Relations and Oxford University Press, 1969.

PRYCE, Ken, *Endless Pressure: A Study of West Indian Life-styles in Bristol*, London: Penguin, 1979.

'RAMPTON Report', *West Indian Children in our Schools: interim report of the committee of enquiry into the education of children from ethnic minority groups*, Cmnd. 8273, HMSO, 1981.

REX, John and MOORE, Robert, *Race, Community and Conflict*, Oxford University Press, 1967.

REX, John and TOMLINSON, Sally, *Colonial Immigrants in a British City, a Class Analysis*, London: Routledge and Kegan Paul, 1979.

SMITH, D., *The Facts of Racial Disadvantage, London: PEP, 1976*.

Racial Disadvantage in Britain: the P.E.P. Report, London: Penguin, 1977.

'SWANN Report', *Education for All: The Report of the Committee into the Education of Children from Ethnic Minority Groups*, (Cmnd 9452) HMSO: 1985.

> *Talking Chalk: Black Pupils, Parents and Teachers Speak about Education*, Birmingham: AFFOR, 1982.

iii) Black Christianity in Britain

ARNOLD, Selwyn E., *From Scepticism to Hope*, Bramcote, Nottingham: Grove Books, 1992.

BROOKS, Ira, *Where do we Go from Here?* New Testament Church of God, 1983.
Another Gentleman to the Ministry, 1985.

BURROUGH, Paul, *West Indians in Britain*, newspaper article, (Birmingham Diocesan Archive).

CHARMAN, Paul, *Reflections: Black and White Christians in the City*, London: Zebra Project, 1979.

HILL, Clifford S., *West Indian Migrants and the London Churches*, London: Institute of Race Relations/O.U.P. 1963.
Black Churches: West Indian and African Sects in Britain, London: B.C.C., 1971.

HILL, Clifford S. and MATTHEWS, D., *Race: A Christian Symposium*, London: Victor Gollancz, 1968.

ESTRIDGE, Sylvia, 'I Came to England: a Testimony', in *Celebrating the Black Family*, Birmingham: Claiming the Inheritance, 1988.

GERLOFF, Roswith, *The Development of Black Churches in Britain since 1952*, paper presented to the History Workshop on Religion and Society, unpublished, 1983.[1]
Blackness and Oneness (Apostolic) Theology, paper presented to the Annual Conference of the Society for Caribbean Studies, unpublished, 1985.[1]
A Plea for British Black Theologies: The Black Church Movement in Britain in its transatlantic cultural and theological interaction with special reference to the Pentecostal Oneness (Apostolic) and Sabbatarian Movements (Studies in the Intercultural History of Christianity no. 77, 2 vols), Frankfurt: Verlag Peter Lang, 1992.

GERLOFF, Roswith, and others, *Partnership in Black and White*, London: Methodist Church Home Mission Division, 1977.

GRANT, Paul and PATEL, Raj, *A Time to Speak: Perspectives of Black Christians in Britain*, London: Racial Justice (E.C.R.J.)/ Black Theology Working Group, 1990.
A Time to Act, Racial Justice (E.C.R.J.)/ Black and Third World Theology Working Group, 1992.

HARVEY: Louis-Charles, 'From Rejection to Liberation: The Development of the Black Church in Great Britain and the United States';
'From Immigration to Integration: The Exodus Experience of Black People in the United States and Great Britain'; in 'Claiming the Inheritance', *Racial Justice*, No. 6, Spring 1987, Evangelical Christians for Racial Justice, 17 Bell Barn Shopping Centre, Cregoe Street, Birmingham, B15 2DZ.
Black Religion in USA and Great Britain, unpublished mss., 1986.[1]

HEWITT, Roderick, *Reflections on the Handsworth Riot*, unpublished mss., 1985.[1]

HOBBS, Maurice, *Better will Come: a Pastoral Response to Racism in British Churches*, Nottingham: Grove Books, 1991.

JACKSON, Anita, *Catching Both Sides of the Wind: Conversations with Five Black Pastors*, London: B.C.C., 1985.

KENDALL, R. Elliott, *Christianity and Race*, London: B.C.C., 1983.

MacROBERT, Iain, 'The New Black-led Pentecostal Churches in Britain' in Paul Badham (ed.), *Religion State and Society in Modern Britain*, Lampeter: Edwin Mellen Press, 1989.

Black Pentecostalism in Britain, Edinburgh: St Andrew Press, 1992.

MOORE, David, 'Black Theology, A Tentative Exploration', *The Modern Churchman*, Autumn, 1980.

OLDHAM, J.H., *Christianity and the Race Problem*, London: SCM, 1924.

PHOENIX, Sybil, *Willing Hands*, London: Bible Reading Fellowship, 1984.

'The Black British Family in the Church', in *Celebrating the Black Family*, Birmingham: Claiming the Inheritance, 1988.

PITTS, Eve, 'Black Consciousness', in 'Claiming the Inheritance', *Racial Justice*, No. 6, Spring, 1987, Evangelical Christians for Racial Justice.

ROOT, John, *Encountering Westindian Pentecostalism: its Ministry and Worship*, Bramcote, Notts: Grove Books, 1979.

SIMMS, Arlene, 'The Church's Task', in 'Claiming the Inheritance', *Racial Justice*, No. 6, Spring 1987, Evangelical Christians for Racial Justice.

> Pilgrims in Progress, Birmingham: Wesleyan Holiness Church, 1983.

TOMLIN, Carol, *Black Preaching Style*, M.Phil. thesis, University of Birmingham, 1988.

WILKINSON, John L., 'Black Christianity in Britain: Survival or Liberation?' *International Review of Mission*, January, 1986.

WORALL, B.G., 'Some Reflections on Black-led Churches in England', *Theology*, January 1987.

iv) British Council of Churches

Building Together in Christ, second report of the joint-working-party between white-led and black-led churches, London: B.C.C., 1978.

Coming Together in Christ, first report of the joint working-party between white-led and black-led churches, B.C.C., 1977.

The Enemy Within (filmstrip and text), B.C.C. & Catholic Commission for Racial Justice, 1981.

Learning in Partnership, third report of the joint-working party between white-led and black-led churches, London: B.C.C., 1980.

The New Black Presence in Britain: A Christian Scrutiny, London: B.C.C., 1976.

Rainbow Gospel, Report of the Conference on Challenging Racism in Britain, London: B.C.C., 1988.

Partners in Practice, London: B.C.C. 1989.

v) Church of England

Birmingham Diocese, documents and publications:[2]

Building a Black and White Church, Recommendations to the Bishop's Council of the Diocese of Birmingham, R.R.G., 1985.

Response of the Bishop's Council to 'Building a Black and White Church', 1986.

Comments on 'The Response of the Bishop's Council to "Building a Black and White Church"', R.R.G., 1986.

Equal Opportunity Policy for the Birmingham Diocesan Board of Finance, Birmingham D.B.F., 1986.

D.E.C. ACUPA Day Conference, Response by Diocesan Race Relations Group (the report of R.R.G. delegates to the R.R.G.), 1986.

Black People's Participation in the Anglican Diocese of Birmingham, Diocesan C.B.A., 1989.

Church of England, Publications:

Britain as a Multi-Racial and Multi-Cultured Society, (GS 328), B.S.R., 1977.

The Church of England and Racism, (the 'Leicester' Report), B.S.R., 1981.

The Church of England and Racism – And Beyond, Race Pluralism and Community Group, B.S.R., 1982.

Anglicans and Racism, (the 'Balsall Heath' Report) Race, Pluralism and Community Group, B.S.R., 1986.

Faith in the City: Minority Ethnic Groups, Report by the Standing Committee (GS 753), 1986.

Black Membership in The General Synod, (GS 844A), report by the Committee for Black Anglican Concerns, 1988.

Racism & Theological Education, B.S.R., 1988.

Report of Proceedings, General Synod, CIO.

Seeds of Hope: Report of a Survey on Combatting Racism in the Dioceses of the Church of England (GS 977), General Synod of the Church of England, 1991.

Church Missionary Society, *Newsletter*, October, 1985.

> *Faith in the City, the Report of the Archbishop of Canterbury's Commission on Urban Priority Areas*, London: Church House Publishing, 1985.

> 'Immigration and Racial Justice, A Christian Statement' – signed by 13 Anglican Bishops, and 3 other Anglican clergy, J.C.W.I., 1979.

LEECH, Kenneth, *The Liverpool 8 Defence Committee*, B.S.R., 1981.

The Fields of Charity and Sin, B.S.R., 1986.

MOORE, David, *Invisible People: Black People in the Church of England*, for the Race, Pluralism and Community Group of B.S.R., unpublished, 1984.[1]

SINCLAIR, Keith, *Theological Reflections on Racism*, paper delivered at Queen's Theological College, Birmingham, unpublished, 1986.[1]

Southwark Diocese Race Relations Commission, publications: *Black Anglicans in Southwark Diocese, A report of a survey of parishes*, 1986.

Where do I Stand? A report of the Summer Youth Conference, 1986.
WILKINSON, John L., *Black Anglicans in Birmingham*, (in the Library of St. George's House, Windsor), unpublished, 1984.[1]
WILKINSON, John L., WILKINSON, Renate and EVANS, James H. Jr., *Inheritors Together*, B.S.R., 1985.
WILKINSON, Renate, *A Chance to Change: A sociological study of the relationship between black Anglicans and the Church of England in the Diocese of Birmingham in 1983*, M.Sc. thesis submitted to the University of Aston in Birmingham, 1984.[1] (abbreviated version published in 'Inheritors Together').

vi) Methodist Church

Methodist D.S.R. publications:
Faithful and Equal', *Agenda of the 1987 Methodist Conference*, Methodist Church, 1987, pp. 156–193.
Holden, Tony, *People, Churches and Multi-Racial Projects*, 1985.
Milwood, Robinson, *Let's Journey Together*, 1980.
Walton, Heather, *A Tree God Planted: Black People in British Methodism*, Ethnic Minorities in Methodism Working Group, 1985.

vii) Roman Catholic

> *Charter*, London: CARJ, 1990.
> *Congress of Black Catholics: Report*, London: CARJ, 1990.
> *Building Bridges: Dialogue with Black-led Churches*, CARJ, 1988.
Pontifical Commission 'Iustitia et Pax', *The Church and Racism: Towards a More Fraternal Society*, London: Catholic Truth Society, 1989.
HUME, Basil, *Racism: the Need for Positive Action*, London: CARJ, 1986.
KALILOMBE, Patrick et al., *Black Catholics Speak*, London: CARJ, 1991.
> *With You in Spirit?* Cardinal Hume's Advisory Group on the Catholic Church's Commitment to the Black Community, 1985.

viii) Theological Education

CRACKNELL, Kenneth, JENNINGS, David and TRETHOWAN, Christine, *Blind Leaders for the Blind? Theological Training the Today's Plural Society*, Birmingham: AFFOR, 1981.
DANIEL, Wesley, *The Question of Race and Theological Education*, paper written at Queen's College, Birmingham, unpublished, 1987.
HARVEY, Louis-Charles, *All Along this Pilgrim Journey: a Paradigm for Black Theological Education*, unpublished, 1989.[1]
HOLLENWEGER, Walter J., 'Interaction between Black, and White in Theological Education', *Theology*, September, 1987.
A.B.M. Working Party on Educational Practice, *Integration and Assessment*, London: A.B.M., 1990.

MOORE. David, *Pre-Theological College Training: A Discussion Paper*, unpublished, 1983.[1]

Queen's College, Birmingham, *Black Christian Studies at the Queen's College, Birmingham and the West Midlands Ministerial Training Course*, 1989.

RUSSELL, Peter, MULRAIN, George, HOBBS, Maurice and WALTON, Heather, *Race and Theological Education, a Discussion Paper*, Methodist Church D.S.R., 1983.

> *Simon of Cyrene Theological Institute*, pamphlet issued by the Governing Body of the Simon of Cyrene Theological Institute (Chairman R.K. Daniel), 1989.

THOMPSON, Maureen, *Church Education: Some Implications for the Inner City*, dissertation submitted to Westhill College, Birmingham, unpublished, 1984.[1]

WILMORE, Gayraud S., *The Historical Mandate for African American Theological Education*, unpublished, 1989.[1]

F. MUSIC

BROUGHTON, Viv, *Black Gospel: an Illustrated History of the Gospel Sound*, Poole, Dorset: Blandford Press, 1985.

HARVEY, Louis-Charles, 'Black Christology: The History and Theology of Black Gospel Music', *Journal of Theology*, United Theological Seminary, Dayton, Ohio, U.S.A., 1987.

JACKSON, Rose C., *The Nature and Role of Black Gospel Music in the Black Pentecostal Worship Service*, dissertation for Doctor of Ministry degree, University of Chicago, 1986.

Lift Every Voice and Sing, New York: Church Hymnal Corporation, 1981.

Songs of Zion, Nashville: Abingdon, 1981.

SOUTHERN, Eileen, *The Music of Black Americans: a History*, New York: Norton, 1983.

WALKER, Wyatt Tee, '*Somebody's Calling my Name': Black Sacred Music and Social Change*, Valley Forge, Pa: Judson, 1979.

G. OTHER BOOKS

i) Theology

BARRETT, C.K., *A Commentary on the First Epistle to the Corinthians*, London: A. and C. Black, 1968.

BULTMANN, Rudolph, *Theology of the New Testament*, Vol. 1, 1952; Vol. 2, 1955, London: SCM Press.

DAVIES, J. Gordon (ed.), *A New Dictionary of Liturgy and Worship*, London: SCM Press, 1985.

DAVIES, Rupert E. and RUPP, E. Gordon, *A History of the Methodist Church in Great Britain*, London: Epworth, 1965.

EICHRODT, Walter, *Theology of the Old Testament*, Vol. 1, 1961; Vol. 2, 1967; London: SCM Press.

FORD, David F., *The Modern Theologians, an Introduction to Christian Theology in the Twentieth Century*, Oxford: Blackwell, 1989.

FREND, W.H.C., *The Donatist Church: A Movement of Protest in Roman North Africa*, Oxford University Press, 1952.

GOLLWITZER, Helmut, *The Rich Christians and Poor Lazarus*, Edinburgh, St. Andrew Press, 1970.

GOTTWALD, Norman K., *The Tribes of Yahweh*, Maryknoll: Orbis Books, 1979. (ed.) *The Bible and Liberation, Political and Social Hermeneutics*, Maryknoll: Orbis Books, 1984.

HABGOOD, John S., 'On Being a Liturgical Reviser', *Theology*, March, 1979.

HOLLENWEGER, Walter J., *The Pentecostals*, London: SCM, 1972.
Pentecost between Black and White, Belfast: Christian Journals Limited, 1974.
'Roots and Fruits of the Charismatic Renewal in the Third World: Implications for Mission', *Theological Renewal*, February, 1980.
Conflict in Corinth, New York: Paulist Press, 1982.

KELLY, J.N.D., *Early Christian Doctrines*, London: A. and C. Black, 1958.

KÜNG, Hans, *Theology for the Third Millenium: An Ecumenical View*, New York: Doubleday, 1988.

MACQUARRIE, John, *Twentieth Century Religious Thought*, London: SCM Press, 1963.

MOLTMANN, Jürgen, *The Open Church*, London: SCM, 1978.

MUDDIMAN, J., *The Bible, Fountain and Well of Truth*, Oxford: Blackwell, 1983.

NEIL, Stephen, *Anglicanism*, London: Penguin, 1958.

NEWBIGIN, Lesslie, *The Other Side of 1984*, Geneva: World Council of Churches, 1984.

RAMSAY, Arthur Michael, *The Gospel and the Catholic Church*, London: Longmans, 1936.

RICHARDSON, Alan, *An Introduction to The Theology of the New Testament*, London: SCM Press, 1958.

SCHREITER, Robert J., *Constructing Local Theologies*, London: SCM Press, 1985.

SHEPPARD, David, *Bias to the Poor*, London: Hodder and Stoughton, 1983.

STROUP, George W., *The Promise of Narrative Theology*, London: SCM Press, 1984.

SYKES, Stephen and BOOTY, John (eds.) *The Study of Anglicanism*, London: SPCK, 1988.

THEISSEN, Gerd, *The Social Setting of Pauline Christianity*, Edinburgh: T.& T. Clarke, 1982.

THOMPSON, H.P., *Into All Lands: the History of the Society for the*

Propagation of the Gospel in Foreign Parts, 1701–1956, London: S.P.C.K., 1951.

TILLER, J. *A Strategy for the Church's Ministry*, London, Church Information Office, 1983.

WELSBY, Paul A., *A History of the Church of England 1945–80*, Oxford University Press, 1984.

WENGST, Klaus, *Pax Romana and the Peace of Jesus Christ*, London: SCM, 1987.

WHALE, John, *The Future of Anglicanism*, London: Mowbrays, 1988.

WILES, Maurice, *The Christian Fathers*, London: Hodder and Stoughton, 1966.

WILLIAMS, Rowan, *Resurrection*, London: Darton, Longman and Todd, 1982.

WOLF, William J., *The Spirit of Anglicanism*, Edinburgh: T. and T. Clark, 1982.

ii) Other

'BRANDT COMMISSION', *North-South: A Programme for Survival, Report of the Independent Commission on International Development Issues* (the 'Brandt' Report), London: Pan, 1979.
Common Crisis North-South: Co-operation for World Recovery, Independent Commission on International Development Issues, London: Pan, 1983.

BROWN, C.H., *Understanding Society: An Introduction to Sociological Theory*, London: John Murray, 1979.

HARALAMBOS, Michael, and HEALD, Robin M., *Sociology, Themes and Perspectives*, Slough: University Tutorial Press, 1980.

MACINTYRE, Alasdair, *Whose Justice? Which Rationality?*, London: Duckworth, 1988.

H. JOURNALS

Caribbean Contact (monthly newspaper of C.C.C.), C.C.C., Bridgetown, Barbados,[3]
Caribbean Journal of Religious Studies, U.T.C.W.I., PO Box 136, Golding Avenue, Kingston 7, Jamaica.[1]
Journal of Religious Thought, Howard University Divinity School, 14th and Shepherd Street NE, Washington D.C., 20017, U.S.A.
Journal of the Interdenominational Theological Center, 671 Beckwith Street S.W., Atlanta, Ga., 30314, U.S.A.[1]

1. In the library of Queen's College, Somerset Rd., Birmingham, B15 2QH.
2. Available from the Diocesan Adviser on Black Ministries, 175 Harborne Park Road, Birmingham, B17 0BH.
3. In the library of Kingsmead College, Selly Oak, Birmingham, B29 6LP.

Index

246

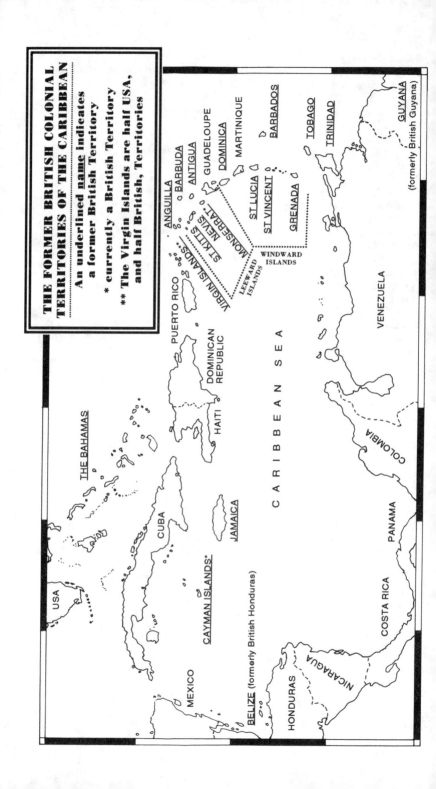

THE FORMER BRITISH COLONIAL TERRITORIES OF THE CARIBBEAN

An underlined name indicates
a former British Territory

* currently a British Territory

** The Virgin Islands are half USA,
and half British, Territories

Board Windows on Theology / Fenster zur Theologie

Windows on Theology / Fenster zur Theology is a charity which aims to promote the publication of theological works. The fact that there is no shortage of theological books on the market today does not necessarily mean that all the voices which deserve a wider audience are heard. Even authors of outstanding ability find it increasingly difficult, if not impossible, to find publishers who are able and prepared to offer them the conditions and terms they deserve. The problem becomes even greater for authors who come from non-western countries. Despite their ability to make outstanding contributions to world theology, they are often unable to overcome the problems of production, distribution and appropriate price in their own countries. What good is a book when it can't be distributed and sold at an affordable price where it is most needed?

Windows on Theology aims to bridge these gaps in two main ways:

a) to produce titles which are accessible to both student and lay person, at prices they can reasonably afford. Windows on Theology will publich two series, a General series which will be of wider interest, and a Students' Series with the sub-titles Insights into Theology / Einsichten in Theologie.

b) Windows on Theology not only wants to produce books as part of the two series but also to offer their services and know-how to authors and organisations, especially in countries where these are lacking, to enable them to develope their own infrastructure and organisation, strengthen and develop the contacts and distribution network and to find access to the European and North-American market. It is therefore necessary that Windows constantly developes and broaden its technical and financial expertise and improves its contacts.

Windows on Theology / Fenster zur Theology.

The series was developed over a period of 2 years. Several publishers, authors, and experts were approached to develop the concept and to secure the greatest possible editorial freedom for the Board and the authors, the availability of the series in all parts of the world, the lowest possible net sales price of the books and the best printing quality for each book.

Pahl Rugenstein Verlag Nachfolger, Bonn, and Saint Andrew Press, Edinburgh, co-publish and distribute the series, which is edited by the Board. This guarantees world wide distribtion.

The editorial board consists of Dr. Eleanor Jackson, lecturer at Saint Martin's College, Lancaster; Dr. John Parrat, Deputy Director of the Centre for the study of Christianity in the non-western World, University of Edinburgh; and Klaus-Dieter Stoll. Every book is separately priced for the country where it is sold. This is to ensure that the books are affordable for students, scholars and lay-people all over the world. Losses which occur through the sale of books in underdeveloped countries because of sub cost price, prices will be compensated for through profits accrued by the sale in Europe and America.

The two series will aim to provide texts which, besides being of wider interest, will be of considerable usefulness for theological students. Each volume will be written with the minimum of technical language and foot-notes, in a style to make them accessible to those for whom English or German is not their mother tongue, but will have extensive bibliographies to enable the reader to follow up points of particular interest. They will primarily aimed at the reader comming to the subjekt for the first time. All books will be written from an ecumencial perspective, in many cases involving cross-cultural encounters, and will explore how the Gospel is interpreted in different cultures and milieux. The authors will present their material from a new and significantly different or original viewpoint. The aim will not be merely to communicate knowledge but to stimulate dialogue with the reader. The editors do not necessarily subscribe to the views of the authors, but do belive that their views should be heard. Encouragement will be given to newer authors who may not have published much, but who have considerable expertise in their chosen field of area. Authors from Africa, Asia, Latin America and Oceania will play a prominent role. Hitherto unobtainable materials by established authors will also be included.

A invitation for co-operation

The Board hopes to co-opt further members as and when necessary, and exept to be aible to avail themselves of advice from other academics acting as consultants for specific works. Everybody who is interested in the work and aims of the charity and also those who are seeking advice and contacts for their own projects are invited to participate.

Finance

These arrangements are only realistic and possible through the fact that the Board works on a non-profit basis and the funding of books through independent trusts. The running costs, the support and developement work of the charity have to be met through donations. Like every charity, Windows is always looking for funds, therefore we are not only grateful for any donations but also for advice and contacts to grant-giving trusts. The accounts of the charity are regularly audited by an independent accountant.

For more informations turn to: Windows of Theology
68 Windermere Road
Lancaster LA1 3EZ
Great Britain